After Autonomy: A Post-Mortem for Hong Kong's
first Handover, 1997–2019

Daniel F. Vukovich

# After Autonomy: A Post-Mortem for Hong Kong's first Handover, 1997–2019

palgrave
macmillan

Daniel F. Vukovich
Comparative Literature Program
University of Hong Kong
Hong Kong, Hong Kong

ISBN 978-981-19-4982-1     ISBN 978-981-19-4983-8   (eBook)
https://doi.org/10.1007/978-981-19-4983-8

© The Editor(s) (if applicable) and The Author(s), under exclusive license to Springer Nature Singapore Pte Ltd. 2022
This work is subject to copyright. All rights are solely and exclusively licensed by the Publisher, whether the whole or part of the material is concerned, specifically the rights of reprinting, reuse of illustrations, recitation, broadcasting, reproduction on microfilms or in any other physical way, and transmission or information storage and retrieval, electronic adaptation, computer software, or by similar or dissimilar methodology now known or hereafter developed.
The use of general descriptive names, registered names, trademarks, service marks, etc. in this publication does not imply, even in the absence of a specific statement, that such names are exempt from the relevant protective laws and regulations and therefore free for general use.
The publisher, the authors, and the editors are safe to assume that the advice and information in this book are believed to be true and accurate at the date of publication. Neither the publisher nor the authors or the editors give a warranty, expressed or implied, with respect to the material contained herein or for any errors or omissions that may have been made. The publisher remains neutral with regard to jurisdictional claims in published maps and institutional affiliations.

Cover illustration: ANTHONY WALLACE/Contributor

This Palgrave Macmillan imprint is published by the registered company Springer Nature Singapore Pte Ltd.
The registered company address is: 152 Beach Road, #21-01/04 Gateway East, Singapore 189721, Singapore

# Epigraph

*No man is an Iland, intire of itself.* John Donne [1623]

"The deepest problems of modern life derive from the claim of the individual to preserve the autonomy and individuality of his existence in the face of overwhelming social forces, of historical heritage, of external culture, and of the technique of life." Georg Simmel [1903]

*For Vicky*

# Acknowledgements

My work on this book began during 2019, and I was spurred on by invitations to write for a political magazine in Germany (*Jungle World*) and then by invitations to submit to *Critical Asian Studies* and *Javnost: The Public*. The results were: "A City and a SAR On Fire" (52.1 (2020): 1–17) and "A Sound and Fury Signifying Mediatisation" (27.2 (2020): 200–209), respectively. While I do not draw on these essays here, I thank the editors and reviewers there for the opportunity and for prompting my further work on 2019 and its meanings from an Asian/China studies as well as cultural/media studies perspective.

Working with Palgrave and commissioning editor Jacob Dreyer for a second monograph has been a pleasure. I would like to thank as well two anonymous reviewers for their constructive criticisms of the proposal and first drafts.

I happily thank some genuine colleagues who have helped keep things humane and professional during these tumultuous times. Thanks especially to Song Geng, John Carroll, Ci Jiwei, and David Pomfret. I also thank several, anonymous supporters in the School of Humanities as well as outside reviewers of my various files, with apologies that my/our employer does not honour their recommendations or its own professional obligations to them either.

Allen Chun, Yan Hairong, Cui Zhiyuan, Daniel Bell, Nurry Vittachi, Zhao Yuezhi, Lin Chun, Barry Sautman, Wang Zhengxu, Ray Jiang, Pan Lu, Zairong Xiang, the Lai crew, Jan Nederveen Pieterse, Liu Shih-Ding,

X    ACKNOWLEDGEMENTS

Tugrul Keskin, Greg Mahoney, Ernest Leung, Jay Schutte, Wang Dan, Jon Solomon, and others based in Hong Kong either offered direct feedback on drafts and ideas, or just as importantly, said or did other things to help me remind myself I am not wrong to read HK and 2019 against the grain. I would also like to thank Lui Tai Lok in particular for his work, which has helped me think through the question of the Basic Law and the handover process/problem. Of course all of the usual caveats apply, and none of these good folks are responsible for anything I say in this book. (Neither is Xi Jinping.)

Thanks also to all those other friends and students, many of them having left the SAR already, who shared the past several years with me. Shout out to Team No Calves as well, who kept picking up heavy things and putting them down.

*   *   *

This, my third monograph was even more of a challenge to write than the first two. First this had to do with the genuine challenges—emotional and intellectual—that the events of 2019 entailed. To call it trauma would be too much (in my own case anyway). But these were not easy months to live through, due as much to witnessing others suffering as from my own uneasiness. From July onwards there was a painful, inescapable awareness that Hong Kong had changed forever. One did not know how, but it did not seem good. In the event it came in the form of the national security law in June 2020. And of course the many changes since, not least under the global pandemic. And yet, from the standpoint of Spring 2022, and despite the mishandling of the Omicron wave of the virus, it is clear that the new law and new era does not mark the end of Hong Kong. But it is certainly the end of Hong Kong as some "democrats" and "autonomists" wanted it to be. This is admittedly a lot of people, whether "lot" indicates a substantial minority or a bona fide majority. Whether this will be better or worse depends right now on who you ask. We shall see.

The next challenges were to academic life and family-life after Covid-19 and the nearly two-year long school-closures (aka online learning) in particular. Hong Kong attempted to micro-manage the virus (still better than the 'let it rip' approach), a process that ended in abject failure with the onset of Omicron and the lack of vaccination efforts and of test-and-trace capabilities. Given the legacies of political colonialism in Hong Kong as well as its anti-state or "neo-liberal" ethos, this failure in governance came as no surprise, even if it was difficult to live through. But having weathered that, it seems now to be back on track and moving forward with that second handover. We shall see. What made the past few years liveable was my family above all, and the unstinting goodness and energy and love from two kids in particular. Ollie was indispensable and made the whole pack hang together. My wife Vicky Lo is the strongest and the wisest person I know, and I dedicate this book to her.

# CONTENTS

| | | |
|---|---|---|
| 1 | **Introduction** | 1 |
| 2 | **In the Event: The Politics and Contexts of the 2019 Anti-ELAB Protests** | 9 |
| | *From the Umbrella to the Fishball 'Revolutions'* | 16 |
| | *From a City-State to a SAR on Fire: The 2019 Anti-ELAB and Its Aftermath* | 25 |
| | *Policing the Crisis?* | 36 |
| | *Colour Revolution and Quasi-Imperialism: Media and Money* | 41 |
| 3 | **Basic Law, Basic Problems: Autonomy and Identity** | 57 |
| | *One System: Everything That Rises Must Converge* | 61 |
| | *Autonomy and Its Discontents* | 69 |
| | *Identity and Its Discontents* | 77 |
| 4 | **Re-Colonization or De-Colonization?** | 97 |
| | *Towards Economic De-Colonization?* | 99 |
| | *Politics Not in Command: Political De-Colonization?* | 108 |
| | *Politics of Knowledge (Brief Reprise)* | 117 |
| | *Can the Parties Continue? Whither Participation?* | 122 |
| 5 | **Coda: The Search for State Capacity After Covid and Zero-Covid** | 141 |
| | *On the State, During and After Colonialism* | 142 |

xiv  CONTENTS

*The Fifth Wave: Incapacitation*                                    150
*Towards a Second Handover, After the British*
*and "Autonomy" Eras*                                               155

**Select Bibliography**                                            167

**Index**                                                          173

CHAPTER 1

# Introduction

This book began first as a follow-up to *Illiberal China: The Ideological Challenge of the P.R.C.*, with a desire to further think through the 'core value' of autonomy within classical liberalism and modernity as well as within Hong Kong's own mainstream, post-colonial, intellectual and political culture, and more specifically within its "democracy" and opposition movements *for* suffrage but—it is true—even more strongly *against* the mainland and/or Hong Kong's integration since 1997. While clearly such a framework does not include every Hong Konger (leaving aside what constitutes a Hong Kong person to begin with), the 'core values' of many in the SAR certainly include liberal economics and politics and general beliefs or values, including autonomy, negative liberties (freedoms *from* certain things and people), and so on. Many of these issues are still engaged in what follows.

But what happened in the interim between this original plan and the real world, between 2014's Occupy movement (discussed at length in the former book) and the pandemic was of course the fairly catastrophic anti-ELAB movement and thence its aftermath in the form of the national security law, and then shortly thereafter the catastrophic global pandemic. In short, as Christopher George Latore Wallace put it, things done changed. It was simply impossible not to focus on 2019 in greater detail, albeit to delve into the theoretical and political issues,

© The Author(s), under exclusive license to Springer Nature Singapore Pte Ltd. 2022
D. F. Vukovich, *After Autonomy: A Post-Mortem for Hong Kong's first Handover, 1997–2019*,
https://DOI.org/10.1007/978-981-19-4983-8_1

1

including those of imperialism and post-colonialism, subtending 2019. A post-mortem was in order.

Not only of the movement but of how and why it came to be, and what this might all mean for understanding the global conjuncture, the colonial past, and the 'first handover period' (1997–2019), as well as how we should interpret Hong Kong politics now and in the future. The new security law dating from June 2020 still enters the conversation here, as it must since it is a direct product of the protests of 2019 and the attempt to solicit foreign powers to intervene into Hong Kong. But it is not the focus, and nor is the pandemic. The latter in particular would lead us into a much larger and different study than the uproar of 2019 and its aftermath. At the same time I wanted to publish this specific project on 2019 before that event recedes further into the past. It was a watershed event for Hong Kong and China, but also an emblematic moment for contemporary, global politics (albeit not in the Manichean way dictated by political orientalism). But the final chapter does engage the SAR's handling of the pandemic, especially the fifth, Omicron wave and the struggle to not only contain this but to find and develop state capacity after colonialism. One reason why the SAR failed to handle the extradition bill *and* the massive protest against it was precisely its lack of state capacity or, put another way, its sheer political and institutional dysfunction. This may well be changing now, and certainly has in regard to policing and the legislative process, but for virtually everything else: We shall see. If the new fruit of 2019 was the security bill, the old fruit of British colonialism in Hong Kong, in political terms at any rate, was the lack of state capacity and a functional ruling/governing class. 2019 was momentous, its roots deep in the colonial past as much as the post-1997, global conjuncture, and the problems and contradictions leading up to it (including but not limited to the Basic Law) have yet to be resolved. But they may well be so, in a difficult and protracted way. We shall see.

What follows continues my now decades-long engagement with the politics of discourse, and the conceptual and discursive as well as historical or contextual dimensions of 'real' politics (and Stuart Hall always reminded us that real politics are always discursive because this is what hegemony is). Any such analysis of Hong Kong or the global conjuncture will behove us, as always, to wrestle explicitly with the crucial dimensions of colonialism or imperialism, or simply of the global conjuncture and the not-so-new Cold War or Sino-US rivalry. It will also have to wrestle with the enormous power of media-sanctioned, media-produced discourse about the event and about China, about Freedom, Inc., and so on (a discourse that often gets reproduced in more academic work and commentary).

My purpose in this book is not to directly counter the mediatization of 2019 (a project more impossible than the "five demands, not one less!" slogan) but simply to offer an alternative analysis. However the reader should immediately know the type of media (and political) discourse I am speaking of critically, as it is too common to need citation. My own view, as will become clear, is that for Hong Kong to de-colonize (and prosper) beyond the 'mere' question of sovereignty and the racial or ethnic composition of its ruling class, it will have to integrate with, not autonomize or immunize itself from the mainland political and economic system. I certainly do not mean this as some type of original hot-take that is warranted by this or that bit of jargon or theory-talk.

But as I have argued previously in *Illiberal China* and again below (albeit differently), the appeal for integration is also an appeal for greater livelihood and indeed greater 'democracy' and well-being resulting from such a momentous socio-economic process and second handover. This can, or could, in turn be construed as anti- or de-colonial in a number of ways, not least in the sense of moving beyond Sinophobia and blind faith in autonomy and laissez-faire liberalism. Hong Kong of course has always been part of the world and of global, capitalist modernity (with all its iniquities), and this has even been part of its appeal to its global fan base (and it does have a fan base), and even to many in the mainland in past decades especially. But at the risk of sounding too Romantic or Hegelian, it now has a chance to live not on borrowed time (the fifty year hiatus of the Basic Law) but *in* history in a fuller and hopefully better way. Swim with the tide and be water *that* way. Why try to stave off the inevitable and live on 'borrowed time' over and over again, which only serves to uphold the current status quo? Who exactly has benefitted from the pursuit of autonomy (be it a high degree thereof, or de facto full, quasi-independent autonomy)? Go in fear of nostalgia. Go in fear of Occidentalism.

Or as Machiavelli put it, Fortune has only fifty percent control of us, and the rest is up to human agency. Even this may be too optimistic, but surely there is something to be said for living in the moment. Having had its imminent death predicted repeatedly since the 1970s, it is worth emphasizing instead that the SAR has always been a city of changes, and if things seem bleak now (as they sometimes do and not least because of Covid and especially zero-Covid), this too shall pass.

At any rate in a post-covid world, should we actually get there in the SAR and China, there *should* certainly be new space not only for protest or 'the streets' (albeit in a very different form than in 2019 or even 2014 and with clear red lines) but for a newfound if more 'loyal' opposition that contests *how* such an integration might happen and whom will benefit. As I detail later, this is a tall order given the—colonially induced—lack of a political class and cadre (civil service) up to the task of integration with the mainland, the rise of xenophobia or nativism locally, and the lack of state capacity in Hong Kong. The Basic Law itself has served as an obstacle not as a lubricant. But now, while the official terms will remain the same, it is clear that the political victory of the 'establishment' (if this is the right word) means that their and/or the mainland's way of interpreting and enforcing the Basic Law will hold sway for years to come. As discussed elsewhere, there was always a battle of interpretations over the meaning of the deceptively straightforward, contradictory Basic Law, one side emphasizing suffrage/voting and comprehensive autonomy, the other emphasising security and integration and a de-limited autonomy. The Law will now be a vehicle of integration and the production of one country, one system over the oncoming years and decades. This much is certain, at least. It must also be said that Hong Kong does still enjoy a large degree of autonomy and second-system in relation to the mainland that only a Western media or expert commenter could deny. Whether this is a good thing or bad thing depends on the details, not on whether it stems from one system or the other.

The blind spots of the Basic Law have always been the silences on de-colonization (aside from handing over mere sovereignty) and on capitalism (or the false premise that there were two separate economic systems, socialism to the north and capitalism to the south, and these could be kept separate even if you tried). It is less certain that these will be addressed in the coming years, but the following pages make a case for how and why they could be. It perhaps goes without saying that there is also a chance—perhaps a strong chance—that not much will change in these ways, just more security-based authoritarianism to go with the iniquitous capitalism already plaguing Hong Kong for decades, despite its wealth. Indeed many would claim (have already claimed) that this is already the case and the real story of Hong Kong after 2019. From the standpoint of those who lost the 'war' or 'revolution' it would be hard to refute this. Rather than try to do so I seek instead to offer an alternate account of what that "war" was and what it means in the light of post-colonial and other types of theoretical analysis.

A productive, beneficial integration between the SAR and the sovereign is easier said than done, given the Basic Law itself and the lack of understanding on both sides of the border. While the mainland arguably has much less of it, both sides have far too high a tolerance for inequality and a penchant for letting 'market forces' hold sway. Much of the economic integration that has happened since the 1990s has benefitted only the few. The language of class consciousness and *that* type of inequality and conflict were never prominent within the oppositional/democracy movement. But there is no doubt that these experiences and lived realities informed the protests and movements anyway, fuelling its anger and affect. This is hardly unique to Hong Kong or the behemoth to the north. What is promising is the rising awareness of economic inequalities and living and working conditions in the city: something noted early on and frequently by mainland state media outlets, and moreover now in some sense a major part of at least the platform and rhetoric of the second handover. The latter is the meaning behind such ambitious projects and 'plans' as The Greater Bay Area network for communication and transport industries, the Northern Metropolis development strategy, the Lantau Reclamation project or other housing initiatives, and so on (discussed in later pages).

Again, it is too early to tell what will come of these (and the Lantau one may be dropped soon), just as one does not know when and in what form political or legislative contestation will fully return. It would be easy to dismiss all of this from the outset as mere words, a distraction from Real Freedom, impossible without 'universal suffrage,' as alarmingly statist, and so on. But people living in Hong Kong and making it their home nonetheless need to take all of this seriously, the dangers but also the possibilities and opportunities.

In what follows I do not attempt to provide a definitive and exhaustive account of the 2019 events or their aftermaths, a project which may well be impossible in any case. This book is not an introduction to 2019 or to Hong Kong. It presumes (hopefully not too much) a basic familiarity with those seven months and moreover with at least some of the histories and realities of colonial and post-colonial Hong Kong leading up to and beyond 1997 in particular. Readers interested in even more detail than I provide here about e.g. police violence and protester violence, foreign funding, and later arrests and security-law developments versus domestic funding, interviews with participants, and so on, can be directed to numerous sources online and off, including in English the *South China Morning Post*'s reports and *Rebel City: Hong Kong's Year of Water and Fire*. The latter tries to give an impartial, non-moralizing account of the movement, and while this is probably impossible, the mission is of value nonetheless. So are the more obviously partisan sources be they yellow or blue, as long as one realizes—despite the struggles over hegemony that seek to tell you otherwise—that there are two or more sides to the entire matter of 2019 and Hong Kong politics in general. And in the end, since the matter of autonomy (in its fullest senses) and a liberal-democratic political future has apparently been settled, it is good to think about the new present and the future; dialectical thinking East and West.

This book is structured by four longer-than-usual chapters The first, long chapter or part offers an account of the 2019 protest movement and what became of it. While I try to be fair and follow the actual time-line and sequences of the protests, I do not pretend to be objective, or 'blue" or "yellow." Let us call this a green book perhaps (combine your primary colors), but one that is concerned with the well-being and livelihood of Hong Kong and all its people, now and especially going forward into this new, uncharted territory. Those more sympathetic or cathected to the aims and methods of the anti-ELAB movement, or of the 'pan-democratic' movement in general, and those many more who think of China as George Orwell's Room 101 ('the worst thing in the world'), may well feel that because I am critical of the former then I am anti-Hong Kong and pro-Beijing. A more intelligent, less belligerent response might be that I nonetheless lean to one side. This is not wrong, as there can be no neutral or free space, and 'objectivity' in political or other deeply human or social matters is always partisanship. But what side am I on? Given my critique of the establishment and the status quo in Hong Kong, and my belief that integration is not only going to happen anyway but can be a good thing, my lean is not towards "Beijing" or say the "loyalist" parties in Hong Kong (e.g. the D.A.B. party) specifically but towards development and livelihood as Hong Kong travels down the road of being a full, hopefully functional, part of the P.R.C. It may be a very difficult path, and certainly has been the last several years, and it has never been a path freely chosen by 'the people.' But I see no good reason to wish Hong Kong to go backwards, or to fail on this new journey after 2019/2020.

After establishing my account and political analysis of the rise and transformation of the 2019 protests, the next chapter deals with the Basic Law and the intimately related problems of autonomy and place-based and localist identity. Both that 'mini-constitution' (in reality an inevitably compromised and expedient treaty more than anything else) and the question of an 'authentic' yet singular Hong Kong identity are more complex and variegated than they might first appear (especially as they appear in media and other discourse).

Thence on to a fuller discussion of the multi-faceted issue of de-colonization in e.g. political and economic as well as ideological/cultural realms. For too long post-colonial studies has elided the question of *economic* de-colonization, perhaps because of the typical academic's class fraction in itself and because so many of the national-liberations never actively pursued liberation from capitalism as a mode of production and development. So too the question of *political* de-colonization not only must take us beyond the mere change of sovereignty but should entail And finally as a Coda and conclusion to this post-mortem, a final chapter on the search for state capacity in Hong Kong, or rather the failures thereof as it sought (and seeks) to follow something like a zero-covid policy. If the future of Hong Kong now is as an increasingly integrated part of the mainland system, even as it will likely retain significant measures of autonomy and difference, then it will have to have a more functional and stronger state and mode of governance than its past reliance on the free market and essentially liberal economic ideology. Of course all of this presupposes the mainland likewise moving in the direction not only towards social control but to livelihood and common prosperity and re-distribution. We shall see.

CHAPTER 2

# In the Event: The Politics and Contexts of the 2019 Anti-ELAB Protests

The 2019 Hong Kong protests were the most broadcasted and live-streamed ones in history. This massive international media attention, combined with the size and scale of the protests (a virtual shut-down of the city) as well as with the direct direct action or collusion of several activists/participants (e.g. Joshua Wong and media tycoon Jimmy Lai) with Western politicians and interests, placed Hong Kong squarely on the map of the new Cold War between Euro-America and China, and hence at the centre of the global conjuncture. This is an outsized footprint even for Hong Kong, itself a "global city" with a large fan base due to its unique visuals (a *Bladerunner*-esque city of skyscrapers and extremely high density), its previous openness to tourists and travellers and even refugees, and its colonial heritage as—for many—the "free" and "cool" and "modern" part of the mainland and the 'greater Chinese' world.[1] The symbolic power attached to Hong Kong, directly stemming from its place within British imperialism and global finance capital, cannot be over-estimated. It is not that Hong Kong is somehow "guilty" of this by virtue of having been tainted by colonialism and by pursuing a generic capitalist modernity. But it is to say that the politics of discourse or knowledge-power are always in play, that these include the problems of orientalism, Eurocentrism, and other forms of liberal universalist pretension, and that

© The Author(s), under exclusive license to Springer Nature    9
Singapore Pte Ltd. 2022
D. F. Vukovich, *After Autonomy: A Post-Mortem for Hong Kong's first Handover, 1997–2019*,
https://doi.org/10.1007/978-981-19-4983-8_2

there needs to be a place for critical scholarship that works against the grain of both media and mainstream academic discourse.

Precisely because of—not despite—such factors of media and 'punditry,' the events and "facts" of the 2019 event are poorly understood, or rather systematically mis-understood. Predictably enough, interpretations of the 2019 event (or of the now-defeated Hong Kong 'democracy' movement in general) are rarely acknowledged *as* interpretations constructed out of facts that are themselves highly selective and always already interpreted. The xenophobia and irrealism of politically impossible demands, for example, are simply ignored or mentioned as very minor, unimportant issues. One can say all of these things about the reification of the 2019 movement (or the one of 2014) and not actually be an apologist for the mainland's handling of the SAR. One will of course get construed just so anyway. But much of our analysis in what follows will also focus on such failings stemming from north of the Lo Wu border, and not least from the Party-state's own Basic Law framework.

Instead with 2019 what we are presented with is the Truth and Reality of, for example, mainland Chinese intrusion into its own territory, the erosion of already-existing freedom, the breaking of promises for free elections and, in short, the smashing of a previously existing, more-or-less full autonomy. In sum, as soon as the first wave of mass protests against the proposed extradition bill happened in June 2019, the one Truth was of a freedom struggle against an undefined tyranny, due to the theft of unnamed freedoms, and because the enemy or out-group was precisely China. It was instantly framed as a heroic and monumental struggle against far more than any proposed and looming extradition law with the mainland. From a standpoint critical of the media, as opposed to those who would merely reproduce its discourse, 2019 was about the imposition of obviousnesses as obviousnesses.

This is especially true of virtually all major English and Hong Kong Chinese news outlets and publications at the time, and up through 2021 when the explicitly pro-2019 protest media began to voluntarily shut down or be shut down by the government authorities. I will leave to one side here the mainland and mainland-identified Hong Kong Chinese outlets, which just as unsurprisingly, condemned the events from the beginning as unpatriotic or 'trouble-making', albeit at times with a noteworthy focus on the deplorable economic and housing conditions within Hong Kong.[2] Here the equally predictable narrative of foreign, regime-change forces and violent, destructive protesters commanded the headlines. As with the case with the many and increasing signs of Hong Kong-mainland integration, from immigration, tourism, and normal business to the arrest of Hong Kong based booksellers for selling and distributing books on the mainland, or to an obvious good like the high speed rail link connecting Hong Kong to the mainland, there is always a rational kernel of something real and empirical beneath the headlines. The imperialistic, foreign-derived aspects of the protests and their descent into violent confrontations and property damage are impossible to deny, as is the larger discontent—and political as well as economic stagnation—within Hong Kong society, including in regard to the mainland-SAR relationship. As we will note later, there certainly was a substantial amount of foreign funding and interference or "help" during and before the 2019 movement; all of which makes the criticism of the protests as imperialistic or foreign have a certain and undeniable if often over-stated purchase on the reality of the situation.

So too it would be impossible to deny that the eventual crushing of the protest movement, especially after the suddenly imposed national security law of June 2020, marked the end of Hong Kong's 'high degree of autonomy' from the mainland in political and legal terms. The aftermath of 2019's event—which must be distinguished from the actual situation on the ground prior to, say, July 2019—does indeed mark the rolling back of certain freedoms in the legislature, of the press or free speech, and of what can be done if and when street protests are allowed again. While only a handful of those successfully prosecuted since 2019 have been convicted under national security laws specifically (and far more from colonial-era laws about rioting and the like), these convictions of course also illustrate the utter political defeat of the pan-democratic movement. And in that sense also the defeat of a certain political autonomy to run clearly anti-mainland-regime campaigns. While the Hong Kong system has been radically changed, albeit in still-emerging ways, as a result of 2019 there is no doubt that the entire mess dates back to the Basic Law itself and its fundamental tensions between being one country yet two systems on the one hand, and the inevitable disruptions and chaos subtending capitalist expansion and integration. While the Basic Law will continue to live on in name, it too has reached its historical end at least in so far as it was interpreted within Hong Kong itself by many. But this particular loss will likely be an eventual gain for Hong Kong, or for its development and, one hopes, livelihood and well being. (We return to this later.)

But our point right now is a simple two-fold one: first, that as compared to the global/English media and 'expert' commentary, few people outside of the mainland (and many within it) take the official media at face value. This includes of course the "Sinophone" or diasporic audience for the most part, particularly those groups whom are a generation or two removed from the mainland. The Chinese diaspora in the United States for example, is historically and famously anti-P.R.C. and anti-communist, or in other words at the level of geo-politics it is aligned powerfully with their actual home government and not that of China. In any case it is clearly the global/English and allegedly "authentic" Hong Kong media that carry far more weight academically and otherwise. For this reason the present study will interrogate some of this discourse and offer in passing an alternate account of the movement itself in 2019 and before. Note too that at the level of discourse and representation, two camps emerged simultaneously with the protests, having already been scripted ahead of time. Let us call these the pro- and anti- ELAB movement, but with the important proviso that the "pro" side was only ever signified (in comparative silence) by the government (and thence later displaced onto the police force in lieu of the government that was in effect hiding) and by "Beijing" (which mostly spoke publicly and obliquely through their own official media). The point is that while there was always by definition two sides, only one counted within the major media.

Again, this is why the "heroic" side of Freedom, Inc. calls out for interrogation far more than the rather obvious and often ham-handed responses from the so-called propaganda press of the mainland or from the Hong Kong government (as if, for example, Reuters and the *New York Times* were less biased on Chinese politics than e.g. *People's Daily*).

To say that the two camps appeared immediately in the mediatized universe, well before the turn to petrol bombs and urban chaos, and were moreover scripted- in-advance by discourses of orientalism, nationalism, and liberalism, is also to gesture, importantly, to the limits we all have in knowing what was going through the minds of various Hong Kong based participants at the time. Even if we agree that the size of the largest protests was grossly exaggerated (being much closer to half a million, say, rather than two million) this is not only still a massive turnout but a considerable slice of humanity and human minds that we have no actual access to. This is worth noting for many reasons, perhaps chief among them that the movement as a whole transformed from something normal and even typical for Hong Kong (with its long-standing and active, post-handover civil society or protest sphere) to a violent and confrontational, riotous and nihilistic clash between protesters and police, and sometimes between protesters and other citizens. The point is that within people's heads it may have been possible, for example, to be against the extradition bill but nonetheless still "for" integration with the mainland in other ways (not least of all economically), or conversely it may have been possible to be fully "for" the right to protest but against the violent and anarchic turn the movement took. The latter would correspond to the present author indeed. But here the point is that when we come to analyse the movement it is not what is secretly or silently going on in people's heads that matters, but what the over-arching discourse and other structures were in play, how the allegedly (or initially) leaderless movement was quickly captured by the usual suspects, from the aforementioned Wong and Lai to long-standing pan-democratic activists and groups like the "Civil Human Rights Front," and so on. (Leaderless movements are never leaderless for long, just as they can offer no exit strategy or viable winning tactics.)

Another reason to begin by noting the absent presence, so to speak, of the range of views and implicit beliefs and feelings of 'the people' in this case is precisely that it might offer some grounds of hope for Hong Kong's future. For many it seems that not only the "democratic movement" is dead but that Hong Kong is, in the aftermath (the national securitization) of the riots and the movement's courting of Western imperialism to intervene. This 'death' is genuinely tragic for many people, but it may help us to recall that while in the end the movement—perhaps even the longer movement since 1997—definitely followed a particular line to ruin, we cannot actually say that all participants consented or assented to all of the movement's demands and behaviours. Perhaps in due course the movement will be seen to have made its own, fairly massive mistakes and failures and should be read as a negative, if tragic lesson of how not to get what you want.

Given the power of political orientalism, or in other words, the ruling intellectual and political discourse about Hong Kong, China, history, and politics that asserts Western liberalism and electoral democracy as universal, absolute goods that the other lacks, this "pro" versus "anti" ELAB protest dyad was and is immediately mapped onto several other oppositions. These include pro- vs anti- democracy (a term never defined aside from 'suffrage'), pro independence (or full autonomy) versus some unnamed capitulation to despotism or self-censorship, yellow ('authentic' Hong Kong) versus blue (pro-police or pro-government/Beijing aka inauthentic). Perhaps most simply, the coding of the protests immediately turned upon a predictable but intellectually specious opposition about "freedom versus authoritarianism," "individuals versus the state", and so on. Or perhaps most tellingly, an opposition between a true "Hong Kong identity" versus a "mainland Chinese identity." All of which will express a certain, undeniable logic of the political or visceral friend/enemy dyad in Hong Kong and global politics (and where China or communism or 'the state' are of course the hated one). The split in Hong Kong is real indeed, and on one level what the events of 2019 and beyond have shown definitively—for those who can be bothered to look closely enough—is that there are now, and always has been, two sides: those aligned or identified with the idea of a liberal/free/democratic aka Western or 'global' Hong Kong, on the one hand, and on the other, far less British hand, those who were always happy with at least the idea of reunification with mainland China and who accepted a certain political, and not just cultural, Chineseness. Those in the latter camp are usually referred to as "the establishment," and not without good reason (even if the liberal democratic camp has long hegemonized the educational and cultural fields); but it also traditionally includes the Hong Kong working class and trade unions as well as many non- or a-political demographics. (It is worth recalling that in Hong Kong, not unlike other places, most people simply do not vote at all and have zero perceptible interest in politics.)

But what the mere fact of the two sides' existence shows us is also that the above binary oppositions, ultimately turning on a simplistic Good versus Evil dualism, are also deeply tendentious and misleading. After all, few in either camp would understand themselves as cruel, authoritarian freedom-haters or as benighted, selfish and imperialistic nihilists. They may get represented and understood as being in X or Y camp, and this has real material or institutional effects, but again we must recall that this is not necessarily the same thing as how people see themselves, just as it leaves out those who do not fit into either camp.

The debate or rather the non-debate and split between the pro- and anti- government/ELAB 'camps' simply cannot be overcome and resolved merely by setting the record straight in some objective way where the facts, images, and videos speak for themselves. As a deeply political and deeply ideological and affect-laden event that spoke to a real societal and interest- or power-based antagonism in Hong Kong as well as to colonial legacies and current geo-political competition between the US-West and China, the 2019 events are irresolvable except by political—and therefore *state*—means. The only way forward would be through some such (political) solution; if not a compromise between the government and anti- government or 'democratic' groups—an option now rendered moot by the legislative and legal changes in Hong Kong in 2020—then by a complete victory for the so-called Hong Kong establishment. This last is, as of 2021, apparently in the works as a result of the 2020 National Security Law and further subsequent legislation and prosecutions. That law, it must be said, is itself a direct result of the violence of the 2019 protests and perhaps especially of the wilful, conscious actions by some Hong Kong activists to court the U.S. government to intervene in Hong Kong on their behalf, against the sovereign state of China.

But if the 2019 movement resulted in the incineration of the very idea of a fully autonomous and 'free' and 'democratic' Hong Kong, then perhaps the crucial question for now is not what will come next in the new Hong Kong, which is too inchoate to know right now. Perhaps the more appropriate line of inquiry right now is to examine how and why the 2019–2020 movement or events took the form they did. What are the connections to Hong Kong's recent and colonial pasts, and the state of liberal and democratic and other politics and ideologies today? What can we learn or better understand now, in the aftermath of these months and of the end of the pan-democratic and localist movement, at least in the forms they have taken since the late 1980s? These and related ones are the questions that this book aims to unflinchingly explore.

We must first begin with a basic account of the 2019 and 2020 events, to help orient what follows in later chapters. As will become quickly clear, this is not an account that glorifies the protests and protesters. But it also does not simply condemn them, and nor does it defend the government's handling of the protests, nor even the sanctity of the Basic Law or mini-constitution co-created by the Party-state to the North and by British Hong Kong and Hong Kongers. Indeed one inescapable conclusion from any analysis of Hong Kong since the handover leading up to the present (and as might have been predicted beforehand if one can think dialectically with Marx about the social dynamics of capitalism) is that the Basic Law, premised in some ways upon de-politization and simply ignoring the effects and legacies of colonialism, is or was the major obstacle to Hong Kong's progress.

16    D. F. VUKOVICH

What this brief account of the events will do instead is to try and point to some of the deeper and more substantial issues that exceed a simplistic freedom versus authoritarianism narrative.

## From the Umbrella to the Fishball 'Revolutions'

The 2019 protests are typically narrated as naturally following from the Occupy Central With Peace and Love movement or what quickly became known as the Umbrella Revolution of 2014. The present author and many others have written at length about the 2014 movement, which at the time and in its immediate aftermath seemed like both a genuine failure as a 'revolution' or as a directly political, demand-based movement but also, nonetheless, as a very significant and substantial social or 'cultural' moment in post-handover Hong Kong's short political history. Its symbolic and social-imaginary or poetic dimensions are best left to others, or to those who believe that these constitute 'real' politics to begin with. Perhaps the key point to make here is simply and importantly that the movement was non-violent and of a piece with classical civil disobedience protests, including the willing, peaceable arrests of those who remained on site in December 2014, when the protests had dwindled to small groups. For this reason the 2014 movement, or at least its principled practice, should be respected by even the most establishmentarian of citizens in Hong Kong and China.

We can call this a failure because it did not 'win' direct civic nomination and one-person, one-vote elections for the Chief Executive (Hong Kong's version of a city mayor), something which in fact is forbidden by the Basic Law's stipulation of a vetting committee for all C.E. candidates. Indeed many of the more seasoned activists and observers likely knew this from the beginning, i.e. that Beijing was not going to give in to the demands to have some type of Western, liberal democratic system in Hong Kong, and not least this would be tantamount to allowing the election of anti-communist Party politicians within one of its most significant cities. What this means, in turn, is that the demand for not only 'universal suffrage' but direct nomination of any city Chief Executive candidate (perhaps outside of any vetting or Party primary system at all) was political theatre, a performative and rhetorical demand. A compelling and seductive demand-as-gesture that might well be part of a powerful, effective political movement but—and here is the rub—in the case of Hong Kong one without an actual political demand or goal that could possibly be realized. If we define politics as being an ideological but practical, material struggle or contentious process over interests and desires and demands that must necessarily be addressed to and ameliorated by the state or government, then it is clear that Occupy/Umbrella was far less political than is ordinarily assumed. It is or was even arguably a depoliticized form of 'politics' that ultimately was far more performative than political.

We may refer to 2014 as a failure, too, not just in itself but for the city as a whole in that the other result, or non-result of the movement was the rejection in June 2015, six months after the end of the Fall 2014 protests, of an admittedly modest and partial electoral reform package proposed by Beijing. That plan was to offer a one-person one-vote election between two pre-selected CE candidates from the Hong Kong establishment. This was first proposed by the mainland in August 2014, weeks before the 2014 movement started, and was itself an obvious No to the pan-democratic and localist demand for direct nomination of the C.E. To be sure the plan would have precluded any pan-democrat or other anti-Beijing candidate from consideration (or if you prefer the phraseology, any pro- full autonomy candidate). But it would nonetheless have resulted in an actual C.E. election of one winning candidate, who would have had to at least distinguish himself or herself from a rival candidate on policy, value, or other presumably political grounds.

This was not to be, as the city legislature at the time was in control of the pan-democrats who unanimously rejected the plan, in the hope of scuttling the government and Chief Executive (C.Y. Leung), and in effect demonstrating the illegitimacy and general dysfunction of the city government. This type of strategy was to later prove fateful indeed when it was tried again after the 2019 protests and riots, in an explicit attempt by law professor and Occupy 2014 leader Benny Tai (among others) to run an unofficial (and debatably illegal) primary before the scheduled 2020 elections. This was to measure and ensure a pan-democratic victory based on who emerged as favourite candidates. Leaving aside the putatively "illegal" nature of this poll, the real offense and aim was indicated by Tai himself, in a published April 2020 column entitled "Ten steps to laam chau [burn with us]." Here the primary's goal was not simply election but the formation of a bloc to bring down the government through filibusters of the budget and all other business, through thereby forcing the C.E. to resign, and through calling for and securing international sanctions against Hong Kong and Beijing.[3] Once the national security law was passed a month later, and then the primary held after that, the stage was set for the arrests not only of Tai but of 50 other activists and candidates. While the filibustering mode (indeed entire basis) of pan democratic politics was well established for over a decade, it was this connection to international and arguably imperialist interference as well as to 2019's burnism that sealed their fates after the June security law.

However it is not the 'failures' of Occupy 2014 and pan-democratism that are typically narrated in relation to 2019 and beyond but the *government's* failure, including Beijing's failure, to grant direct nomination and elections of the CE, and perhaps to grant full autonomy in general. This failure, in turn, led to the rise of localism and the desperate actions, including violence, and the courting of President Trump and the US Congress to politically intervene in Hong Kong, that resulted in 2019. Such an analysis, which will be familiar to most Hong Kong or China watchers, places responsibility not on the violent or saboteur-like activists but on the government. This may or may not be ethically defensible and persuasive. But what it elides is that under the Basic Law the government could not simply 'give in' and institute direct nomination or full autonomy even if it wanted to. Such revisions to that mini-constitution— such as scuttling the CE vetting procedure—would have to go through Beijing.

In sum, then, both supporters and sceptics of Occupy 2014 would have good reason to see Occupy as something of a failure, or at least radically ineffective, even as they differ radically on the causes and responsibilities. Clearly the tactic of occupying the streets (which was somewhat disruptive to traffic and the like to be sure, but very weak tea compared to what would come in 2019) and demanding the impossible seems to have resulted in little to no change, politically and practically speaking. The legislature was still highly dysfunctional and ineffective, not despite but because of Pan-democratic hegemony there. It had never been a dynamic government and legislature, in part because there is no tradition of social democracy and institution-building even on the "left" in Hong Kong (the democrats generally speaking), let alone by the laissez-faire establishment. Recall that Hong Kong's economic ideology and minimalist state has long made it the fetish of neo-liberals and libertarians such as Milton Friedman and the Hoover and American Enterprise Institutes. But in the years after Occupy, not just the proposed popular run-off election of two selected candidates but most other legislation was brought to a virtual standstill. In 2014 the Legco passed only 8 bills, and by 2016 was back up to only

29. What is more, even these fairly non controversial bills were delayed by countless hours of filibustering, as this has been the single strategy of the democratic opposition.[4] From 1997 onwards, the city has been stagnating in terms of improving people's livelihood and simply from benefitting from being part of China and its booming economy. That is has not done so is the fault of many, starting with the so-called establishment. But clearly the filibustering has benefitted no one, and Hong Kong like anywhere else needs development and governance, not their absence.

All the same, Occupy was still a principled non-violent movement overall, and if not directly political (as argued above) it still registered both popular discontent within a large demographic and sent a message to a government that might well have ignored the impossible demands in favour of addressing livelihood.

But from the standpoint of 2019 and beyond, Occupy itself seems very distant indeed, and not just because of the National Security Law and the now greatly increased powers of the government to battle 'terrorism' and subversion. There is no good reason why 2019, with its riots and extreme xenophobic elements and fascistic, nihilistic affect and energy (as if they took it upon themselves to burn down the city in order to save it) should be connected with 2014 except by way of moral and sociological contrast. But there is plenty of connection with the Mongkok Fishball Revolution of 2016 and the emergence not of localism and Hong Kong identity but of an ardent nativism and a particularly strident xenophobia that, were it not for the shared Chinese ethnicity, would be a very clear instance of a racist backlash or superiority complex.

What began as a conflict between hawkers and hygiene officers who were trying to restrict unlicensed and illegal food stalls at a lively night market quickly escalated on February 8 and 9, 2016 into a violent protest and riot, replete with arson, vandalism, and explicitly xenophobic, anti-mainland and nativist sentiments. These two were the qualities not of Occupy but of the later 2019 protests, or what they all too quickly became by midsummer. Such stalls often appeared around the city during the lunar new year in the evenings, and until recent years (circa 2014) were usually tolerated by the authorities. Efforts to shut them down had failed for two years before, as the hawkers would simply close up shop and return the next evening. In the context of popular discontent with the government, and with newfound anger towards the police (due to the use of tear gas during Occupy and the eventual removal of the final occupied spaces) this year's lunar ritual was to prove different. What had happened in the interim was the rise of a strident nativism or Hong Kong nationalism, this time in the form of one group among others that called itself the "Hong Kong Indigenous," a post-1990s, younger generation of some former Occupy protesters and other activists. As part of its nationalist bent, the group was explicitly for the independence of Hong Kong. This was—as we have argued elsewhere—a small but significant step from the misleading but traditional pan-democratic notion of full, not just a "high degree" of political and social autonomy for Hong Kong to begin with. Since the end of the 2014 protests, Hong Kong saw the rise of younger, localist, and/or nativist politicians and activists who are vociferously anti-mainland and for this full autonomy, if not independence explicitly. While this new generation of activists quickly derailed itself or later 'burned' themselves down during 2019 (e.g. Joshua Wong and the former 'Demosisto' youth group), the days after Occupy there was some hope, even amongst those of us who are not anti-mainland integration, that the new generation of activists and politicians, should they prove able to adjust to Chinese sovereignty, might help lead Hong Kong forward and help the older pan-democratic generation of liberals exit the stage gracefully. Such was not to be the case, however, as the pull of nationalism/nativism and anti-communist or political orientalism were to prove too strong, and the tide of history too fast.

Anti-mainland views also pre-dated Occupy of course, as in the infamous "locust" rhetoric and images published in various media (e.g. in the now defunct *Apple Daily* 'pro-democracy' tabloid) and directed against mainland immigrants giving birth in local public hospitals. Other objects of nativist or anti-immigrant desire, and protest, have been mainland tourism generally, new Hong Kongers living in Shenzhen but bussing their kids into schools in Hong Kong, and so-called "smugglers" aka parallel traders who cross the border to buy goods in Hong Kong and re-sell them back across the line. To take two technically non-violent but exemplary instances from the summer of 2019, during the July turn to fire and bricks and police attacks there was still time enough for two such protests against "mainlanders." As Martin Purbrick notes in his remarkably well detailed account of 2019:

> On Saturday 6 July, a protest took place in Tuen Mun, New Territories, against "dancing aunties", middle-aged mainland Chinese women [who

may well be actual Hong Kong citizens] who dance in public parks, illustrating deep anti-mainland feeling amongst Hong Kong people. On Saturday 13 July, a protest in Sheung Shui, New Territories, against cross border "parallel-trading," which was impacting on local residents, led to violent clashes with Police.[5]

After 2014, the Legislature saw a handful of new elected officials from the Occupy movement and/or from the localist/nativist surge; some of these were, in turn, disqualified from keeping their seats because they refused to take their Oaths or otherwise mocked and insulted Beijing and the government during their swearing in. (One highlight was the use of an anti-Chinese slur from the Japanese imperialist war.) In any case within a year or two of Occupy it already seemed that Hong Kong politics had tuned a page. Away from the traditional pan -democrats— as anti-Communist Party as they were and are—and towards a more localist, autonomist or even independence ideology that pulled even fewer punches in antagonizing Beijing and expressing their hatred of mainland immigration and influence on Hong Kong. One can also—a la mainstream English media and even China Studies—frame this not as hatred of immigrants and of the Communist Party and of the mainland generally but simply as love of freedom and the desire for democracy (both terms forever remaining undefined). But even if we were to take such rhetoric as real, sincere rhetoric, and a wise appreciation of the superiority of liberal capitalist democracy, this would still leave the xenophobia and chauvinism firmly in place, as the elephant in the room. At the very least we must insist that both aspects exist, and are allowed to co-exist because the elephant must not be named and shamed. Or at least, it could not adequately be until the aftermath of 2019. At any rate the rise of nativism and xenophobia, a sense of desperation or frustration over Occupy's failures, combined with anger at the government and police, are the contexts of 2016, and of Hong Kong through 2019 and 2020. Such a brief description is far from exhaustive but must be born firmly in mind as one tries to make sense out of 2019.

After the hygiene officials closed the Mongkok stalls, then, the Hong Kong Indigenous group issued calls online to go there and 'defend' the hawkers and moreover to confront the police. Earlier a local district councilor had been arrested for working in one of the illegal stalls after the food-and-hygiene officers ordered it to close. There were no crowd estimates but most reports indicated a few hundred or more. What was striking about the protests was precisely their violence and arson, which had not been seen in decades in Hong Kong, and only rarely before then during the entire British occupation (particularly in Hong Kong's brief cultural revolution episode). In a clear foreshadowing of 2019, the protesters quickly clashed with the police, arguably even starting the violence, including by throwing rocks and by acts of arson. The police initially took the brunt of their attacks, also for the first time historically. Of the 130 people hospitalized, 90 were police.[6] In fact with the 'Fishball revolution' the government had not only a crisis with the protests but another with police morale, again in a foreshadowing of what was to come in a far greater magnitude three years later. There was strong discontent amongst the frontline police (many of them simple traffic officers), who felt that their superiors left them under-manned and under-prepared for the confrontations, and they were moreover under initial orders *not* to in turn confront or physically stop the violent protesters/rioters. They were, initially, placed in a defensive position of having to absorb the rocks and violence without responding in kind (and without, for example, helmets).

Hong Kong police ordinances, like those elsewhere, are detailed and seek to specify when police can and cannot use force in the name of public order and security. As Hong Kong has rarely had violent or severe disruptions to public order or security, these ordinances were largely mothballed until 2014 (with the use of tear gas) and especially 2019. Likewise the type and amount of protective armor and tactical weaponry of the police have been more normal and 'tame' than the heavily militarized and lethal equipment of, e.g., the United States in particular. As a result of 2019 (and not Mongkok), anti-riot gear and tactical equipment have all been upgraded in the city (albeit not carried by regular police). But the police ordinances have remained the same since 2019, and they have not noticeably changed since the handover. As the "Policy on police use of force in public order events in selected places" indicates, the ordinances for use of force follow UN recommendations and are comparable to UK guidelines (they are not drawn up to mirror the mainland system).[7] The ordinances, in sum, stipulate great control and selective use of force by the police, and only when absolutely necessary. Of course the proof is in the pudding, but in this case of 2019 and an increasingly violent and brick and petrol-bomb throwing sector of the protesters, it must be said that the police did not use force or 'attack' protesters pre-emptively until they were themselves first physically confronted. The protesters clearly knew, or thought that they knew, that the police would not attack them back due to the ordinances. Their actions may also be due to the absence of any such previous police violence in their knowledge of Hong Kong, or due to the many promises made on social media and chat groups that lawyers would be provided from donors and dedicated funds, that the charges would not be serious, and so on.[8]

Throwing petrol bombs or rocks from a distance—emerging from the cover of large crowds of 'normal' protesters and dozens or hundreds of 'citizen reporters' or 'citizen paramedics' grouped behind a police line or barricade—and then running off was not only strategically wise, so to speak, but had a certain 'legal' rationale. Put another way, Hong Kong's police ordinances made the force into something like a 'free' target, and prevented them from aggressively going after protesters and dispersing them until they were themselves palpably attacked, or until the projectile throwers stopped and ran away. What was no doubt seen by many observers as either great restraint on the part of police or great bravery on the part of confrontational, even violent protesters, actually comes down to local police ordinances and a certain tactical 'culture' of violent protest. This was not in other words about the police being afraid or buffaloed by the teeming masses, nor about the 'radical' protesters with petrol bombs and bricks being heroically brave martyrs driven only by Freedom. Everything has its roots, after all. After June 2020 and the national security law, it remains to be seen if or how such ordinances restricting the use of force to restore public order or security will change. Again, one can consult the official documentation and watch the tape, so to speak, and draw one's own conclusions about who did what first and to whom during 2019. The point here is that one must contextualize not moralize.

Reading the ordinances and observing the restrained approach of the police in the city during the 2016 riots and 2019 months of greater chaos and violence (again, in comparison to, say, the French forces during the "Yellow jacket" protests of the same time), helps one understand why the sudden charge of extreme police brutality during 2019 was so jarring.[9] Jarring to protesters and some other Hong Kongers whom had never seen any police-violence before in the city (even the use of tear gas in 2014 was controversial to many), and jarring to those of us whom have seen all too much, and far worse, lethal violence in for example the United States. In seven months of protests—some of them clearly riotous and violent or 'radical'—three protesters were shot by Hong Kong police, and all survived.

This essentially urban guerilla style of hit-and-run warfare (sometimes at different sites or times of day in the city) and the petrol/brick bombing of police to keep them at arms length (the fire bombs rarely got close enough to hit police, but bricks sometimes did), might be seen to resonate with Maoism or some simulation of 'people's war' from a long gone era. As if this middle-class movement in Hong Kong were the equivalent to the streets and alleys of the Casbah in colonial Algiers.[10] This would however leave out the actual politics of the movement (and of Maoism). In an arguably self-orientalist—or, if you wish, *inspired*—moment of image-marketing, this was instead articulated to the name of Bruce Lee, the diminutive but legendary Chinese/Hong Kong- American movie star of martial arts flicks. It was said to be Lee's command for us to "be water"—aka fluid and formless and existing in great volume/numbers yet potentially powerful—in life and in fighting. (These lines actually hail from scriptwriter Stirling Silliphant, uttered by Lee on the television show *Longstreet*.)[11] Whatever the merits or demerits of Lee/Silliphant as intellectual or tactical genius, the argument here is that all of this has more to do with the nitty gritty, technical details of legal police ordinances, fairly meticulously observed, and financial support and/or misinformation from civil society support groups, including barristers.

Such 'be water' street tactics, should they re-appear some day, now have new stakes with the national security law. With that on the books, the police now have more legal grounds from which to take the offensive and disperse crowds and potentially arrest suspects, such as those shouting for Hong Kong independence or liberation or waving such a banner. (Note that crowd dispersal is a separate issue from the use of violent let alone lethal force.) It was precisely the main slogan of 2019—光復香港, 時代革命—usually translated as "Liberate Hong Kong, revolution of our time" that was coined in 2016 by Edward Leung, the leader of nativist political group, *Hong Kong Indigenous*. The other possible translation is "*Reclaim* Hong Kong, revolution of our time," which has interesting shades of meaning in regard to the colonial or even pre-colonial past, a la anti-colonial movements in South Asia and elsewhere that sought in part to restore a certain primordial yet national greatness before the depredations of modern colonialism. 'Reclaim' then could signify a fantasy and nostalgia for the British colonial era when things were good or better, paradoxically enough for an independence group, or could signify a certain 're-colonization' of Hong Kong by Beijing: as if 'native' or 'indigenous' Hong Kongers—whatever these might be—were once free in or by nature and natural law. Or perhaps just in the late 1970s and early 1980s.

But in any case, whatever literal or figurative sense we make of it, the separatist or independence stance of the group, as well as others at the time like the now equally defunct *Youngspiration* and *Civic Passion* parties, is undeniable, as are their various anti-immigration and anti-integration positions. After the end of this 'independence struggle' in Mongkok—it was never really about the hawkers or the doughy fishballs—was not successful, Leung was eventually jailed for rioting and observed the 2019 events via prison. His slogan however took on a second, far greater life during the anti-extradition/anti-government protests where it was a common chant. It is now specifically banned in the city.

## FROM A CITY-STATE TO A SAR ON FIRE: THE 2019 ANTI-ELAB AND ITS AFTERMATH

The extradition law proposed by C.E. Lam was vociferously opposed by pan-democrats from its inception, but the government in turn refused to drop it and instead proposed further tweaks to the bill, which—perhaps ironically—even included new language that would conceivably help prevent white-collar criminals (or corrupt officials) from being easily extradited. The mainland had long wanted such a bill, and there had also been little progress since 1997 within Hong Kong in passing some type of national security law. (In fact the bill had never been allowed to come to a vote, partly through filibustering but also through government or establishment party ineptitude.) Hong Kong, part of China yet ambiguously so thanks to the Basic Law, lacked an extradition with its own sovereign country as well as other countries, including Taiwan. One such murder case by a young Hong Kong male (Chan Tong-kai) who fled to Taiwan was the specific case cited by Lam for needing the law. However rational such a law would be, it was immediately objected to by politicians, activists, and lawyers within the opposition camp and who were also, in effect, for the full political and legal autonomy of Hong Kong from China. Rightfully wary of the Chinese legal system in terms of its handling of dissidents or anti-regime critics, these specific groups as well as many others in the city whom were paying attention (Hong Kong being famously apathetic to politics for some of it population) opposed the bill. There was a large street-level protest at the end of April 2019, a typical Legco meeting (aka a debacle) around the bill on May 14, and then the first of many rallies and marches on June 9 and June 16.

While almost certainly nowhere near as large as the organizers themselves claimed (the faintly ridiculous number of 2 million to be repeated verbatim by mainstream media), they were nonetheless very large and significant even by Hong Kong annual march standards. This is an important point because it has implications for how we might understand or interrogate the rest of the movement that was to follow. How fateful was the de facto decision, or rather the lack of a decision/deliberation for the movement to go forward and escalate into violence and 'revolution.' The march organizers (the Civil Human Rights Front, founded in 2002) claimed two million protesters for June 16 and one million for July 1, whereas Reuters news agency, drawing on the work of professional, academic researchers into such estimates, has suggested 227,000 for the July 1 march. June 16, in some ways the high water mark for the protests before they were transformed by violence, by policing, and by their capture by both outright reactionaries and pan-democratic, traditional leaders, was still the largest of them all. But here estimates even amongst the sympathetic 'experts' (e.g. the pollsters) were 500,000 or more, but far closer to the police's estimate of 338 k.[12] Even the latter reveals a rather clear if not definitive answer as to whether or not the government should have scrapped the bill.

While it may seem odd to treat the math as crucial, I would suggest that the numbers matter a great deal. If nearly half of the able-bodied adults and youth of Hong Kong were in the streets against the bill (as 2 million would suggest) then the rest of what followed, from the impossible demands for the government to dissolve itself as well as the Basic Law, to even the 'just' use of violence and arson and smashing of public transportation, *might* be said to have some type of 'democratic' justification or popular mandate. If the biggest march was 300–500 thousand this would seem less apparent, at least to the present author. And in any case we should not assume that every person on the street held the same ideas about anything other than the bill being a bad, objectionable development. So too none of this should over-ride the dark sides of the uprising or its fatal 'burnism' strategies.

But by the end of June, specifically by June 17, the extradition bill was dead in the water, even if C.E. Lam would not formally withdraw it until October. She had announced it was 'suspended' the day before the second large march, and also apologized for how she handled the bill on the day after it. But in a gesture that was too prove characteristic and costly, she refused to formally bin it and thereby give the protesters some face and tangible recognition. Complicating the matter, the movement—as an ad hoc formation without organization or leaders—had no exit strategy to begin with, and not by its end either. But formally, officially withdrawing the bill might have helped one to appear.

Still there would be no way the bill could pass now, even if it were ever tabled again, when it had already been more or less shot down in Legco. In short, this would have been not only a major success for those against the bill (and oddly good for actual criminals), but an extraordinary demonstration and reproduction of the power of civil society. The mainland had always insisted that Hong Kong must pass its own laws— even those it badly wanted itself, like the national security law, the 2014 electoral reform proposal, and presumably this extradition bill. This after all was their commitment to 'one country, two systems' and the process of integration over five decades; Hong Kong people ruling Hong Kong is actually *their own* moral high ground even if, while literally true, this was unconvincing to many Hong Kong people in a political system which has or had very little legitimacy or 'buy-in' because for many non-elderly generations it was another country's system.

Seeing Lam fail with this specific bill, as with earlier city leaders failing to get anything passed a filibustered Legco, is something the mainland *could* have accepted in the face of such massive discontent. (Whether it *should* have done so is a different matter.) Such, alas, was not to be the case. The movement itself, perhaps due to it lacking a clear and accountable leader or set of leaders (it was fairly quickly co-opted by traditional pan-democratic groups like the Civil Human Rights Front, and localist youth leaders like Joshua Wong and 'Demosisto')[13] and appearing to be 'spontaneous' and 'authentic' and 'leaderless' also failed to claim victory and live to fight another day against what was, even in 2019 with a slow and weak governmental and police response, a far greater and more organized power. What was to come was a massive escalation replete with police and protester violence (though mild in comparison to the contemporaneous 'yellow jacket' protests in France) and at best a politically ambiguous, sometimes nastily xenophobic radicalization. There was ugliness and bad thinking on all sides, resulting in a genuine tragedy in the sense that both major sides of Hong Kong (the establishment and the opposition, let alone the rioters and 'valiant' aka violent 'radicals') were and are culpable for it.[14] (We will return later to the foreign funding and imperialistic aspects of the movement.) It is also something that has not killed Hong Kong and the Basic Law—their deaths are greatly, if frequently exaggerated—but certainly begun to transform them forevermore.

What were some of these darker sides that I have alluded to? I would not include a peaceful, hand-holding, human chain protest (of perhaps 30 miles length and going up the famous Lion Rock hill in the northern New Territories) in late August.[15] This was modeled on the 1989 protests against the Soviet Union in Estonia, Latvia, and Lithuania, and while obviously a deliberate affront and signification of Cold War anti-communism to the mainland, and therefore arguably unwise if the aim is to persuade anyone in the mainland government or committed to it, the chain also signified a certain moral high ground and even peaceful message compared to the chaos of the previous two months. Coming in late summer however it was also the exception that proved the rule of the violent and full-frontal confrontation with the police, and by extension with the very existence or sovereignty of the Beijing and Hong Kong governments in toto. We might even exempt the large marches of early-mid June as well, as these were, during the daytime or initially at any rate, mostly free of violence or strong clashes with the police. On June 9 there was a large march that, while resulting in some clashes with police (eight were injured but no protesters were), ended with only 19 arrests out of a crowd of well over one hundred thousand; this stemmed from some activists refusing to leave after the peaceful march and insisting on staying nearby the LegCo building in the city center. Clearly most of the protesters, en masse and marching earlier, were not violent and had not suddenly become quasi-fascistic 'radicals' who wished to destroy not only the police but Hong Kong itself. However the latter forces were in the end to effectively co-opt and control the movement as well as its narrative within the government, the establishment, and Beijing (as opposed to the opposite narrative in the liberal and foreign media for the most part).

The large marches on the 12th and 16th escalated more quickly and earlier in the day. On the 12th afternoon, hoping to disrupt the LegCo meeting over the bill, activists attacked the police cordon and blocked roads, by throwing eater bottles and bricks. The police responded with tear gas and, for the first time in Hong Kong's history, with rubber bullets. The police commissioner referred to the clash as a riot, a la the Mongkok event of 2016 (and which would therefore potentially carry a

## 2 IN THE EVENT: THE POLITICS AND CONTEXTS ...  29

major jail sentence, not just a misdemeanor). There were 11 arrests, 82 injured protesters, and 22 injured police.

The 16th proved less violent while also being the largest. The march contained hundreds of thousands of protesters over six hours. The pan-democratic officials called for Lam to formally withdraw the bill and not just suspend it. Demands emerged as well for Lam to resign, for the 19 people arrested to be freed, and for the "official" designation of June 12 as a "riot" to be revoked. Again, aside from the bill being potentially withdrawn (very much in Lam's power to do) these demands were largely performance or theatre, as is often the case with protest politics. This is not a flaw of social movements but a feature. But just as rhetoric is never mere rhetoric, this does not mean all messages will get the answer they want or that it is smart politics to ask for what you can never realistically have. The 16th must be counted as a huge success from the protesters' standpoint. It was after that that Lam apologized publicly in addition to suspending the bill. The police themselves seem to have been under orders to adopt a low key strategy during the 16th and early hours of the 17th, just days after the violent clashes on the 12th.[16] The small groups of protesters occupying nearby streets (nearby LegCo) were allowed to remain. All seemed well, relatively speaking. Even as wildly inflated as the organizers' figure of two million is, had the 16th proved to be the model or logic of the anti-ELAB and anti-government movement, Hong Kong may have remained largely the same (and without the extradition bill).

But it was the logic and practice of the 12th that proved more decisive and became, in effect, and with or without the conscious leadership of anyone in particular, the movement's basic strategy. In the ensuing months, and leaving aside the many other events and actions such as campus occupations and traffic and transport shutdowns, the logic remained the same: after the large, mostly peaceful rally the more militant and more clearly anti-government factions (aka the 'black shirts' organized online) would take cover and physically confront the police and commit various acts of violence, most notably throwing petrol bombs (in the thousands), bricks, setting fire to or destroying businesses and public transport stations, blocking roads, and so on. This was to prove a pattern over the course of the next several months and was hardly anomalous each and every time: a large rally is organized and is held, usually by the Civil Human Rights Front (CHRF), whose leader at the time, Mr. Figo Chan, is now held in jail pending trial for organizing several marches which turned violent. Without fail, each march ended with a contingent of the marchers breaking off and throwing bricks and petrol bombs, tearing down police barricades or crossing police lines, and so on.

It is not the case that the CHRF (and its many NGOs and other member-groups, e.g. the Civic Party and so on) was the mastermind of the protests or the main author of their derailment (which in any case they would not see as having derailed but as having been beaten down by Beijing and Lam). The various acts of violence, such as the infamous setting on fire of an elderly mainland Chinese immigrant, or the death of another pedestrian by a brick thrower, are far more numerous than the acts at the end of large organized marches, which like the CHRF itself can be seen as a traditional pan-democratic 'thing.' But they happily embraced the violence, refusing to denounce it and moreover refusing to call off the marches even while knowing the 'black shirts' and violent contingent would be fully present in them, getting cover from the larger crowds. In a rather questionable 'revolutionary' mentality and practical ethics—given the decidedly non-Marxist or liberal-Occidentalist ideology of the movement—the CHRF, like the older pan-democrats and the localist/xenophobic youth leaders all refused to voice even the mildest criticism of the movement, or to criticize the violence or xenophobia or anti-communist (anti-CCP) rhetoric of the same 'radicals.'

So too they would remain largely silent on the later solicitation of the US Government to intervene into Hong Kong against China. Whatever moral high ground they might have occupied before and after June 16, it was—for some observers, including those not in the anti-mainland camp already—abdicated for occupying the streets. Thus on the annual July 1 rally, the large march went off peacefully but by afternoon escalated—or devolved—into the storming of the LegCo building at last (recall that the disruption of the meetings was an initial, and properly political, objective of the protesters). Over a year later, when an unruly mob stormed the Capitol Hill buildings in the United States after then President Trump's electoral defeat (some of them with Hong Kong flags, *a la* the US flag appearing in various 2019 protests in Hong Kong), the Chinese media would have a field day recalling the American and global celebrations of the protesters on July 1 and afterwards. The offices were empty but a group of masked protesters stormed the building, smashing through glass doors, and entering and vandalizing the interior, smashing screens, tearing down the Hong Kong and China flags, and so on. However the protesters were also allowed to leave, and the total arrests were only 12, with 54 and 13 injured protesters and police respectively.

This event not only shows a return to the violence itself (by which we primarily mean to injured people not property) and—in effect—the movement's choice of strategy. While the affront to the Chinese and HK flags and the seat of government may have shocked some, and was a rather deliberate, political gesture, it seems to have emboldened the protesters even further, and to move from what were at least political, governmental targets to anything and anyone not deemed to be on their side, from airport passengers to public universities to Mandarin speakers to perceived undercover police to public infrastructure to private 'blue' or non-yellow businesses. From July 1, the violence and clashes would escalate, as well as the deliberate goading of the Beijing government not just through flag-burning and the usual anti-China graffiti and messaging but—far more fatefully, even tragically—through courting its super-power rival the USA to save Hong Kong. Following the "success" of 'occupying' Legco, the clear and explicit ethic or logic of the movement emerged on its own terms, or rather Hollywood's: as Joshua Wong (and older activist Alex Chow) put it to Lam and Beijing in the protesters' second great ally newspaper, the *New York Times*: "if we burn you burn with us." This slogan from the adolescent *The Hunger Games* movies came to be known as 'burnism' ('laam chau,' 攬炒), and tried to give an ethical foundation to the escalation of the movement to bring down the government by literally and figuratively burning down the city they claimed to be saving.

Likewise this analogy to a movie tried to give such a foundation to the anti-self-criticism, 'movement discipline,' and likewise said nothing about the truth-content of what they were saying and trying to do. So too for the silence and complicity of those who, while not committing violence or xenophobic hate-speech or attacking "blue" people were nonetheless silent about such behaviour or anti-immigrant, nativistic ideology; such partisans should also take responsibility for what followed. Had Hong Kong really lost freedom (whatever this means) and if so who? Certainly the five booksellers whom were arrested for publishing tabloidesque tell-all books about Chinese leaders and their alleged sexual and other immoralities. Whom else? How? And was it via Beijing or some not-so-secret proxies in the city, and are these secret agents or 'underground Communists' (as they are imagined in the city sometimes) or simply Hong Kong people with sharp differences in political and other views and values?). Other than the usual depredations of capitalism in the city—a city long-constituted by two of the worst forms of capital indeed, i.e. finance and property—the common refrain that the 2019–2020 protest were about "freedom" vs "tyranny" or neo-colonial "encroachment" only makes sense if you believed that Hong Kong was and is supposed to be fully autonomous from the mainland, and was in terms of "freedom" somehow better under British control.

The 'burnism' desire and fantasy—coming on top of the original one about\Beijing stealing "freedom"—worked powerfully not only on the youth and others involved on the ground, but also on the long-distance nationalists of the Hong Kong diaspora and other foreign admirers of the movement, like Verso author and UCLA sociologist Ching Kwan Lee, who suggested that not just Hong Kong but the whole world would burn if Beijing was not stopped.[17] For others on the ground or at the end of screens it may have seemed like live-action-role-playing (aka LARPing), a real-life simulation of the recent Joker movie, or for the more internationalist, anti-imperialist set, as something akin to the infamous logic from one fire-setting American Vietnam-war soldier who infamously claimed, 'we have to burn down the village in order to save it.' In fact such a nihilistic, atavistic, ultimately narcissistic or selfish desire to 'exterminate the brutes' is an old story that predates the movies. One can see the logic in other expressions of nationalism, of modern colonialism (c.f. Joseph Conrad's *Heart of Darkness*), of fascism, and more generally and perhaps most aptly in what Freud tried to explain as the occasional failures of civilization to repress and transform the worst of human instincts.[18] Thus it is not the slogan or even the anti-communist 'liberal' anti-communist ideology at stake—the former is merely marketing PR and not a thought-out strategy with a plausible, let alone realizable goal, and the latter is simply part of Hong Kong culture. As many have noted, while Hong Kong is certainly a Chinese city with its own, pre-Communist or pre-P.R.C. culture, it is also deeply informed, ideologically and politically and economically, by 'classic' British liberalism, with its emphasis on laissez-faire economics and libertarian, individualist sentiments and beliefs in natural rights and so on. Or put another way, there is no pure or authentic Hong Kong culture that is separate from its colonial past and its antagonistic relationship to the mainland. This hardly calls for moralizing in one direction or another but it does mean that Hong Kong cannot be immune from the same historical and worldly forces that have formed and malformed politics and ideology and social movements over the course of the last and current century.

What is at stake with 'laam chau'—essentially nihilistic, anarchistic rioting with street-level violence—is the easily-foreseen self-destructive effects on the city (and the individuals eventually arrested) and the realization that the government and mainland China would both eventually strike back in some way. *Burning down the city in order to save it, mutual destruction, is not simply nihilistic but an assault on the public and the political as such.* Instead of politics as war by other means, one is simply left with war, with a painfully obvious winner lined up in advance. It is also a rather telling way to express one's love for the city or one's home; perhaps that love isn't as pure as alleged. What is fascinating about the burnism phenomenon, however, is not just its self-destructive and authoritarian logic but that it seemingly produced—in a dialectical reversal—exactly what the so-called radicals and nativists of the movement said they feared the most: the full-on incorporation of the city within the mainland, the loss of the city's autonomy, its fate to become 'just another Chinese city,' the paranoiac, bad Orwellian vision of Hong Kong under China as seen is the anthology-film *Ten Years* (十年). But we can say 'seemingly' here because not all of the SAR's autonomy is lost (clearly some was however), and for other reasons that will be discussed later.

But if burnism was indeed a fantasy in thinking that it would ever succeed in bringing down the P.R.C. or 'saving' the city, it was also something put into practice. Public transportation (mass transit rail) was badly damaged and shut down; streets and pedestrian spaces were destroyed, albeit temporarily; private businesses (deemed to be "blue" aka not sympathetic to the protests) were set on fire or smashed; two public universities were vandalized during 'occupations,' and one (Polytechnical University) was massively damaged in what was arguably, aside from the killing of the 70 year old street cleaner (who was taking photos of some of the protesters as he worked) and the near-death by burning of another man, the ugliest weeks of the movement. The two-week long siege of the university in November 2019 involved over 1400 canister of teargas, 1300 rubber bullets, hundreds of other soft rounds, over 4000 petrol bombs (600 tied to propane canisters and therefore potentially deadlier), countless bricks, some arrows shot by bows, over 14 kg of explosive chemicals, and eventually 100 arrests.[19] The occupation, most of it not by students but other residents, was preceded by the protesters shutting down the important cross-harbour tunnel connecting Hong Kong Island to Kowloon. The siege of Polytechnical University was precipitated by the occupation of the Chinese University of Hong Kong to the north, which likewise began as a road and traffic disruption, this time by protesters throwing bricks and obstacles onto the nearby train/transit tracks. More

34 D. F. VUKOVICH

violence ensued when other, counter-protesters arrived to try and clear the roads and tracks and were met by bricks from the anti-government people. When police cleared the campus scene, much to the chagrin of students who assembled to decry their alleged 'invasion' of the publicly funded campus (as are PolyU and the other major universities of Hong Kong), some of the CUHK protesters moved south to PolyU. (During this month other universities also had brief occupations and were cleared by police, but the scale was much smaller than these two.)

The two campus occupations were the high watermark of the "black shirt" or "radical" or "be water" wing of the movement, which is to say of the post-July 1 transformation of the movement into a violent or otherwise 'radical" or extremely anti-government, nihilistic anti-regime movement, its descent into full-on confrontation with an enemy in the Schmittian sense. The 'burnism' was now to be called the "blossom everywhere" strategy whereby the 'radicals' attempt to distract and disperse the police force by creating chaos and destruction around the city, trying to exhaust the policing capacity in general. (Again such actions often immediately followed from 'peaceful' or non-violent marches or protest gatherings.) Thus fires and bricks and petrol bomb throwing on campuses is matched by street blockades, property-smashing, and fires elsewhere across town: the point was to literally attack the police (as opposed to government buildings, it must be said) in hit-and-run confrontations as well as to distract them through other actions, all while occupying the universities and having this all live-streamed and boosted by local 'volunteer' or 'citizen' media as well as by the usual foreign media outlets eager to speak with the protesters.

All of this certainly worked to exhaust and even demoralize the police, whom themselves frequently warned that the city was on the verge of collapse. On its own terms the blossoming and flowing may be said to have succeeded. It was certainly not business as usual in a city dedicated to business, and to spending as much time as possible outside of cramped flats. The police and related institutions (emergency rooms, courts, firefighters, and the like) were certainly exhausted and stretched very thin over the summer and through November. University campuses were largely closed down for the last two months of their terms, or moved online. Many international and mainland students fled the city. The airport industry was disrupted briefly and even witnessed the beating of one mainland reporter. While foreign, sympathetic observers of Hong Kong tend to downplay the xenophobia and anti-mainland sentiment in the city, it was rather obvious to the mainland people targeted as such. The attacks on 'yellow' businesses (which could range from the public MTR to small shops) were pulled off "successfully," and certainly not only were roads and transportation systems disrupted but it prevented or at least delayed millions of people from going to work.

But of course all of this costs money, public money at that, and also represented one movement's own will-to-power and desire to 'burn' or destroy the city, i.e. bring it to the final crisis and either achieve "suffrage" or go down in flames. Even leaving aside what is 'democratic' about this aside from the call for elections, and leaving aside the intolerance of others' views (as represented by the elderly street cleaner and counter-protester), the very idea of the public would seem to go out the window here, or rather get damaged as much as the public transport system did. How are we to evaluate and judge this movement and its blossoming/burning guerrilla violence and anarchy? If one is anti-violence on principle, e.g. a pacifist or religious, civil disobedience thinker like Mohandas K. Ghandi or Martin Luther King, the answer should be clear enough. It should always be morally and analytically difficult to justify violence, especially in a non-war scenario. But there has also long been political-ethical justifications of it in the name of some higher principle or calling, be it anti-colonialism or anti-slavery or communist movements against massive inequalities and injustices.

The classic work on this question of justifiable political violence, aside from older sources like Franz Fanon and Georges Sorel (writing in very different contexts to that of Hong Kong in 2019), is that of political philosopher Ted Honderich, who has argued forcefully and in scholarly fashion for many years that political violence can be morally just (as in the case of Palestine or Apartheid South Africa).[20] But while a qualified justification for political violence is certainly possible to make, in an ends justify the means fashion (connected for Honderich to eliminating distress and inequality), it is hard to see how this would apply to the case for 2019. The ends were unclear and unstated at best, or simply impossible and irrealist (amnesty even for violent offenders and in in effect overturning the Basic Law), and moreover were never generated and promulgated by consensus within the movement (despite the 'five demands' becoming a slogan by the end) or aimed at social and economic equality. (This is not meant to be damning or dismissive so much as honestly descriptive.)

One must also factor in the specific goals and exit strategy of the movement or the lack thereof, as well as their desirability, and whether they were achieved or could be. In other words, violence must be seriously justified or it must be condemned. This is precisely what did not happen, for example, when one Hong Kong activist (and American citizen) was interviewed by the major international outlet, *Duetche Welle* about the increasing violence of the protests: only the government can be blamed, no splitting, no admission of remorse or regret.[21] And while one would not look to the streets on fire for such a rationalization and justification, it is nonetheless stunning that the broader pan-democratic movement or its intellectual pundits in the media were so silent on the issue. At least some of the protesters/rioters were crystal clear in their affirmations of their own violence, pointing to it as self-defence (and not the original provocations or attacks they were).

Obviously in this case, in comparison to the 2014 or 2016 events, the 2019 movement was a much greater failure, even a catastrophic one, for both the nativists and pan-democratic causes, or indeed for any of its stated goals beyond the mere withdrawal of the bill (which again was more or less secured by June, and certainly by October when it was officially withdrawn by the C.E. Lam). What is more, the movement in effect ushered in a far harsher, more strict and encompassing National Security Law than what was originally proposed by the extradition bill. Subsequent changes have been far reaching, seeing the dissolution of the LegCo for the time being, the end or evisceration of most of the pan-democratic parties as well as the localist ones, the outright banning of independence-rhetoric in the city or the "liberate Hong Kong" slogan, and equally large changes to the city's mediascape (e.g. the popular tabloid Apple Daily) and various politically oppositional NGOs and groups.

## POLICING THE CRISIS?

But at least two other crucial areas of the movement—again what I have called the dark sides or highly questionable values, beliefs and tactics—must be discussed here: the question of imperialism and the foreign funding of the movements, and its larger transformation, from July onwards, into a confrontation between "the people" (as represented by the movement of course) and not the government or Lam specifically but the police. Let us deal with the latter first. By virtually any international comparison (e.g. from the mainland or USA or Europe/U.K.) the police violence in Hong Kong was of a much smaller scale than even, say, the Yellow Vests riots happening in France around the same time.

## 2 IN THE EVENT: THE POLITICS AND CONTEXTS ... 37

As with the Fishball event in Mongkok, the police were both deliberately restrained and even unprepared or outmanned for much of the summer and fall. Hong Kong police have traditionally been held in high esteem locally; and in the absence of much violent or major crime compared to other cities and territories, had even operated more like a social service branch than a 'hard' and violent police force. This had begun to change with the use of tear gas in 2014 and then in the *eventual* striking back by force in 2016 (c.f. above). (We leave to one side here the cultural revolution era riots and colonial era in general.)

*In many ways, Hong Kong's protests-turned-riots telescoped years if not decades of change into a handful of hot and sweaty and tear-gassed, petrol-burning months.* Once the mainland decided, apparently in November 2019 during the NPCC conference, to do something not militarily but legislatively and politically, and then instituting the national Security law the following June 2020, we can say that protests kick-started the full-on process of the city's integration into the mainland. Whatever Lam's mistakes in responding to the protests or in trying to get the extradition bill passed (hardly controversial in itself unless you are in the full-autonomy camp) there is no doubt that that ill-fated bit of legislation likewise sped up Hong Kong's integration, which is to say its future. Policing is a case in point for this telescope effect, in that by the end of the riots the police force in Hong Kong was becoming militarized in many respects, especially in using force (i.e. violence albeit without live ammo) and proper anti-riot police and gear and tactics. Gone are the days of a police force that is akin to a social service organization with an entirely unsullied (and idealized) reputation and that has no major crowd control or street-violence to deal with. Here are the days where the Hong Kong police force, and with it the courts beforehand, can and will act authoritatively to supress violence or 'sedition' or 'terrorism.' Is this a good thing or a bad thing? History will judge, aka those victors who get to write that history.

There is certainly a case to be made—not just for something repressive and authoritarian—but for all of this helping make the city and even China safer and more 'normal' compared to other advanced, developed cities and countries. Few would deny the rise of bomb threats and genuine 'terrorism' possibilities in the city during and after 2019, even if the charge of terrorism can and has been used and abused by governments and legal systems the world over. More generally, the transformation of the city by the national security law codifies reality, namely the reality that the PRC has sovereignty over Hong Kong but also that full-on anti-governmental confrontations with the state conducted in a manner meant to destroy it, are simply not feasible or desirable, even for a small state like Hong Kong's laissez faire government and the heretofore *distant* authority and arm's length 'repressive state apparatus' possessed by the PRC. Whatever form opposition and protest take in the future of Hong Kong—as elsewhere—it will have to work around this cold and unforgiving, brute reality.

How did the protests so quickly become a contest between the 'radicals' (with their silent supporters) and the police? There should be no denying that *much of the violence from the police was directly instigated by the rioters or radicals attacking them with bricks and petrol bombs*. Even the one police shooting during the movement—widely circulated on video—seems a clear case of self-defence or standard police protocol (which is what it was ruled to be at the time). In early November 2019 a group of protesters in Sai Wan Ho district gathered to block a road and challenge police there. A lone traffic policeman was "approached" by one protester wielding a pipe, in turn drew his gun and thence began grappling with the protester; at this point another young male, Mr. Chow Pak-kwan, attempted to grab the police's gun and help his 'comrade.' The officer shot Chow in the chest. This was a momentous event across the city. Fortunately Chow survived, albeit without part of his liver and kidneys. Now one can condemn or glorify the protester's or police's actions, but the violence was clearly started by the protesters.

Of course this specific instigation and the clear pattern of it in general amongst the "radicals" is rarely acknowledged in media and expert commentaries, which take the protesters' cue and speak only of the extreme police violence in Hong Kong, the desperation of the protesters against tyranny, and so on. But the use of non-lethal force throughout the movement must be acknowledged. The protesters' and citizenry's outrage at the use of—by American standards—mild police violence must also be noted. The point is neither to praise nor to morally condemn either group but to show the Hong Kong scene in its complexity. Hong Kong was, and remains, a safe and 'civilized' big city.

It must also be said that the police did at times use violence indiscriminately, i.e. not just against the direct bomb throwers and the like (who would hit-and-run) but also on other protesters "innocently" standing by but catchable and therefore beatable. It is easy to see how an exhausted and angry and frustrated and overwhelmed police force, only some of whom are trained in crowd/riot control, but all of whom, as noted above, ordinarily have to wait until being directly attacked or approached, would react indiscriminately and violently in some, even in many cases. Again this is not to justify the excessive or unfair use of violence. One can easily find video examples of police continuing to hit protesters even after they have been subdued and held down. We must also note the infamous Yuen Long train station incident, which took place in the north end of the city during another major protest (and tear gas scene) back on Hong Kong island. In harrowing video footage later circulated widely, protesters returning home (and having changed out of black clothes) were beaten by a gang of stick and metal-rod wielding white-shirted thugs from the Yuen Long district who knew at least some protesters would be passing through. They beat others as well, indiscriminately. The police arrived only after thirty minutes of the attack, and worse yet there were photos of police vans sitting idly by while the white-shirts assembled beforehand. This harmed the police's reputation during 2019 tremendously, and no doubt added fuel to the brick and petrol-throwing fires.

The nature of the "blossoming" or "hit and run" strategy also added fuel to the fire, alongside the heretofore unprecedented (and therefore, to the protesters and their supporters, outrageous) use of police violence. As was frequently noted at the time, at some of the hotspots protesters would change clothes quickly, removing their black shirts (and gear) for normal clothing, and/or quickly donning one of the ubiquitous yellow reflective vests worn by the hundreds and thousands of "citizen journalists" and "citizen emergency helpers" and easily purchased at stalls across the city or online or distributed amongst the protesters themselves. In fact the violence against the police and then their retaliation point to the anti-extradition quickly becoming more akin to war and the mutual embrace of "collateral damage" or of a Hobbesian 'state of nature' than to a civil society protest. The eventual focus of the movement—and of the media— on the police was not a positive development from any perspective. That specific institution simply cannot provide a political solution. While the police are of course an arm of the state or government, it must also be said that attacking them and obsessing over them comes at the expense of struggling against the chief executive (the office) and legislative branches for that matter. i.e. of the directly political parts of the state. Surely, even on the protesters' own terms, the government—i.e. the executive and legislature powers—should have been the main focus, including appealing directly to the liaison office or "Beijing."

In a way, the focus on the police and their alleged brutality was not only a battle they could not win (as if the chief executive would just dissolve the forces, or the forces would quit) but a sign of the political naivete and nihilism of the movement, and its deformation into a series of acts of aggression. Of course it also took on a very traditional, "democratic" rhetoric of Hong Kong civil society past: the "five demands, not one less" talk, liberal use of the words "suffrage" and "democracy" and so on, crossed with a great deal of anti-communist and xenophobic rhetoric about invasion, take-over, encroachment and so on. Also as with the past, self-proclaimed leaders or spokespersons of the movement, were you to ask them, would be sure to claim that they all knew full well that they would never get these grand demands beyond the withdrawal of the bill.[22] As noted many times, it is not even in the power of the C.E. to change the Basic Law and any of the fundamental governance structures. But they would nonetheless demand the impossible and stick to their ideals/demands, perhaps in the utopian hope that someday it might become true, that the mainland system would whither away or implode (or fall by mutual destruction aka burnism), and so on. This utopianism or irrealism is also part of what constitutes Hong Kong colonial culture, unfortunately exacerbated by the Basic Law's fifty year 'grace period' itself: the idea of living on borrowed time, putting everything off until the future and so on. But apart from what the politics of such gestures are, beyond signalling one's own virtue or faith, remains a question that goes begging. And the virtue signalling and role-playing opportunities (the arm-chair, tweeting revolutionary 'sharing' the Truth) are no doubt part of what made the movement so popular to foreign watchers.

Why indeed would a political movement insist on 'demanding the impossible' not during one summer, say, but for well over two decades? The old, dated slogans from May 1968 in France—"Be realistic, demand the impossible!," and "Underneath the paving stones, the beach!"—have gotten lots of play in cultural studies circles, and they are certainly poetic, but they also make for terrible political thinking. Such utopianism or playful energy may be fun and inspiring for awhile but at some point, movement's need achievable goals and exit strategies and a struggle not only for state power but for political structures and institutions. Fantasies such as total liberation into a brave new world can be wonderful, but only in so far as you suspend critical thinking and the power of negation.

But to return to Hong Kong and not the mythical May'68: if the movement was not really, or not primarily about "democracy" and "freedom"—*or rather about these primarily as signifiers*—and there was virtually zero chance of "Beijing" falling and thereby somehow freeing Hong Kong, one must ask what else it was about. What were "we" trying to free Hong Kong *into*? If everything means something else, so do "suffrage" and "democracy" and "freedom." This, in turn, in the specific context of Hong Kong, leads directly to questions of colonialism and its aftermath, including the mega-problems of political orientalism, liberalism, and identity politics. These will form the subject of the rest of this book.

## Colour Revolution and Quasi-Imperialism: Media and Money

As a segue to that larger discussion, we must finally acknowledge the decisive, even fatal dark side of the 2019 protests, namely the direct and "successful" solicitation of, or indeed collusion with the United States government and other powers in an attempt to 'save' or "protect" Hong Kong by intervening in it's own and China's affairs. These efforts resulted in the "Hong Kong Freedom and Democracy Act" and various sanctions (for indefinable 'human rights violations') on Hong Kong officials, as well as a certain embarrassment or angering of the mainland by protesters blatantly waving American flags and pictures and slogans of President Trump, appealing for help at the US Consulate office in the city, and so on. The Act also requires an annual review of whether or not to grant Hong Kong its usual, favourable trade relations with the United States or instead—and rather ironically—treat as just another city in the mainland (which used to be the localists greatest fear). While the genuinely pro-Trump supporters in Hong Kong (and they existed in China as well as other unlikely places) were never a majority within the movement, the active solicitation of US Congressmen and women, for example, for their help and assistance in somehow "fixing" or influencing the two governments, was conducted by several leaders within the larger democratic movement, such as Joshua Wong and Jimmy Lai. The general tactic of pleading for, even inciting the West and/or anti-China forces and feelings to 'save' the movement and Hong Kong—which is what the movement's attempted mediatization of itself amounts to—must also be accounted for as an ill-fated decision to use (cultural) imperialism in an allegedly progressive way.

The appeal to the US and other foreign governments to intervene in the city against Beijing, something unimaginable in any space under Chinese sovereignty, was obviously sincere, if also desperate and remarkably unwise, even for eminent personages schooled in American civic/political ideology. These global, virtually live-streamed media appeals and these direct solicitations (e.g., meeting American Congress and White House officials people in Washington, DC) were not sideline matters of the 'real' movement or tangential to some demand for Freedom and Suffrage and an unconscious 'desire to participate' but were instead the main show in realist and real-politik terms. Hence the live-streaming, the cameras, the fake media vests, and so on. The direct appeal to international media—American and English media—to support the protesters' anti-government movement, even as some of them act violently or nastily towards other citizens, was the real action of the movement, aside from, again, the nihilistic burnism strategy.

It was an attempt to *mediatize* the 'democracy' movement within Hong Kong, deploying the 'fifth estate' in an effort to secure its autonomy or freedom-from the specific bill but moreover from the mainland in general and the process of Hong Kong's (inevitable) integration.[23] Hence the thousands of yellow-vested cameras and broadcasters, who often outnumbered not only the police but the non-vested, black-clad protesters. For awhile it may have seemed this would work. Beijing sat back and did nothing while it itself waited for Lam, and then the police, to quiet down the movement and bring it under control. This may or may not have been to Beijing's specific credit, and can be read as negligence or as peacefully upholding the Basic Law and Hong Kong's autonomy. (This was to change in June 2020 with the National Security Law and all the subsequent arrests and new legislation making it impossible for the pan-democratic and nativist camps to continue in their same forms.) This attempt to employ the media, print, online, social and virtually all media to win the hearts and minds of the "whole world" raises new, complex questions as to what constitutes imperialism today, i.e. imperialistic practice. If the case of Hong Kong activists directly enlisting the United States government and others into their cause is a clear case of an attempted, if ultimately feeble 'regime change' operation familiar to critics of 'velvet revolutions' and 'humanitarian interventions' then it is hard to avoid seeing the mediatic appeals differently. This is all not only a miscalculation of one's potential benefactors being capable of helping (let alone being altruistic) but a misrecognition of what all such forceful, uninvited interventions by one (usually Western) country into another have historically amounted to: a political if not also economic imperialism or quasi-imperialism. And moreover a disaster for the majority of the 'native' people involved, regardless of where they might fall on the political spectrum.

The point is not that borders and patriotism and nationalism are intrinsically important or part of something called 'human nature' (they are not). The point is that in a world of competitive nation-sates based upon a global, capitalist system of sovereignty and nationalistic, imagined communities, when other powers—be they states or foreign NGOs—intervene and attempt to change other countries, regimes, or peoples, only harm is done. (This applies as well to China invading Vietnam in 1979 as it does to American imperialism world-wide, not to mention the modern French and British empires themselves.) This used to be common sense on the post-war, post-colonial, and pre-World Bank era of developmentalism (one can easily recall the Bandung Conference, global Maoism, and so on here). That it is not common sense today, speaks to the eclipse of such progressivism and the rise of a powerful neo-liberalism and 'human rights imperialism' that eventually triumphed after the Cold War. Thus even if one wishes to ascribe naivete or a more innocent or perhaps tragic desperation to the Hong Kongers wishing to bring, say, the United States government squarely into Hong Kong politics or to simply win over global public opinion (which is already mostly hostile to the P.R.C.'s politics) in order to 'revolutionize' Hong Kong via social media, the end result is the same. Like the xenophobia and the violence in the movement, it must be noted and evaluated negatively, not dismissed as a side-show. As for borders specifically, Jon Solomon has recently argued at length over how the struggle in Hong Kong since the handover, and culminating in 2019, is important not because it illustrates the politics of Freedom against Authoritarianism but because it illustrates the pitfalls of what he calls "bordering practices."[24] By seeking to defend the Hong Kong border from the mainland invader, and yet simultaneously inviting American and other foreign power and money inside, the movement actually *proliferates* borders and thereby works in a reactionary, conservative fashion to keep everyone in their 'proper' places and enclosures.[25]

One does indeed have to attend to the money and explicit regime-change operations behind the 2019 event (starting years earlier), and that have since been uncovered and are still ongoing, well into 2021 and 2022. We do not need to dwell on this here as it has already been well documented and is publicly available information.[26] Even American governmental websites admit to 2 million USD being provided for Hong Kong via the notorious National Endowment for Democracy. Much of the arguably imperial or quasi-imperialist activities connected to the Hong Kong movement have been out in the open; this is a far cry from the infamous COINTELPRO operations within the USA itself (e.g. its various operations against the Black Civil Rights and anti-war movements) or from traditional, covert spy agencies (e.g. the CIA funding Tibetan resistance operations before and after 1949, including the Dalai Lama himself until the 1970s and the Sino-US detente). Thus there is no conspiracy here, and the funding and resources devoted to (non military) 'regime-change' operations in what has been termed hybrid-war is well known. Likewise there is no secret that the United States government not only sees itself as the leader and defender of the free world, but that it seeks to contain and constrain China even while it maintains a close, if ambivalent and co-dependent relationship with the Chinese economy. To take another important example, the "human rights" and "individual freedom" aka 'regime change' or 'velvet revolution' organization called the *Oslo Freedom Foundation* hosted several Hong Kong activists and opposition figures before Occupy in 2014 and up through and beyond 2019. It hosts instructional 'how to overthrow your regime' workshops in Norway, and is mostly funded and run by the New York-based non-profit *Human Rights Foundation* (financed in turn by an elite Venezuelan-Norwegian-American entrepreneur, Thor Halvorssen). Here we have a technically non-governmental organization, highly visible and occupying the moral high ground 'beyond' left or right wing states and ideologies. Such groups are untroubled by any sense of potential complicity in the global machinations of empire, East and West, or in acting in a way that they may think is heroically anti-tyranny and pro-freedom but that ends up doing harm (a la Graham Greene's *Quiet American* and countless colonial-era officials and global capitalists like George Soros).

According to Hong Kong writer Nury Vittachi, American groups like the "Oslo" one, the N.E.D., the Albert Einstein Institute, the Centre for Applied Nonviolent Action and Strategies, the Open Technology Fund, and the Agency for Global Media provided at least 4.99 million HKD to protesters in 2019, and the NED itself sent 170 million HKD to the mainland and/or Hong Kong in order to "advance the cause of democracy."[27] From within Hong Kong there was likewise no shortage of money to fund the protests. The "612 Humanitarian Fund" was established during the protests (by several high profile activists like Cantopop singer Denise Ho and Bishop Zen) for legal and other financial aid, and named after the first use of tear gas on June 12. It recently closed (having reportedly spent 243 million HKD on legal costs) due to its parent organization dissolving under pressure from the new security law. While the fund and the group's bank accounts are now being investigated, such monies may well have been virtually all from within Hong Kong. (In fact there were several such funds during the movement.) Opponents would argue that they were nonetheless caught up in the imperial game between China and the U.S., a la the protest leaders and the movement itself by late summer.

Finally, one cannot tell the story of the protests and indeed the democratic movement of the last decade or two without mentioning the role plaid by media tycoon, Catholic fundamentalist, devout Donald Trump and Republican Party booster, owner of the now defunct, madly xenophobic and anti-communist but adamantly "pro democracy" tabloid *Apple Daily*, Mr. Jimmy Lai Chee-ying. A former penniless immigrant now imprisoned and likely to face many more charges, Lai has funded the democracy movement for decades, often flirting with illegal, grey boundaries in his business empire and anti-regime activism, and also working in cahoots with a former U.S. Navy intelligence and Republican Party employee, Mark Simon. This is not to scapegoat Lai, who after all is just one individual, albeit a wealthy and powerful one. But it is to underscore the very obvious yet, outside of Hong Kong, mostly unknown links between Lai (as well as the larger movement) and American power and money, and the shared beliefs and rhetoric between the 'democratic' movement and imperialistic or colonial ideology in general vis a vis the mainland.

Lai was always an unabashed and vocal critic of all things Beijing (except of course its cheap labor when he was a textile tycoon), and for Hong Kong's de facto independence or full autonomy despite the obvious, intractable barriers to this. Tolerated for years in the free-market 'paradise' of Hong Kong, what seems to have finally tripped him up was not only violating laws against illegal assembly (in 2014 and 2019) but certain strictly financial dealings with his companies (e.g. zoning requirements of some of his offices) and now, after the security law, his direct involvement in collusion with foreign governments and powers. It is not surprising that his efforts became so brazen, as he had gone scot-free for decades despite his constant provocations of the local and Beijing governments. Had the 2019 movement not engendered that law by enlisting the US in particular and calling for global sanctions and 'anti-regime' laws—a movement he has had a huge role in building through his impressive propaganda efforts at *Apple Daily*—he, like all the pan-democratic stalwarts, may well have survived. But now Lai has recently been accused, via testimony of a noted Hong Kong independence activist (Andy Li of the "Stand With Hong Kong" group), of spending over 13 million HKD to lobby UK anti-China groups, to bring their leaders to the city during the protests, to pay for articles written in favour of the movement, to hire consultancy firms, and to organize rallies; all of this, to produce sanctions and suspend previous agreements between Hong Kong and the international community.[28]

This last goal of Lai (and others lobbying the USA and UK) was indeed the one concrete outcome of the movement, after stopping the extradition bill itself: the American law and sanctions noted above, and perhaps now also the extension of the British National Overseas visas for Hong Kongers who wish to leave the SAR. A pyrrhic victory indeed, at least from the 'democratic' perspective, as the real political resolution of the movement was precisely the new national security law and the ushering in of a new era for Hong Kong, what some have called the city's "death" but others call the second-return to the mainland. The 1997 'return' clearly failed to either win hearts and minds, or to de-colonize the former colonial enclave. In point of fact the new sanctions and laws and even the out-migration of B.N.O 'refugees' have and will affect the city itself very little. There is no shortage of talented and hard-working people, nor of money in the city. Cities and their inhabitants by definition are always changing, not dying or being reborn but shifting and transforming, as has Hong Kong since 1860.

Thus the regime-change effort or 'colour-revolution-of-our-time' failed spectacularly at its stated goals. But whatever we call 2019 and its resolution/transformation, surely it must tell us something about imperialism and the new Cold War today, assuming these are the right critical terms. To begin with, we must begin with the painfully obvious: that this was indeed a concerted attempt, funded in part by American and other foreign monies and people, to not only defeat one particular bill but to bring the Hong Kong *and* mainland Chinese governments to crisis, even to the point of 'mutually destroying' or 'burning' both. That bringing down Beijing via Hong Kong may seem even more absurd today than in

2019, and that the Hong Kong government itself was in retrospect never on the brink of collapse, does not make the imperialistic intention any less clear. It was certainly and understandably *understood* as a would-be colour revolution, precisely because of the violence, petrol bombs, and US lobbying and not only the protesters' "liberate Hong Kong" chant.

But what should be equally obvious, and is the far larger problem, is that the movement, warts and flags and Trumpism and all, as well as the deep passions and discontent of the protesters, was home-grown more than anything else. It was not instigated or created by any foreign power or agents but was decades in the making. Those decades certainly included N.E.D money and who knows what else before, but even tens of millions of self-righteous Hong Kong dollars cannot produce such a 'revolution.' Had there been zero American or otherwise illicit funding and "help" involved, the two or three decades of Hong Kong protests, and Hong Kong democratic opposition, would still have happened and still been strong. 2019 (and 2014 and other events) may well have looked different but Hong Kong was always going to be a difficult situation in relation to the mainland or mainland politics specifically. This has more to do with the contradictions of the Basic Law (of which more later), the colonial intellectual political culture and educational hegemony of the pan-democrats ("liberalism" in short), and the undeniable social and economic problems—housing, cost of living, and so on—that subtend the city's discontents. Certainly "Beijing"—even at a full arm's length from the actual government before 2019—must bear some responsibility for the rise of the movement and indeed for not doing more to benefit Hong Kong or learn from it. The general inattention to Hong Kong— aside from doing business of course—has been a bad choice, evident a decade before 2019. But of course it is the Hong Kong establishment in general that must be blamed: the series of ineffectual C.E.s, the lack of ideas and political skills amongst the "pro-Beijing" parties, and also the pan-democrats themselves. The cramped living conditions, the lack of a robust economy with decent jobs, the high costs of living and so on speak to a global condition under capitalism, surely, but also to a failing if not failed state within the city. With any luck, after 2019 failure will not be an option for the mainland.

In this sense, the 2019 movement was not imperialist if by that we mean it is something like a foreign plot or organized force to start and overthrow another country or regime, or 'merely' to trigger the local system to fall apart, a la the missionaries in Chinua Achebe's *Things Fall*

*Apart*. The foreign money and workshops and so on may well have had an important influence in producing and reproducing the movement's ideologies (human rights, anti-communism, liberal democracy/voting as a panacea) and providing talking points and other tactics. But it is important to note that Hong Kong is the author of its own history, its establishment and elite opposition (e.g. all those barristers and well-heeled democrats) mutually responsible for ruling the place, even if that place has been constrained by the post-colonial Basic Law itself. The anti-communism and general anti-mainland orientation also stem far more from the colonial background of Hong Kong, and the hegemony of a particular Hong Kong identity inculcated by the British and thence by myriad 'authentic' Hong Kong educators, intellectuals, media figures, celebrities, culture industries, and so on. We will attend to the colonial question in more detail in a later chapter. We restrict ourselves here to the imperialistic or regime-change aspects of the 2019 events.

It must also be said that the mainland refused to intervene until after the Hong Kong police and therefore the Hong Kong government—and again, we must note the transformation of the entire movement into de-politicizing confrontation between the police and the protesters—were able to restore order on their own. At no point was there any credible threat of tanks and troops entering the city from across the border or from their own barracks in the city (where they do serve/reside in limited numbers). What this means is that "Beijing" did not think Hong Kong was actually going to fall from petrol bombs or demonstrations, and that they had no need to role-play the *Hunger Games* or *Joker* movies. Of course they were fully aware of the lobbying efforts from Hong Kong to get the US involved. But they did not seem to have the same fear of imperialism or colour revolution that others did (or that others greatly desired). That they were annoyed and constantly provoked is also certain. But they waited until such time as they could intervene quickly and force-fully with the June 2020 security law and made amendments to the city's Basic Law/mini-constitution. Put another way here was no real colour-revolution or imperialist take-over because the P.R.C. is now far too strong and stable for such a thing to happen, and the US far too weak or unable. It is shocking that even the veteran, old time pan-democrats could not recognize this. But nihilism, like fascism, can be powerfully seductive. In this sense it must also be said that the analysis of 2019 as a genuine threat to Chinese sovereignty in general, not just a desire but a major,

## 2 IN THE EVENT: THE POLITICS AND CONTEXTS ...     49

concerted, feasible plan of the U.S. to break up China, stands as a major exaggeration.

In sum, then, where does the failure to burn, or mediatize, or have the US et al. 'save' Hong Kong leave the question of imperialism today? It would seem to be greatly weakened, especially in political terms. It is worth recalling here that this was the most live-streamed protest movement in history, and the well prepared and tele-visually genius and English-speaking protesters of Hong Kong have no peer elsewhere in the world. China was in a tense "trade-war" with the US at the time. The protesters, however we differentiate them, massively outnumbered the mostly unarmed police-force that was itself unprepared for such a major, city-wide, "flowing" guerrilla style event. And yet it failed. Does this mean that imperialism, to return to our subject, is a mostly irrelevant or useless term to understand the Hong Kong protests? Is this why even the avowedly left-wing China studies experts refuse the term—and indeed any difficult comparative or evaluative analysis—in relation to 2019 or to contemporary China in general? (Leaving aside of course conventional media and academic commentary which construes it in terms of mere political despotism or allegedly extreme mainland nationalism and so on.)

And yet even if we were to dismiss the category of imperialism as outmoded in today's world (though ironically, there is no shortage of media and academic talk about 'Chinese imperialism in Africa and Asia') there is not only the strong conviction among others that this *was* such a colour revolution, there are also the massive effects of this same attempt: new laws, emigration, even a rewriting of the Basic Law in its appendices. We can debate whether or not this was 'real' imperialism, or something more amorphous or simply weaker, or even a tragic farce, something which had no chance of working (a la the 'five demands' themselves) but which would certainly have consequences. But to dismiss the question would be not only to dismiss the obvious and concerted efforts at regime-change (via the N.E.D, the professional activists, etc.) it would also miss the very palpable effects: new laws, new jail sentences, new legislative systems, and thence a new Hong Kong. If imperialism is not an issue for the case of post-1997 Hong Kong (in 2019, and before and after) then why would China see it as so? And why would the 'democratic' anti-government activists try to summon it forth?

In short, after 2019 we can say that imperialism lives on in a subtler or amorphous sense, albeit not in this case as a credible threat to political sovereignty (at least not to China's or strong-enough states). If certainly

50   D. F. VUKOVICH

much weaker than in the age of colonialism and hot wars of invasion, it is always-already available at the level of discourse (e.g. in the guise of human rights and democracy -rhetoric nowadays), at the level of tactics (mediatization via the fifth estate and new technologies), and at the level of legal-yet-illicit monies from this or that Human Rights Foundation, this or that George Soros-like tycoon, and this bag or that other bag of cash from the N.E.D or the like. It is highly unlikely to work in the sense of direct regime-change, but it can certainly make trouble for the status quo as well as for other people and other institutions within a society who then become collateral damage. Alternatively, we can also say that if you want to overthrow your own domestic regime, this is your one option: which is exactly what organizations like the Oslo/Human Rights Foundation will tell you and coach you up on.

Another consequence of 2019 may well be that at least in the Hong Kong context a "democratic" or oppositional politics of sovereignty—liberate/reclaim Hong Kong!—may well turn quickly into its opposite: not something democratic and humane and all things good, but something rooted in an intense, dyadic, friend/enemy identity politics of recognition, as opposed to a politics of re-distribution.[29] One that ends up worse than that which it understands itself as attacking. One that is less about the stated goal of self-rule or sovereignty and "suffrage," and ultimately about identity politics and an obsession with autonomy, and the will-to-power. After all Hong Kongers are not an oppressed minority within their own city, or within the confines of the Chinese nation-state. Hong Kong has in some notable ways benefitted from its special relationship to the mainland, whereby it and not Shanghai is given a certain priority as a finance capital centre for foreign investment, and whereby Hong Kong, while part of China, pays no tax to the mainland (while admittedly getting little social benefit either).

Rather than seeing Hong Kongers in general, or the city itself, as some type of victim or subaltern, victimized and marginalized by the mainland, we would do better to see it/them as a different and at times contentious or even "anti'" part of China that has definite grievances and discontents over its own, literally colonial system in relation to the mainland's one-party system.[30] The Basic Law, while lauded as a wise diplomatic solution for Hong Kong and even Taiwan, is much more the problem than the solution. Though it should also be recalled that the original sin here, so to speak, is the British's empire's and their local collaborators. Hong Kong is also, it must be said, powerfully privileged in relation to the mainland, not least in terms of its relative wealth and education and living standards per capita, but even in its "autonomy" prior to at least 2020. (If one assumes this to be a good thing.) Put another way, any analysis of the city or its populace that treats them like a victim of modern Chinese colonialism, or of conquest, or of systematic racism a la African-Americans throughout their history in the United States, is at best unhelpful towards understanding history and reality.

The denouement in late 2019 of the Hong Kong democracy movement begun late in the British era before the handover, thanks to the last-minute manoeuvres of the last Governor Chris Patten, must itself be analysed, neither mourned nor celebrated. (Though both reactions are to be expected.) We must analyse more than its tactics, multiple though these were: the violence or anarchic/nihilistic approach of burnism, the mediatization, the fluidity/guerrilla style, the solicitation of foreign powers, the foreign as well as domestic funding. So too we must account for more than the lack of patriotism or the "right" type of nationalism, the lack of police professionalism or preparedness, or the surfeit of an increasingly nasty nativism/localism. We have to understand why the movement took the form it did, including its colonial legacies.

## NOTES

1. I wish merely to signify Hong Kong's pre-1997 connection not only to colonialism but to the mainland here, as opposed to, say, the sovereign state of Singapore or the de facto independent and, it must be said, very different, sovereign state of Taiwan.
2. See for example a report from Xinhua news agency, "Start by Solving the Living Problem," on living standards in the city, from September 2019: Xinhua News Agency. 2019. "从解决居住难题入手破解香港社会深层次矛盾," September 13. http://www.xinhuanet.com/2019-09/13/c_1124992983.htm?fbclid=IwAR29aa3Ryr0vqftuSlBblD4Bx_4-sgYbND SMzHODc_J0fsW7YJ8ArboF9dc. Accessed 29 November 2020.
3. See the report in Hong Kong Standard, "Explainer: What Is Benny Tai's '10 Steps to Burn with Us,'" https://www.thestandard.com.hk/breaking-news/section/4/162727/Explainer:-what-is-Benny-Tai's-%2210-steps-to-burn-with-us%22. Accessed May 2022. His original Chinese article has been expunged from the now-closed *Apple Daily* website. While still ambiguous to a certain extent, Tai's and others' rationale for the 'burnism-primary' does posit—and seemingly welcome—an eventual violent crackdown from the authorities.

4. See "Andrew Leung Aims to End Filibustering in Hong Kong's Legco," from CGTN network, June 2017. https://news.cgtn.com/news/3d676a 4e354d444e/share_p.html. Accessed May 2022.
5. See Martin Purbrick, "A Report on the Hong Kong Protests," *Asian Affairs* 50.4: 465–487: 472.
6. See the long report on the 2016 incident by the SCMP's *Hong Kong Magazine*, "The Wake of Hong Kong's Fishball Revolution: The Aftershock of a Bloody Clash Reveals the City's Deepening Hatred of an Overwhelmed Police Force." https://www.scmp.com/magazines/ hk-magazine/article/2037641/wake-hong-kongs-fishball-revolution. Accessed 15 March 2022.
7. See "Policy on police use of force in public order events in selected places," Research Office of the Legislative Council Secretariat, IN14/19–20, 2020. https://www.legco.gov.hk/research-publications/english/192 0in14-policy-on-police-use-of-force-in-public-order-events-in-selected-pla ces-20200713-e.pdf. Accessed 4 May 2022.
8. The most notable example of such funds, now dissolved and whose trustees have been arrested as of Spring 2022, was the *612 Humanitarian Relief Fund* (founded June 15, 2019, early on in the protests), which at one point had a total of 173 million HKD in donations, most of it dispersed to about 19,000 people. For more information, see their own website, https://612fund.hk/zh/fund-info, as well the usual social media platforms. Accessed 4 May 2022.
9. It is always worth noting that during the 2019–2020 protests nobody was killed by police, but one 70 year old counter-protester was by an anti-ELAB brick-thrower, and another man was nearly burnt to death by another in a truly gruesome incident captured on video. Police did fire their weapons and shoot protesters three times, though no one died; one HKUST student did fall to his death at a rally (after a jury deliberation the coroner ruled it an open verdict); another protester committed suicide after hanging a banner downtown, at an early, July 1 stage of the movement. We leave to one side here the entirely uncorroborated rumours of secret killings inside Admiralty MTR station and other such reports. As I note elsewhere, and just to be clear, this is not to condone any unnecessary or excessive use of violence, and the oft noted beatings of some protesters after they were subdued by police in the course of physical altercations. But one should not condone or deny the amount of violence committed by some protesters as well. For information on the latter and post-2019 protest violence, see the archival website *Truth-HK*. https://www.truth-hk.com/about. Accessed April 2022. For more on police violence and errors, see Pubrick, 2019 and Shek, D.T.L., "Protests in Hong Kong (2019–2020): A Perspective Based on Quality of Life and Well-Being," *Applied Research in Quality of Life* 15 (2020): 619–635.

2  IN THE EVENT: THE POLITICS AND CONTEXTS ...    53

10. For some demographic information, see "Young, Educated and Middle Class: First Field Study of Hong Kong Protesters Reveals Demographic Trends," *South China Morning Post*, 12 August 2019. https://www.scmp.com/news/hong-kong/politics/article/3022345/young-educated-and-middle-class-first-field-study-hong-kong. Accessed 4 May 2022.
11. See the article on this by an anonymous reporter from 2018, "How Bruce Lee Classic Quote 'Be Water' from Fictional US TV Series Came to Be Attributed to Him." https://www.scmp.com/culture/film-tv/article/2155586/how-bruce-lee-classic-quote-be-water-fictional-us-tv-ser ies-came-be?module=perpetual_scroll_0&pgtype=article&campaign=215 5586. Accessed 15 April 2022.
12. See the fascinating research-based comments from demographic experts in the following reports: "How Reuters Counted a Quarter Million People at Hong Kong's Protests," July 2019. https://www.reuters.com/art icle/us-hongkong-extradition-backstory/how-reuters-counted-a-quarter-million-people-at-hong-kongs-protests-idUSKCN1UD0ZT; and "How Many Protesters Took to the Streets on July 1?" July 2019. https://gra phics.reuters.com/HONGKONG-EXTRADITION-CROWDSIZE/010 0B05W0BE/index.html. Accessed 9 May 2022.
13. I return to this 'leaderless' question below. Strictly speaking, few protests are ever spontaneous, and in this case we are dealing with a seven-month long event for which many emerged from the woodwork, so to speak, and unsurprisingly.
14. I owe the formulation of Hong Kong 2019 as a "tragedy" to Kerry Brown, who is as always lucid and succinct. See "China's Turbulent Year: 2019" at *Strife*, an academic blog from King's College London. https://www.strifeblog.org/2019/12/27/chinas-turbulent-year-2019/. Accessed December 2019.
15. See "Hong Kong Protesters Join Hands in 30-Mile Human Chain: Event Inspired by Anti-Soviet 'Baltic Way' Across Estonia, Latvia and Lithuania in 1989," *Guardian*, 23 August 2019. https://www.thegua rdian.com/world/2019/aug/23/hong-kong-protesters-join-hands-in-30-mile-human-chain. Accessed 3 May 2022.
16. Here and elsewhere for the timeline and 'casualty' figures, I refer to the following report from the SCMP, information that can also be found in the paper's later book, *Rebel City*. https://multimedia.scmp.com/infogr aphics/news/hong-kong/article/3027462/hong-kong-100-days-of-pro tests/index.html.
17. See Ching Kwan Lee, "Op-Ed: Hong Kong Is the Front Line of a New Cold War: If It Burns, the World Gets Burned Too," *The Los Angeles Times*, 28 May 2020. https://www.latimes.com/opinion/story/2020-05-28/op-ed-if-hong-kong-burns-the-world-gets-burned-too. Accessed 19 May 2020. It is hard not to read this op-ed, from a distinguished

scholar of labor conditions in China, as nonetheless a clear example of the type of yellow-peril, Cold War discourse that is dominant today in many circles, including those of the so-called Western left.

18. Sigmund Freud, *Civilization and Its Discontents*, Trans. James Strachey (Norton Press, 1989 [1929]).
19. "14 kg of Dangerous Substances and Improvised Bomb Found at Abandoned School Site in Hong Kong," *SCMP*, 2 May 2020. https://www.scmp.com/news/hong-kong/law-and-crime/article/3082594/three-suspected-bombs-found-abandoned-school-site-hong. Accessed 11 May 2022.
20. See Ted Honderich, *Violence for Equality: Inquiries in Political Philosophy*. 3rd edition (Routledge Press, 2014).
21. See the famous/infamous video interview of Joey Siu in November 2019, by Tim Sebastian at *Deutsche Welle*: https://www.dw.com/en/hong-kong-will-violence-kill-the-pro-democracy-movement/a-51134455 and https://www.youtube.com/watch?v=V9nNeO0yWyk. Accessed May 4, 2022.
22. See the ending comments from Joseph Cheng Yu-shek to this effect—'we have no chance of getting what we want but still we ask it anyway'—at the end of an article by the late Arif Dirlik, "The Mouse That Roared: The Democratic Movement in Hong Kong," *Contemporary Chinese Political Economy and Strategic Relations* 2.2 (2016): 665–681. Note that this refers to the 2014 Occupy movement.
23. See my article on 2019 and mediatization in: "A Sound and Fury Signifying Mediatisation," *Javnost: The Public* 27.2 (2020): 200–209. For an introduction to the term (which is not akin to mediation), see John Connor, "'Mediatization': Media Theory's Word of the Decade," on the *Media Theory Journal* website, 21 May 2018. https://mediatheoryjournal.org/john-corner-mediatization/. Accessed 4 May 2022.
24. See Jon Solomon, "Hong Kong, or How Social Struggles Can Reinforce the Cartography of Capitalist Enclosure," 14 January 2020. *Critical Legal Thinking*. https://criticallegalthinking.com/2020/01/14/hong-kong-or-how-social-struggles-can-reinforce-the-cartography-of-capitalist-enclosure/. Accessed 4 May 2020.
25. See Solomon, 2020, as well as his recent Chinese book, Solomon, Jon. 2022.《香港反送中左翼敗北的系譜：翻譯、轉型與邊界》*Xianggang fansongzhong zuoyi baibei de xipu: fanyi, zhuangxing yu bianjie* [*A Genealogy of Defeat of the Left: Translation, Transition, and Bordering in Hong Kong*] (Taipei: Tonsan Publications, 2022).
26. See Nury Vittachi's detailed but highly readable book, *The Other Side of the Story: A Secret War in Hong Kong* (YLF Press: Hong Kong, 2020). Vittachi is a well known novelist and writer based in Hong Kong for decades, as well as the editor of Fridayeveryday.com.

## 2 IN THE EVENT: THE POLITICS AND CONTEXTS ... 55

27. See Jasmine Ling's report in *The Standard*, November 2020. https://www.thestandard.com.hk/section-news/section/4/225024/Writer-reveals-CIA-funding-in-HK-protests. Accessed 4 May 2020.
28. See Vittachi's report on the court case of Mr. Li. https://threadreaderapp.com/thread/1428524044152807427.html. Accessed October 2021.
29. We are speaking specifically here of Hong Kong. Politics is the "science" of the concrete. How this lesson might apply to Taiwan, to take a seemingly parallel example, is a very different and very open question that would need addressed on its own.
30. For an analysis of Hong Kong as a "subaltern" city, and not as a privileged space with an outsized global footprint and ubiquitous media presence, see Chiu Yiu Wai, *Found in Transition: Hong Kong Studies in the Age of China* (Suny Press, 2019). Needless to say I do not think modern Hong Kong can fit either Gramsci's notion of the subaltern (marginal social groups) nor Spivak's post-colonial one, which spoke—ambiguously—to the gap between people and discourses, or in other words the subaltern both has agency and is yet denied that agency via discourse/power. Perhaps one can see the protesters of 2019 as subaltern in that they did not get what they wanted but something far worse than the proposed bill. But this would be a rather different meaning.

CHAPTER 3

# Basic Law, Basic Problems: Autonomy and Identity

If Deng Xiaoping's "Southern tour" and China's massive acceleration of 'opening up' to capital and globalization (as a response to the political crisis of 1989), spurred the PRC towards epochal, if dislocating economic growth and urbanization as well as 'superpower' status within the capitalist world system, Hong Kong's 2019 protests-turned-riots and their resolution—their teeth gritting harmony—via national legislation and the re-assertion of mainland sovereignty will prove as eventful for the city-SAR itself. Once again, this will not be a happy story for those hoping for a liberal-democratic transformation of Hong Kong (or of China via Hong Kong, as older Hong Kong liberal-democrats like Martin Lee wished). But like the PRC of the 1990s and beyond, it will nonetheless be a remarkable story of change and adaptation to difficult and complicated circumstances in part brought on by the history of imperialism and now a new Cold War. These are, not coincidentally, the same general historical and political conditions that subtended Hong Kong from its inception in the Opium Wars up through the present. More importantly to the people living in the SAR, i.e. to their lived experiences, the next phase of Hong Kong will hopefully also be a story of development and improved livelihood (not simply consumerism) for a city that has over the last two decades been politically and economically stagnating, not benefitting, from the 'return' to the mainland. Socially, as the undeniably nihilistic

© The Author(s), under exclusive license to Springer Nature Singapore Pte Ltd. 2022
D. F. Vukovich, *After Autonomy: A Post-Mortem for Hong Kong's first Handover, 1997–2019,*
https://doi.org/10.1007/978-981-19-4983-8_3

57

and nativistic dimensions of the final, actual 2019 "democratic" movement indicates, the city's discontent, alienation, and general unhappiness as a whole could not have been more evident, if also undiagnosed by the same media and intellectual commentariat.[1]

Or, put another way, this was a large, visible, and foreign-media sanctioned demographic. Other Hong Kongers need not apply. It must also be said that not everyone in Hong Kong feels or felt this way in 2019 or 2022 or in 1922. We know this on principle (Michel Foucault among others would tell you we cannot get inside people's heads), and we know this from other signs (e.g. counter-protesters, self-identified 'blue' people, crowd sizes). But given the smallness of Hong Kong's academic or research sectors (outside of corporate science), there is a great dearth of social science, empirical research into, e.g., demographics; it is or *should* be very difficult to make sense of something like the anti-ELAB movement and the politics and sociology of contemporary Hong Kong. The lack of such information and opportunities also explains why "culture"—films, often made by outsiders, visual imagery, slogans, 'netizen' comments posing as ethnography, etc.—becomes the dominant medium or area of inquiry. Likewise, what such cultural studies show is that 'the people'—the protesters—are "creative" and "imaginative" and, in a word, *cultural*.[2] Rather than asking hard questions and pursuing difficult lines of inquiry into the actual, contextual politics and dynamics of the movement, one gets academic journalism extolling the—somehow surprising or remarkable—creativity and imaginativeness of 'the' Hong Kong people, i.e. protesters. This may be well meaning praise but it is bringing coal to Newcastle, or chopsticks to China, and can be read as condescending if not an orientalist fetish.[3]

The chance for Hong Kong to not simply integrate into China legalistically but to improve people's livelihood, perhaps to become less intensively individualistic and neo-liberal/entrepreneurial, and to live in history—the irresistible rise of China and all the problems and opportunities that presents—as opposed to its colonial era mode of living on 'borrowed time.' If there is one thing that can be said not to redeem so much as to dialectically resolve and take-away from the 2014–2019 protests it would be that it represented in some fashion a desire and demand not for "freedom" or "democracy" in some reified sense but a desire and demand to live differently (despite the actual status quo politics of autonomy) or in a different temporality: a No to the present, and a Yes for an unnamed future.[4] The tragedy of this lies precisely in the way that such an implicit or inchoate demand was articulated in reality: through intense xenophobia and anti-mainland bigotry and anti-communist gore, through a very narrow and conventional language of "suffrage" and "democracy," through an obsession with police violence that was substantially triggered by the movements own tactics and black-clad fringe, and by appealing to (and getting funded by) American and other foreign powers and interests. Any honest reading of 2019 has to acknowledge and synthesize both dimensions of the protest and of Hong Kong politics. And while it may in the end be too much to ask of the Hong Kong government, certainly in its current largely-colonial Basic Law formation, it too will have to learn how to read the movement in just this way. This does not need to be explicitly stated so much as done, much like the movement away from the Basic Law itself (which will certainly stay on the books until at least 2047).

This will not be an easy adjustment, and it will not be the time of an independent or de facto autonomous Hong Kong understood as a distinct and separate "identity" that is somehow locked in mortal combat with, or simply yet militantly *other-than* the P.R.C. Had Hong Kong generated an anti-colonial movement in its time under the British (which it emphatically did not do, as a largely refugee and, conversely, elite and conservative diaspora), or had the mainland decided by the end of the Mao era to simply cede or "let go" of Hong Kong after 1949 or as soon as the British vacated the premises, then the typical reading of 2019 (or 1997–present) as being about re-colonization or broken premises about "suffrage" and "autonomy" would be spot-on. Instead what Hong Kong received was The Basic Law. What 2019 ushered in, in turn, was not what the protesters wanted ('five demands, not one less') but in a fantastic, dialectical reversal into its opposite, what the localists and pandems always *said* they feared the most: that Hong Kong would become "just another Chinese city."

Now, Hong Kong will indeed become in a sense 'just another Chinese city' with clear red lines over what can and cannot be said and done, most specifically about overthrowing or even subverting the government and/or advocating an explicit or de-facto independence. The danger here will be how seriously 'subversion' is taken, legally, as a real threat. But also, more helpfully, it will no longer be possible to filibuster the legislative and executive branches into permanent crisis and stagnation. Of course they very idea that all Chinese cities are the same, or equally dreary and devoid of freedom and happiness and so on, is itself nothing but more of the same old Sinological- orientalism. Indeed in some ways Hong Kong would be *fortunate* to become just another Chinese city, if that meant what is called a Tier 1 city *a la* Shanghai or Beijing, and increasingly even its near neighbour to the North, Shenzhen (all of whom have weathered the global pandemic better than the SAR). Certainly its health and education system would be dramatically improved in size and accessibility, if not also quality.

Why then did Hong Kong—defined, for the sake of argument right now, as pan-democratic or "oppositional" Hong Kong—insist until recently that it was supposed to be autonomous and de facto independent from the sovereign behemoth to the north? That it was supposed to be on the road to a western or liberal style of political democracy, and 2019 was somehow the last stand of such a noble cause, one worth virtually if not literally burning the city down for? Let us rule out two things: a simple failure, due to colonialism (or U.S. imperialism) or an alleged Cantonese/clan mentality, to be sufficiently and authentically "Chinese" or patriotic; the problem of an essentialist identity politics is real, as we will argue later, but this applies to both sides of the border. Secondly, let us rule out the explanation that 2019 embodied, or manifested in specific and distorted form, a universal, innate desire to actualize our common human rights and pursuit of natural or universal "freedom" that was most despotically crushed by an evil regime that is always trying to do exactly this, and to expand its power. In short neither the patriotic gore nor the human rights narrative (and its political orientalism) help further understanding. Both takes are superficial at best and would not hold up to criticism, even if they nonetheless continue to inform much media commentary on different sides of the border. In place of "freedom" we should rather say "power" or "will-to-power" and then have the entire conflict make much more sense. Such a transcoding would not make any group's struggle objectionable on principle, but it would make it specific and more visibly, explicitly political.

What we further need to attend to are some of the roots as well as conditions of possibility for the Hong Kong opposition in general, and for 2019 in particular. Certainly we must therefore attend to colonialism and the lack of de-colonization in the city SAR, and to the Basic Law and indeed the post-Mao Party-state's de-politicizing ambitions, i.e. the foreclosure of meaningful public/social/political participation in one's society. Of course the latter is also a global problem plaguing virtually all political/social systems today, as writers as diverse as Mark Blyth and

Wang Hui have discussed, among others.[5] This inquiry into the historical conditions of possibility for the protests and for Hong Kong's opposition to take the forms it has are the subject of the rest of the second part of this book. There are three basic problems at hand, and all of which are also embedded into and expressed by the city's mini-constitution, The Basic Law. These are: the false promise of autonomy, the question of Hong Kong identity, and de-colonization. De-colonization is arguably the largest question of the three, and will warrant a separate chapter.

## One System: Everything That Rises Must Converge

To understand Hong Kong politics from the 1970s onwards, we have to understand The Basic Law, and the problem with this is that it is a contradictory, ambiguous document born—like all such diplomatic treaties—of expediency and compromise.[6] Moreover it is also one that unlike other such documents also stands or stood—for many pan-democrats or localists—as an almost sacred, talisman-like "mini-constitution" for the city. As one Hong Kong academic put it, the document means more than what it specifically stipulates (wonkish policy statements) but somehow contains a whole vision or poetic/symbolic power that expresses Hong Kong's virtual power and even its ability to potentially change the mainland itself as it internalizes and digests this magical bean of a free territory.[7] Whatever the merits of such a view, it suggests a hefty psychic investment in the symbolic powers of the document—or of Hong Kong itself—as a type of virtual or imaginary political totem that will either change China or refuse to become like it. This belief or more accurately this faith in the power of Hong Kong and/or the Basic Law not only ignores mainland views of both things but is in the last instance not really about the actual document or the actual politics of the Sino-UK-Hong Kong settlement; nor is it about the city's historical realities in in the 1990s or the present. Like the idea that the anti-government movement of 2019 would bring down or mutually destroy the local government and the mainland, it testifies to the power of wish-fulfilment more than anything else. There is also a pro-integration version of this psychic investment, which sees the Basic Law as a virtual perpetual motion machine that can work perfectly if not disrupted. This too ignores the political.

That the Basic Law is in any case often called a *mini* constitution is apt, since for several reasons it simply cannot well serve as a founding governmental document that expresses both sovereignty and vision and core values for all time, especially when it is clear that integration from 1997 onwards *will* happen one way or another. It is not a document born of war and liberation struggle or any mass movement against either a reactionary class system or colonial-imperial power, and drawing on, say, communist or radical democratic rhetoric and professed values. It is an expedient, pragmatic document hacked out between two nation-states who didn't care for one another, born out of the necessity for the colonizer to give up the goods and for the absentee motherland to get them back. The Basic Law speaks to colonialism not at all, aside from duly noting Chinese sovereignty over its former territory. One would be hard pressed to prove that a lot of thought and care went into the document, which is not to say it will be officially abandoned either.

The document was always going to be too "mini" to deal with the burgeoning Chinese economy and the power of the PRC. For many in Hong Kong during the 1980s and 1990s, due to the city's own relative strength or economic power compared to the mainland, and very much due as well to its own, inescapably colonial sense of cultural/intellectual/ideological superiority and "advanced-ness,' there was little fear of the mainland overtaking the city in economic terms. As Lui Tai Lok has noted, at the time of its drafting and early release, the Basic Law was (and remains) mostly about the protection of private property and personal freedom as well as keeping the pre-existing legal system in tact.[8] These three areas occupy the lengthiest and most numerous Articles in the document. The political arrangements or political reform, again aside from unequivocally stating mainland sovereignty and control of national security, were given very little attention. Like the issue of colonialism or rather de-colonization these were deemed unimportant or best not spoken of, left to the future, since the order of the day was compromising in order to ensure for both sides an acceptable and peaceful handover of sovereignty. This is all in keeping with a colonial regime that always said it was really doing philanthropy or assuming the white man's burden, and a Dengist Communist Party that was actually trying to de-politicize its own society and system after Mao, whilst also "borrowing" the energies and tools of capitalist accumulation and profit. As Lui has discussed at length, the main concern and hence "grandest' statement at the time of composition was to preserve Hong Kong's then-dynamic "capitalism" (system 1) and keeping it separate from China's "socialism" (system 2). This was what supposed to last for a period of fifty years and this (including the three sets of capitalistic Articles above) was apparently to be the bulwark of the "high degree of autonomy" in the document. The fear of system 1 ending, seen as incompatible with system 2/socialism, was what prompted the arch-propagandist of neo-liberalism Milton Friedman to chime in on the "death of Hong Kong" in 1995.[9]

Little did anyone foresee that the Chinese economic miracle—aka tsunami—would quickly outpace and overwhelm Hong Kong's capitalism. (The Law's notion of two separate yet mutually involved economies also did not account for the idea of a truly global or world system not just of politics but economy.) Not only did the small manufacturing base within Hong Kong quickly disappear as the city's capital went north (as did most of its organized, triad crime) but Hong Kong's centrality within finance capital and within shipping and port business likewise receded. After the escalation of the mainland's "opening up" to global capital in the wake of Tiananmen 1989, it rapidly became difficult for the city to play its legendary role as "gateway to China." This role was effectively over—or radically reduced in leadership and symbolic terms— by 1997. The gates were wide-open and multiple now, from Shenzhen just across the border through Shanghai and up to Beijing. (Relatedly, this can be seen to induce a crisis within mainstream Hong Kong identity, just as the rise of the wealthy and middle class of China was to do.) Quickly enough, the flow of capital started going in both directions: not just from south to north, but from the mainland into Hong Kong to stay, and not just in hidden or fuzzy banks accounts. As Lui notes, by 2003, in an effort to pull Hong Kong out of its economic crisis due in part to SARS, two-way capital traffic increased significantly.[10] This two-way flow (which is to say the new flows from the mainland into the south) in many ways is the true watershed in Hong Kong's relation to the mainland, as the city both needed the help economically (due to SARS) and, once started, it would be difficult and even politically impossible to reverse. One striking sign of this can be seen in the figures for "tourism" from China principally, which is less about tourism *per se* than a euphemism for consumption and doing various types of business in the city. Lui sums it up nicely:

> Inbound Chinese tourists rose in number from almost 8.5 million in 2003 to 51 million by 2018. The pace and scale of this regional integration is illustrated by incidents such as the run on baby milk powder and subsequent shortages caused by Mainland consumers eager to find a safe alternative to Mainland sources. Births to non-local mothers rose drastically and the SAR Government found this unmanageable given that such

64   D. F. VUKOVICH

babies would be entitled to have Hong Kong resident status. In 2012, measures were introduced to end the granting of resident status in such cases. All in all, the scale of the new influx of people and money from the Mainland was simply overwhelming.[11]

In sum, whether we call it Chinese socialism or Dengist capitalism, the Chinese economy and Chinese mainland was always going to dwarf its post-colonial capitalist enclave in the South. Even by 1984 (the signing of the Sino-British Joint Declaration or treaty), but certainly by 1997, the idea of somehow "containing" or warding off the Chinese economy—as if Hong Kong were some type of autarkic self-sufficient economy itself!—should have seemed absurd, and the Basic Law should have been seen as just a ready-made, sheerly pragmatic document meant to grease the wheels of an awkward transition from one regime to the next. It is remarkable that Deng-era Party members as well as other intellectuals involved in Hong Kong and elsewhere would have thought they could manage or contain the laissez-faire style of Hong Kong capitalism meeting up with—integrating with—mainland style "to get rich is glorious" socialism. Whither Marxism? It was, and to an extent remains, much more Friedrich von Hayek than Karl Marx or Mao Zedong. The global capitalist or world system cannot be neatly divided up like this, into discrete national spaces. The genie of creative destruction under modern, global capitalism cannot be kept in its bottle. This also sheds light on why, especially for a small city actually dependent on the economy and grace of the mainland (note that Hong Kong pays zero taxes to China), an oppositional politics of sovereignty like Hong Kong's 'autonomist' localism or nativism, let alone it's (now defunct) explicit independence groups, are irrealist and hopeless.

And yet, as noted above, such bits of Marxist or world-systemic political-economic wisdom had no purchase at the time, or up to the present. If the Basic Law was from its origin set on a crash course of two not-separate economies and societies (China and Hong Kong), it was nonetheless understood for some time as being something like a blueprint for the future and a guarantor of either Free Hong Kong—a space free *from* the mainland or even its influence—or a magically peaceful, slow but sure integration. It has proved to be neither. Precisely because the document does not detail the political transition of Hong Kong into either China or a "real" Western-style democracy, and precisely because it mentions colonialism and de-colonization not at all, the problems of history and politics were inevitably going to come to the forefront. The

Basic Law simply took the "borrowed time" of colonial Hong Kong and jerry-rigged a delayed fuse, bequeathing future, post-97 Hong Kongers *another* time-bomb. The political aspirations of at least some Hong Kong people—those wishing a more Western, liberal democratic form of governance—as well as those wishing Hong Kong to become *more* a part of the Chinese nation and its imagined community/nationalism were bound not only to conflict but to want to be realized.

When the Sino-British treaty was signed off in 1984, it stipulated that Hong Kong will be under Chinese authority and sovereignty and yet also enjoy a "high degree of autonomy."[12] This implicit tension—'degree' is ambiguous but 'sovereignty' never is—became by the time of the far more important Basic Law document a full-blown contradiction. As I have argued elsewhere about the 2014 Occupy protests the very real and intense conflict in Hong Kong at that time can actually be seen as a battle of interpretations over the meaning of, and the blueprint implied by the Basic Law. This conflict arose not from two well-considered, fleshed-out interpretation of the letter versus the spirit of the law, or any other deep hermeneutics, but from two sides digging in their heels and wilfully ignoring the other side's reading of the Basic Law. And therefore of the future. More specifically, we can say that if understanding or interpreting the Basic Law is the key to Hong Kong politics since the 1980s, then within this it is the conflict or rather contradiction between Articles 23 and 45 that are the heart of the matter. Article 23 is the one that stipulates that the government of Hong Kong must pass a 'national security law' that specifies the illegality of collusion with foreign powers to subvert the regime, to secede, and so on. It reads: "The Hong Kong Special Administrative Region shall enact laws on its own to prohibit any act of treason, secession, sedition, subversion against the Central People's Government, or theft of state secrets, to prohibit foreign political organizations or bodies from conducting political activities in the Region, and to prohibit political organizations or bodies of the Region from establishing ties with foreign political organizations or bodies." After trying once to launch this bill in 2003, six years after the handover but immediately generating large protests against the very idea of 23 before or after 45, it was shelved for 18 years.

Reading the Article today and now knowing the multiple sources of foreign funding, tutelage, and ideological guidance behind the movement and many years before, and then seeing the attempted mediatization of the event during 2019–2020, the solicitation of the American government to intervene legislatively, and the very explicit demands for independence and full autonomy, it is easy to see why the Beijing-imposed national security law of 2020 happened. It must have seemed, across the border in the fall of 2019, an obvious case as to why Article 23 was on the books in the first place and certainly should have been in place already. For Beijing, the 23rd was always the most important Article, and it wanted to see progress on that more than any other one. This security concern is certainly something that had been exacerbated in recent years with the trade-wars and geo-political competition with the United States and its allies. It must be said that this begins or rather intensifies under the Obama administration (2009–2017) and its militaristic "pivot to Asia," a very clear ambition to contain China via guns and boats as much as by trade blocs.[13]

In this sense, the nativist and imperialistic wing of the 2019 protests actually bequeathed Hong Kong a far more draconian set of security and subversion laws than those originally proposed in early 2019 by the government. So deep did the protest leaders—and quickly enough there were indeed several leaders who stepped into the breach after the popular movement emerged—cathect American intervention and would-be protection that even a non-Trumpist pan-democratic politician like Eddie Chu Hoi Dick would pronounce on Twitter that China's National Security Legislation of June 2020 was its first, pre-emptive attack on the President-elect Biden administration.[14] This would seem to show the extent of concern for China's sovereignty and national security, as compared with that of the USA's. As noted earlier, it was—arguably— always highly unlikely that the US would or even *could* effectively intervene in Hong Kong, let alone in the mainland, try as it might through legislative actions as well as NED and other fundings. But for the actual people on the ground in Hong Kong and in China, anti- and pro-government alike, as well as in the Party-state, it may have seemed entirely plausible. Certainly Chu and others seemed to have genuinely believed this. From the pivot to contain China under Obama to the explicit racism and trade-war threats under Trump, the United States has clearly shifted from a Sinologically-orientalist view that it could change China via capitalist market exchanges to a view that simply sees it as a direct rival if not enemy. It is impossible to imagine any other actually existing state acting much differently than China here—i.e. forcing a security law onto the books—in this context.

For their part, the Hong Kong opposition—the 'establishment' parties being mostly inert and ineffectual on securing 23 or much else—was likewise dug-in on achieving suffrage, i.e. not only the election but the direct nomination of the city's C.E. This in their view is promised by Article 45, which is worth quoting in full:

> The Chief Executive of the Hong Kong Special Administrative Region shall be selected by election or through consultations held locally and be appointed by the Central Peoples Government. The method for selecting the Chief Executive shall be specified in the light of the actual situation in the Hong Kong Special Administrative Region and in accordance with the principle of gradual and orderly progress. The ultimate aim is the selection of the Chief Executive by universal suffrage upon nomination by a broadly representative nominating committee in accordance with democratic procedures.[15]

This clearly stipulates moving towards "universal suffrage" as an "ultimate" aim; it also says "the method of selection" will be determined according to the "actual situation" in the city and done in an "gradual and orderly" way. This last gloss constitutes the primary case for the pandemocrats, according to the Basic Law and their own stated core value of the 'rule of law.' However it must be said—even assuming the letter *or* spirit of the law matters as much as 'real' political forces and interests in society at the time—that this is not a strong case at all, given the equally explicit "power of appointment" by Beijing and moreover the stipulation that that selection may be by election *or* consultation, and that a "nomination committee" is going to be in charge of the "nomination." When one recalls that even in the 1980s China had elections within its own party system at a local level, and that the entire Politburo is nothing if not a select, nomination committee, it is easy to see that for Beijing at least, not all "democratic procedures" have to follow a generic Western method of multiple parties. It has always been hard to see the PRC—not least the Party as remade by Deng Xiaoping of 1989 infamy—allowing much more than some version of its own electoral system in Hong Kong, barring some sudden transformation. In any case they have since 1997 always been dug-in on not just Article 23 but the pre-screening process for prospective CE candidates. Again, the implicit red line here had always been that Hong Kong cannot elect a CE who will be anti-communist or anti-Beijing, which would obviously be taken as a secessionist project or simply too insulting and aggressive.

One of the other major overhauls of the political system after 2019 has been to greatly expand the number and type of representatives on the C.E. Election Committee while simultaneously reducing the number of reserved spots for long standing local tycoons and their families (i.e. in their businesses). The total seats are now up 300–1500, and include more sectoral interests from business, industry, and society. Known as the "patriots governing Hong Kong" reform, the aim is dual: reduce the influence of local yellow-tinged or too narrow elites, and to come up with a better, more competent C.E.s. Will this work? We shall see. The other major reform has been to expand the amount of available seats in the legislature (from 70 to 90) but also to reduce the proportion of these that can be directly elected.[16] The District Council functional constituency, as well as other traditionally pan-democratic strong-holds, was also eliminated.[17] As if to prove the point of the pan-democrats actions since 1997, it would *now* seem impossible to reform/transform Hong Kong through electoral means, and a perceived loophole to 'colour revolution' has been foreclosed. The problem of Hong Kong capitalism remains, and was never on the electoral agenda. (We return to the economic dimension in the next chapter.)

The upshot of all of this, for our purposes, was simply zero progress on either Article 23 or 43, neither security nor electoral reform, and hence the continuation of the status quo. Both sides saw themselves as staunchly upholding the Basic Law, though as noted these were very selective readings of the whole document and the general situation in the city, split between an "establishment" content to integrate with China at one pace or another, and an "opposition"—itself part of the mainstream and arguably a majority of people in at least the media and educational industries—wanting to ward off any and all manifestations of national integration. This is, or was, the basic, unresolved conflict and quagmire of Hong Kong politics. There were never any good faith gestures towards compromise within the city's power holders in both camps, and as noted, the 2014 electoral reform proposal from the mainland (which was meant in earnest) was shot down immediately by the pan-democrats albeit (not without some dissent within public opinion).[18]

What has likewise remained consistent until recently is the belief that the city's politics must remain rooted in the Basic Law. From Beijing's perspective, it is *they* whom have defended and now rescued the Law from its capture and destruction by independence activists, rioters, and anti-state, pro-Western subversives funded in part of the USA. This is neatly, diametrically opposed by the pan-democratic opposition to the mainland and the C.E., who have long accused Beijing of violating the Basic Law and delaying the implementation of Article 23 (interpreted, if that is the right word, as mandating 'universal suffrage"). In the wake of 2019 and the dissolution of the pan-democratic movement as well as the national security law appended to the Law (by fiat, via the National Peoples Congress), the "conflict of interpretations" is resolved, for better or worse. It is already clearly worse for those arrested and now prosecuted for their roles in the 2019–2020 protests and aftermath (not least the entire pan-democratic camp, and of course those arrested for their roles in 2019 or for violating the national security law). But regardless of one's views on the fate of the electoral-democracy movement and the actors therein, it is nonetheless too soon to say who else will benefit or lose as Hong Kong goes through another handover process, and integrates more directly. Clearly, development is on the agenda of Hong Kong at last, from big if longer-term plans to alleviate its infamous housing crises to creating a Greater Bay Area for 'technology and innovation' across the Shenzhen-Macau-Hong Kong border. At some point in the future, Hong Kong may get some version of the 2014 political reform package proposed by Beijing before the Occupy movement, but subsequently rejected by the pan-democrats (i.e. the chance to vote city-wide on a choice of two pre-selected candidates). There may be some role to play for a "loyal opposition" that seeks to further democratize or re-direct the government's will, provided it does not cross the red-line of regime-change and de facto independence.

## Autonomy and Its Discontents

If 23 and 43 are the key numbers, so to speak, we nonetheless have to discuss another part of the Basic Law that arguably formed, for the opposition or broad pan-democrats, a far more powerful and compelling part of the perceived political, social contract between it and the mainland: the plank for autonomy. Debate and rhetoric about the articles (i.e. agitation for 43 and suffrage) were indeed part of the legalistic and 'wonkish' culture of the pan-democratic movement. Indeed from one perspective (which may be called "liberal") this legalistic specificity and focus on *procedural* democracy or voting is the chief virtue and distinguishing trait of the former opposition, and its repeated incantations of "the rule of law," the binding nature of the Basic Law and Sino-UK agreements, and so on. From another, socialistic or communitarian perspective this may seem narrow and technocratic, if not neo- liberal, and to be distinguished from robustly state-focused movements, collectivism, the commons, and majority rule (a la some form of Rousseauian mass democracy). The recognition of this wonkishness or rigorously if narrowly liberal character of the Hong Kong democracy movement from its origins until its apparent end by 2021 can itself explain, as a type of compensation-formation, the creative academic acrobatics sometimes used to show that, for example, the Occupy movement was not narrow and legalistic but rather a brand-new type of politics altogether and an illustration of a virtual or imagined or somehow "theoretical" revolution, social imaginary, and so on.

But this legalistic nature notwithstanding, we would do well to avoid *over*-estimating the importance of the Basic Law and related documents. Indeed the weak, facile quality of the interpretations (on both sides) of the 'mini-constitution' itself suggests that it was less the legal and procedural issues that mattered, or the empty signifier of the word 'democracy,' than larger, even existential appeals and phenomena: namely the ideal of autonomy and the construction of a specific Hong Kong identity that is defined against, or at least entirely separate from that of mainland China or mainland "Chineseness." The political as a realm is not after all policy and legality driven so much as deeply ideological and a field of passions, desires for recognition, and profound "interests" that are often if not always in conflict and in now open, now hidden contention.

Let us deal with autonomy first. The "high degree of autonomy" first stated in the Agreement is carried over into the later Basic Law and mentioned several times, albeit always with certain limitations even beyond that "high degree." The pledge to grant autonomy remained vague, as again most such diplomatic documents must do. Yet aside from those who quickly out-migrated from the city to other parts of the former British commonwealth before 1997, it apparently sounded good enough at the time. Here the (misleading) references to the two systems of "socialism" and "capitalism" being kept apart, and just as importantly for the barrister and finance class, for the specific plank that the British legal system would continue, were no doubt of utmost importance. Thus the "Guiding Principle of Drafting the Hong Kong Basic Law" states

## 3 BASIC LAW, BASIC PROBLEMS: AUTONOMY AND IDENTITY

that, via the Sino-UK Agreement, the city "will exercise a high degree of autonomy" and moreover that all the "principles and policies regarding Hong Kong will remain unchanged for 50 years."

And yet, the rest of the document also stipulates that this autonomy and the city "come directly under the Central People's Government," that it is the National People's Congress which authorizes the Hong Kong courts to adjudicate certain matters, and that this autonomy does not apply to matters of defence and national security. Again this at the very least already contains a strong tension between mainland authority/sovereignty and final say, versus Hong Kong not changing and being highly autonomous. The "pan-democratic" view, or what seems the majority view of youth and many adults in the city, is that the "high degree of autonomy" *was and should be* a *de facto full autonomy* (arguably therefore a de facto independence in all but name) from the mainland: from its Party-state but also virtually from everything else except perhaps where business and profitability might supersede. Since there was never any real possibility of keeping Hong Kong capitalism and Chinese socialism apart, as 'local' capital quickly fled into the warm embrace of China's Dengist "reforms" from the get-go. There is also something palpably ridiculous in the plank for even *policies* to remain unchanged for five decades in an always already changing urban centre and a port city of many flows of people and things. From New York to Singapore to Berlin to Tokyo, cities are always changing as if by definition (and via immigration and migration), and Hong Kong itself was certainly this way under the British occupation. Here it would appear that what was sold to Hong Kong is precisely a bill of goods. "High degree" of autonomy could indeed be inferred to suggest a de facto independence or full autonomy, although this obviously leaves out the meaning of political sovereignty and so on. "High degree" can also be reasonably inferred to imply a comparison with the sovereign's/mainland's way of managing and incorporating, say, Guangdong, Shanghai or even Shenzhen as dependent yet federated regions and municipalities.

The question then becomes, Why did this ideal of autonomy—something very much at odds with traditional Chinese intellectual and political culture, let alone state communism—become so powerfully cathected within Hong Kong, beyond its invocation in the Basic Law? Perhaps more to the point, what explains the near-obsession with the "core value" or belief in autonomy that, in turn, was "violated" by Beijing? After all, the so-called "deaths" of the Basic Law and therefore of Hong Kong have turned on this very notion of a loss of autonomy, well before even the 2014 protests let alone the riots of late 2019. (Even the creation of a high speed rail link in the New Territories—to connect the city more readily with the mainland's famous high speed networks—as well as the creation of the Hong Kong-Zhuhai-Macau Bridge were perceived by many groups in the activist/democratic camp, as assaults on the city's autonomy.) Clearly some—as in 'many' and perhaps 'most'—Hong Kongers felt that Hong Kong *had* autonomy and that this was somehow being eroded as if from 1997 onwards.

Was this belief or faith in autonomy simply wishful thinking on Hong Kongers' parts, the flip-side of mainstream mainland views that the integration would just happen naturally because, after all, everyone was Chinese and therefore going to adopt, willy-nilly, a common identity of Chineseness or way of seeing the nation-state?[19] So we have on the one hand, in the unprecedented historical circumstances of the "return" of a colony not through revolution or liberation but through a document worked out by state elites, a high degree of wish fulfilment, of fear if not paranoia about integration, and a powerful disavowal of a sociological problem and antagonism from Beijing's point of view. There is certainly explanatory value within these types of basic psychoanalytic explanations, as "vulgar" as they may be to some ears. Clearly the world and its humans often move in vulgar ways, as Hong Kong 2019 shows. Recognizing this is not reductive so much as an argument for *redefining what counts as complexity* when there are no objective truths in certain, social contexts.

But autonomy is also something sacred within the ideology or discourse most powerfully exemplified in Hong Kong more than other parts of Asia: political and economic liberalism. Autonomy (i.e. personal independence or 'freedom' if not negative liberty specifically) and liberalism (as political system based in preserving or maximizing the former) are not identical concepts even if they are also intimately related and historically articulated together under capitalism. In the work of its deepest thinker and advocate, Cornelius Castoriadis, autonomy is said to be rooted in human nature (or the psyche, in his reading of Freud) and was first developed politically in ancient Greece via its democratic practices.[20] And yet to say that autonomy is ultimately rooted in the psyche or unconscious, and that political society must somehow be organized democratically to respect and foment this, is in the end a deeply romantic and essentialist position. It is unprovable and an *a priori* moment of faith.

3 BASIC LAW, BASIC PROBLEMS: AUTONOMY AND IDENTITY   73

This does not make it bad or necessarily undesirable. But it does raise the familiar problems of Freudian or psychoanalytic discourse, which despite its best efforts to be dialectical, reifies "the" unconscious or desire as something prior to and somehow more important than social, historical determination. Even the Freudo-Marxism of the last century (and which can include Castoriadis well enough) can never quite escape its beginning moment: from the individual psyche and thence to a certain model or image of society or future-society that is built upon this, as opposed to being built on classes or groups or collectivities. So the social is the product of the individual. Surely after Foucault's contributions to radical historicism and the dynamics of 'incitements to discourse,' it should be difficult for us too see the development of society or politics as flowing (or ideally flowing, in theory) from the natural development or natural freedom and independence of the individual (as the politics of autonomy would stipulate as the ideal). To say nothing of Marx. This is simply not the real story and history of capitalism and modern colonialism, despite it being narrated that way from within the dominant discourses of modernity.

As for psychoanalysis and the putatively real, psychological basis to autonomy and its proper political expression, Freud's most political and sociological book, the classic *Civilization and Its Discontents*, makes this *a priori* of the individual id (or 'drives') most clear.[21] But it is also the one text that surely belies any faith in autonomy as something actually feasible. We may be separate from the other obviously enough, but are dependent on it throughout our lives, and it is desire (for Jacques Lacan or Gilles Deleuze and Felix Guattari any rate) or the id or the drives and pleasure principle which rule; they trump any notion of autonomy as something real or feasible. Of course one could nonetheless understand autonomy as an important belief or value nonetheless—that we liberals can proceed *as if* it were true and feasible and so on. But then this— our global conjuncture—is not the early 20th, let alone the 18th century. And it is always worth remembering that for Freud at any rate (or others) we always have to deal with the inherently aggressive and 'selfish' quality of the drives. Freud was writing about Europe or even specifically the Germanic world of the early twentieth century and the spectre of fascism, even if he did not call this by name. This was not the context of Hong Kong in 2019–2020 but there was no lack of aggression, hatred, and the worst parts of human nature/human drives at work. The issue here isn't proper names (be it Freud or Foucault) but that autonomy (or creativity,

74    D. F. VUKOVICH

or aggressiveness for that matter) cannot be an *a priori* 'fact' of human nature that is outside interpretation. Ontology is metaphysics; life and politics are historical.

Furthermore the "project of autonomy" (as Castoriadis puts it), is predicated upon and reinforces liberal individualism. This should not be a controversial thing to say of the concept, nor of the history and reality of liberalism, which always presupposed and depended upon market relations being the model of politics and of society or social relations. Writing at the same time as Castoriadis but from North America and not Europe, C.B. MacPherson, in turn, theorized how liberal individualism led in his own lifetime to the phenomenon of *possessive individualism*, or the illusion that our abilities and skills (and fates) are all our own, like commodities we own, and owe nothing to others or to society.

Even the "workerist" or romantic/anarchic version of Marxism (e.g. the Italian Autonomeia movement, the "libertarian communists" of various internet-based sects) that draw on the concept of autonomy would not escape the predication here, at least not towards liberal individualism and the romantic or 'autonomist' notion of the natural self. They merely radicalize it, conceptually, to the democratically-controlled, "self-managed' workplace. Workplace democracy is anathema to capitalism, and one wants to insist on it, on principle alone. Marx, for his part, saw workers' struggles—the labor movement and strikes—as part of the ultimately rational historical development of capitalism and the proletariat, much like his and Engels's early polemical point in the *Communist Manifesto* that "the working men have no country" and also no ideals to realize within the movement of history towards communism (or towards a direct democracy for Castoriadis).

But the larger problem with the valorisation of autonomy is precisely that it ignores—as in proceeds blithely unaware of—the powerful abstract, emotional, practical, and material dependencies we have on other people, other groups, and on the institutions of society (or the lack thereof). As Tom O'Shea has put it, drawing on the work of political theorist Wendy Brown among others:

Feminist opponents have decried autonomy as — 'a thoroughly noxious concept' which shares in a —myth of masculinity that requires disavowal of relationships that sustain us. Radical critiques of psychiatry lament an illusion of autonomy which suppresses social explanations of action and emotional distress, leading to a 'magical voluntarism' vastly exaggerating the power of the human will. Moral philosophy, in its valorisation of individual and rational autonomy, is said to admire 'a naked Emperor of questionable legitimacy.' In medicine, an autonomy cult has been accused of tyrannising patients and medical staff alike. Similarly, commentators on social policy have bemoaned an uncompromising and rigid worship of personal autonomy and warned that the 'mythology of pure and rational autonomy' leads to a false image of ourselves which is naive, out of touch with an adequate understanding of human motivation, and, ultimately, philosophically and morally untenable.[22]

This catalogue of objections is worth quoting at length since it provides conceptual as well as sociological or practical grounds for questioning "autonomy" as either a progressive political (e.g. feminist) or ethical ideal. This would necessarily apply to Hong Kong as much as any other contemporary society. The city is after all dependent on China and global capitalism yet far too small and 'weak'—if this is the right word for a privileged place—to ever become relatively, let alone fully autonomous in economic or political terms. And what of global warming? Even within the city there is much to it that actually contradicts this alleged "core value" of autonomy. Hong Kong families are Chinese families: by which we mean that they are often multi-generational either in living quarters or also in terms of elder and infant care. There are no day-cares in the city for example, and much is done by grandparents and especially by foreign domestic workers both for children and for the elderly. Hong Kong literally reproduces itself and lives off of such labor and people. There are over 400,000 overseas workers ('helpers') in the city, none of whom will ever be eligible for permanent residency in the city (though they do have access to the public health system and are governed by labor laws). In the absence of a decent and humane welfare system there are private philanthropic businesses of course, but also many underfunded and heroic charities and unofficial organizations, tending to everything from the city's amazing banyan trees to orphans, the disabled, and so on. It is clearly, in large part, the discourse of liberalism—bequeathed to Hong Kong via British colonialism and 'global modernity'—as well as a certain anti-communism or antagonism towards the mainland politically that underpins the power and appeal of autonomy within the city's political and intellectual culture. Everyday life shows little evidence of autonomy in reality. "Autonomy"—as 'core value' and later a battle cry— was not a 'free' rational choice of Hong Kongers so much as something

## 76 D. F. VUKOVICH

that, while certainly scripted into the Basic Law, was the result of a certain incitement to discourse: a discourse of freedom and individualism and 'heroic' struggle against an allegedly despotic, communist Goliath to the North, but also even more importantly a discourse of Hong Kong identity. It—along with freedom and choice and so on—came to define what it meant to be a Hong Konger as opposed to a mainlander, i.e. for those who took up this particular Hong Kong identity. (We leave to one side here, other important but less directly political things like Hong Kong Cantonese, the food, the Christianity relative to the mainland, and so on.) A laisez-faire political identity if you will, to go hand in hand with the free-market ideology and myths of entrepreneurship. The colonial and contemporary governments' commitment to free-market, free-trade (while perhaps undergoing changes now, after mainland tutelage) are well known. But it is much larger than government ideology. For example, one can read "high brow" Hong Kong political and intellectual magazines like the influential and bilingual *Hong Kong Economic Journal*, and see a certain militant if not "vulgar' commitment to liberalism that is defined against populism, collectivism, indeed anything that is not an Ayn Rand, von Hayek type of libertarian or neo-liberalism (a type that is globally dominant now since the 1970s it must be said):

> What are authoritarian-populists? They advocate prioritizing collective security over liberal autonomy of the individual. This is combined with rhetoric that "questions and opposes legitimate authority of the "establishment" as well as developing an "us" vs "them" framework to scapegoat groups for the problems suffered by the populist supporters.[23]

"Autonomy" folded into a place-based rootedness and no doubt mixed with many other affective elements, worked together to move people to not simply protest but construct and participate in laam chau, to literally and metaphorically 'burn' the city in order to save it. Such an outcome cannot appear overnight, but had to be hard-wired into the local intellectual political culture. And it certainly was just so engrained into the anti-government and/or anti-mainland 'democratic' camps and moreover into the media, educational, and cultural sectors. The city's youth, as youth, were ripe for the taking, so to speak, precisely because they had no other identity that the "yellow" or "anti'" one to take up. In a commercial society of wealth and consumerism yet real precarity and a dreary economy of business, real estate agents, accountants, and "event promotion," they also had plenty to fear about their own future and their abilities to fund a bourgeois life or find an alternative, better one. Thus in place of the localist 'yellow' identity that will continue to be boosted by some cultural studies and long-distance nativists in the diaspora, in Hong Kong the government and ruling class needs to offer a genuine chance of redemption and second chances for those youth whom have been arrested and for those many more who were deeply impacted by 2019 as well as by the rise and fall of this form of identity politics.

## IDENTITY AND ITS DISCONTENTS

The question of identity is a complex one, and our critique of Hong Kong's identity politics as expressed in or rather pushed to its extreme in the 2019 movement-turned-riot, where overall it took a radically anti-mainland and anti-communist form, should not be taken in one of two tendentious yet predictable ways: as a dismissal of all identity politics/identity formations (as if identities were always false consciousness) or as a failure of proper, patriotic Chineseness (as if this requires political passivity). Relatedly, the problem with the anti-communism so deeply rooted in Hong Kong's liberal/democratic culture (and perhaps the culture at large), is not that the mainland is authentically communist or is even trying to be. The problem is that the so-called anti-communism is directed at a chimera on the one hand and on the other works in this context to delegitimate egalitarianism and the welfare state, not unlike American fantasies about the "socialism" of the palpably neo-liberal Democratic Party. But even more to the point here, the anti-communist rhetoric is but a mask for a nativist yet by Western ("universal") standards also a politically correct Hong Kong identity that underscores its difference from the mainland and *its* political identity. In short, the anti-communist politics of the Hong Kong opposition are an identity politics more than anything else. This does not make them wrong or trivial; indeed it is crucial for mainstream Hong Kong intellectual culture and anti- or non-mainland group identity. But it does make them contextually specific yet ambiguous and thoroughly subjective. And not actually about specific politics or policies or political structures.

We need a critical understanding of the place of "identity"—of the production and uses of particular identities—during the late colonial period in Hong Kong, from the 1970s up to the present. This means, in turn, we must dismiss a third, unhelpful yet predictable way of seeing identity. A way that Jean Baudrillard insisted was very American: that it is perfectly natural and just, even a right as well as a duty to "express" it politically and emphatically. You have an identity and you must actualize it.[24] The point is that identities are not natural in the way that, say, John Locke wrote about freedom and rights and acquisitiveness and so on. Identities are not only always multiple and sometimes even jarringly contradictory, they are also *made* (albeit not simply under conditions of our choosing, as Marx might have said). They are to be contextualized and studied sociologically, and also as part of global processes. Here is where the work of Allen Chun on Chineseness and identity is so important in pushing us beyond seeing identity as natural, authentic, synonymous with social justice, existential, and so on, (or scientific *a la* the work of Erik Erikson) but bound up in group politics and geo-politics as well as what he usefully calls "pragmatics."[25]

We might also suggest that this multiplicity and historicity of identity also suggests that it may well be wise for a people to not put all their existential eggs in one particular basket. If one formation of a local, Hong Kong (or other) identity only ends in discontent, still others can be—and eventually will be, one hopes—made or re-made. Or one might, *a la* the work of Chinese novelist Wang Anyi, suggest that too much introspection, search for self-identity, and interiorization is the problem to begin with and not the solution.[26] We hasten to add that this would apply to all identities, in varying degrees of intensity, from Kowloon to Krakow. Here the idea or ethic of "selflessness" within historical communism—as opposed to, say, national or nativist revolutions—may have lessons for us all, if only as an ideal. At any rate, if the politics and dynamics and historical actualities of identity always involve 'pragmatics,' to adopt Chun's phrase, then we need not despair over the death or banishment-in-exile of 'the' Hong Kong identity.

Hong Kong studies have long noted that it was not until the late 1960s, specifically in response to the city's small but symbolically important radical and violent (bomb throwing) outbursts during the mainland's cultural revolution years, that the colonial government got actively involved in the Hong Kong identity business. It was out to promote an authentic or official *Hong Kong* identity (or Hong Kong Chinese identity) as distinct from "the" or rather a mainland Chinese one. (Again it is only a popular or dominant culture that asserts that there is only one, true identity, be it in China, this city, the USA, etc.) Small though the outburst was, the local government and elite did not want to see a national liberation movement break out. Hong Kong based historian John Carroll (among others) has covered much of this ground in his monographs, and there can be little doubt that the colonial government made concerted efforts to foster a local identity (via schooling, official literary and cultural festivals, music, the usual propaganda efforts).[27] Law Wing Sang, writing in a avowedly post-structuralist register, also argues persuasively for the collaborative nature of colonialism and colonial power in Hong Kong, and for the multi-faceted way in which Hong Kong identity eventually arose.[28] My own point here is that while this place-based, localist identity was not directly imposed in a top-down, rigorously planned way, it was nonetheless created in large part by such British-regime efforts and moreover was generated in a particular time and context, and which inevitably includes discourses from, for example, the Cold War, colonialism, and orientalism.

As Michael Adorjan, Paul Vinod Khiatani, and Wing Hong Chui have argued in a richly detailed article within critical criminology studies, 2019 revealed how effective the colonial-era project of localism was in the past (i.e. the identification with Hong Kong in itself as opposed to China) and how much it had changed further since the 1990s and leading up to 2019.[29] Thus the changing attitudes towards the local police force cannot be separated from the belief amongst protesters that they were in effect agents of China, an essentially foreign regime, and the anti-mainland views were used by (some) protesters to justify the movement as legitimate civil disobedience.[30] As has been noted many times elsewhere, Hong Kong identity, especially but not only for younger generations, moved swiftly from something mostly place-based and cultural (i.e. connected to Chinese culture broadly speaking) to a greatly politicized—as in anti-communist and anti-P.R.C. politics—one that turned on a fundamental incompatibility between being a Hong Konger and being Chinese. Gordon Matthews, writing in 1997, had already noted that Hong Kong identity was becoming unmoored from being- placed-based to something more in-flux and perhaps becoming more independent and autonomous.[31] In the event, what it become by 2019 to an unfortunately decisive extent was something less autonomous but, again, politicized in a particular, negative and nativist-xenophobic way. Again it is worth noting that the latter form did not speak for all. The main take-away here is that this rather short but rapidly changing history of identity since the 1970s shows us that identity is fluid and historically malleable and fungible, even if it understandably does not feel that way to specific people elbow-deep in it at the time.

In public education, a crucial arena of identity formation, modern Chinese history was usually taught not at all, or later only up to about 1911. This was after all part and parcel of the colonial project in, for example, British India where it was done far longer and on a much larger scale than in the port city south of China. One way in which the colonizer ruled was through inculcating identities. Of course they could and would remain fluid and be taken up in necessarily individual and therefore diverse ways. But the larger point is that it remained a place-based one, not just separate from but opposed to another, allegedly dominant place (Beijing, not London). And also a colonial one, as even some partisans for the Hong Kong autonomy cause have admitted. It is easy enough to affirm Hong Kong identity as a good thing in itself precisely because it is not the allegedly oppressive, monolithic mainland one and because, after all, you must have an identity and you must use/celebrate/extoll it. It is easy precisely because there is such a powerful discourse of Sinological-orientalism ready to hand.

The promotion of a true Hong Kong identity was all to de-politicize or circumvent anti-colonial sentiment and politics (but which were never terribly strong to begin with), and to legitimize further colonial rule. Here Hong Kong Chinese culture could be special and superior to the perceived degradations to the North, and moreover Hong Kong the city or place, as a growing, global, capitalist dynamo fully connected to the West would likewise stand out as the exception: fashionable and trendy (discos, bell bottoms, 'style') yet traditionally Chinese in other ways (e.g. spiritual, familial) and of course allegedly free or more free than the hundreds of millions of other Chinese. Put another way, Hong Kong identity would itself be premised upon *autonomy*: not from the British empire or what was left of it, but from the mainland, the P.R.C., and from—it must be said—any substantial state regulation in its defining free-market system. Hence Hong Kong as the epiphany of a "liberalism" that would inspire anti-communists like Milton Friedman and the like as well as countless fans that love things Chinese but not the mainland political system and society and the actual existence of the P.R.C.

Additionally it must not be forgotten that it is the late 1960s and 1970s Hong Kong-born-and-raised generation who were at the heart of this project and, again, ripe for it. They were the first generations to grow up in Hong Kong fully under a stable British colonial government, with

3 BASIC LAW, BASIC PROBLEMS: AUTONOMY AND IDENTITY    81

little connection to a mainland that likewise seemed either a total mess of revolution and poverty and despair or, alternatively, stable and walled-off (compared to the revolutionary or Civil War periods with a more precarious border). This too should be familiar to observers of second- and third-generation 'immigrants' to other countries, but of course here in a fully colonial and Cold War context.[32] You cannot have localist identity without being a local.[33] But who counts as a local, and why?

Let us also be perfectly clear that the fact that this occurs in a colonial context and was used instrumentally by the British regime (and later by localist teachers, intellectuals, and so on) does not mean that such identities are somehow traitorous vis a vis the mainland (which was after all not remotely interested in retaking Hong Kong) or merely false consciousness. Those post-war generations coming of age in Hong Kong simply had no deep knowledge of or experience in China to identify with. Vis a vis China, they were the proverbial blank piece of paper upon which anything could be drawn. Likewise, many Hong Kongers (residents) who identify with the mainland are often blank in the same way but may draw from more traditional mainland "things" (language, family, literature or music, etc.) to maintain and develop a "Chinese" identification.) Identities matter to many people, and arguably especially so under colonialism or other forms of subjugation or marginalization. Though clearly unjust, Hong Kong's 150 year occupation was hardly an oppressive colonial situation compared to, say, South Africa, South Asia, Vietnam, and so on; but nonetheless the dynamics of identity, of being deprived of a 'native' or local one whilst also being 'not quite, not white,' would certainly have been in play. Deprived of being fully Chinese in the way of their forbears and the millions to the North (or wanting to distance themselves from them), and yet being colonized and not-white, and yet part of a real, global city dedicated to free-flowing global capital, it is easy to see why a new, place-based identity could and would be cathected by new generations.

What matters for our analytical purposes is the particular form that such identity-productions take, and how they are articulated politically. There is no *necessary* dimension of being anti-China or anti-Beijing or anti-mainlander while being 'localist' or Hong Kong Chinese, and even here we might note at least two or three different versions of hate/fear/dislike (the government, the people, the entire combination). But having said all of this, it is clear that by the 2019 protests the Hong Kong identity being actualized on the streets and in the local and global media was, overall, vehemently anti-China in a broad way. As noted in the first part of this book, the protests quickly became much more than a rejection of one specific extradition bill, but rapidly flowed into an anti-HK government, anti-police, and ultimately an anti-mainland integration—or pro-autonomy—movement. Even moments of "cross-community" support of the protests by some South Asian Hong Kong residents also opposed to the bill from Beijing show us as much: such momentary unity in a Cantonese city that has a record of discrimination and racism towards brown-skinned residents and especially foreign domestic workers was achieved precisely through an opposition to Beijing's (or C.E. Lam's) bill and legitimacy to rule. It was a (fleeting) unity predicated upon an exclusion, but moreover an exclusion that was based on a lie or at least a dubious truth claim, namely that "Beijing" and "mainlanders" were oppressing them all and taking over "their" city. Even participants' own responses indicate as much: that these were the first times in their adult lives that they ever felt that they, too, belonged to the city and could claim being a Hong Konger.[34] Of course the protest or the day ends, and things go back to a depressing 'normal.' Furthermore, it is hard to pin the blame for the city's structural racism and lack of inte-gration on the mainland here, as it is a Hong Kong problem due to Hong Kong people and society, admittedly one bequeathed by the British.

And speaking of dubious truth claims, it is indeed telling that one protest event on July 7, 2019 targeting mainland arrivals from the West Kowloon rail station (to 'demonstrate' in front of them and shout the usual words), set up by noted anti-communist, pro-independence politi-cian and activist Ventus Lau, has been white-washed in a progressive academic publication as an example of the movement's cross-border solidarity and inclusiveness towards mainland citizens/victims of the Party-state. Fortunately enough, the rail company closed 80% of its routes beforehand, and the ensuing crowd of protesters for the entire day peaked at about 56,000 (but predictably boosted by Lau as numbering 230,000). While the late evening saw a few clashes with police (and a few arrests), the confrontation with mainland tourists and arrivals never happened to any notable degree. Nor did any "exchange of views" happen of course. But it would be a leap of faith to think that Lau et al. had good intentions here, given their track record. Lau had previously organized "anti-smuggler" aka anti parallel-trader demonstrations as part of his inde-pendence activism. This was a minor moment of the summer of protest perhaps, but also a telling one. Rather than white-wash this as a moment of solidarity with mainland compatriots against Beijing (as if thousands of Hong Kongers turned out to dialogue with mainlanders), a la Hong Kong "Trotskyist" activist Au Long Yu, it would be better to simply appreciate that it did not ignite xenophobic attacks or violent police responses. Explaining away the movement's problems, or greatly exaggerating the "leftist" elements of it, romanticizes it all and only serves to perpetuate a nationalistic/localist Hong Konger identity in opposition to a totalitarian mainland one. It will not help de-colonize the intellectual political culture of Hong Kong, or of China, or the West.

At any rate both of these minor, seemingly progressive moments of cross community protest (and there were others) actually tell us something about the real content and structure of the Hong Kong identity at work. As noted before, the rise of independence and of—far worse— xenophobic and aggressive anti-mainland nativism reached a crescendo in 2019. This in itself would only be news to Western media and their devotees, and it represents a culmination of how Hong Kong identity went from being predicated on autonomy (and difference and, for many, superiority) from the mainland to being, politically and existentially, in a "hidden" friend/enemy war with a colonizer. Clearly the promise of autonomy meant far more than a legalistic issue of perceived rights and incursions. It somehow reached people bone-deep, and activated intense, dyadic, group-identity thinking and affect.[35]

It seems fair to surmise that this type of extreme commitment to autonomy (even at a political and economic level, beyond cultural autonomy) would be impossible to imagine without a deeply felt (or sincere and "authentic") and yet deeply problematic Hong Kong identity itself predicated, from its very beginnings, on that identity being defined as one autonomous from mainland/Chinese identity. It was not the relation to the British, to other Asians or Caucasians that Hong Kong identity was defined by. Furthermore, given the vague connotations of what Hong Kong (or any) culture is defined by that is truly unique or specific to itself, it is the autonomy *from* (and the difference and separation *from*) mainland China/Chineseness that stands out as the most specific, clear demarcation and detail about whatever Hong Kong identity is, or was. Part of the problem here is that this autonomy is not after all some "civic virtue" that everyone pulled off the pages of J.S. Mill or a liberal political theory textbook. It is coded in impossibly exceptionalist terms of superiority, a la American "leadership" of and for the free world. Even the city's mainstream propaganda takes part in this: Hong Kong is "Asia's Global

City." As if Hong Kong is inarguably the most "global" and presumably "cosmopolitan" city in the Chinese speaking world, let alone in Asia. Meanwhile its foreign domestic workers are precluded from becoming permanent residents.

The affect and desire built into Hong Kong autonomy and its attendant localist identity can also be measured by the now-banned film *Ten Years After*. While predictably hailed by the usual suspects in the city and abroad, this baldly propagandistic, yellow-peril "independent" film from 2015 does indeed possess sociological value.[36] Not as some type of truth-telling independent cinema-verité or powerful dystopia—which is what it was taken up as by the above demographic, and renewed again after its release on Netflix in 2019 before—but as a striking expression of yellow peril discourse and of the fear and loathing of the mainland invader by the post-1970s generation (i.e. a large chunk of it). In short, if you want to know what Hong Kong localist identity became at its extremes by 2014–2019, and especially its panicked nihilism, watch *Ten Years After*. In place of a narrative let alone a rational depiction of Hong Kong's various and complex problems stemming from the Basic Law arrangement and colonialism, one gets a series of chapters that simply turn on fear if not horror over what will happen by 2025 (the banishment of Cantonese language, Red/youth guards attacking bookstores, bulldozing of houses at will, and so on). Most strikingly, it also depicts a Hong Kong where a staged assassination takes place in order to legitimate a pending national security legislation. One may wonder if the petrol-throwing anarchists/nihilists of 2019 may have read the film too literally. Primal fears indeed.[37] As Liu Shih Ding and Wei Shi note in their analysis of the film and by extension of the dysfunctional Hong Kong-mainland relationship:

> Hong Kong is constructed as the injured and victimised subject under threat and unable to maintain their ways of life or dignity, ultimately unable to control their own destiny. Articulated with hatred for the enemy, such politics of fear leads to the cultivation of a rebellious subject who is self-determined and uncompromising when fighting against the enemy. The self-other relation is defined in absolutely moral and antagonistic terms of binary opposition that makes reconciliation impossible.[38]

In this scenario, which became all too real by 2019, the antagonism can only be decided by radical, i.e., fundamental and confrontational means: one side will win, and one will lose. There will inevitably be a moment of decision, a decisive socio-political turn, and for better and worse the anti-ELAB movement and C.E. Lam finally made this happen after many years of a difficult and stagnating status-quo in the city. This is, again, the tragedy of the pan-democratic or broadly oppositional, autonomist movement of Hong Kong that is now finished. One can perhaps call it a revolution after all, but if so it is one that failed (obviously) and moreover it was not admirable or even especially progressive in its ideology (or absence thereof, outside of colonial-liberalism).

One can certainly agree with Ip Iam-Chong's earnest defense of Hong Kong localism or nativism as a complex sociological formation in its own right, one that often has no directly political beliefs or positions, one that indicates participants' existential struggles, one that is replete with fantasies deriving from cultural crisis, and so on.[39] We can hope that more such studies, perhaps more critically and psycho-analytically inflected, of 'the movement' will be produced in the future. But as even Ip readily admits (despite being sympathetic), this is still a right-wing nativism. If anything Ip underplays the size and scale of Hong Kong nativism and xenophobia as opposed to a more 'neutral' localism. But the problem with Hong Kong cultural studies, in its efforts to not only understand but to literally be part of 'the movement' for 'democracy' since the 1990s, has long been that the 'neutral' spot between explanation and endorsement is bewitched. It repeats what Lenin called the partisanship of objectivity, and therefore also gives short shrift to the ethically and politically problematic aspects of the movement, and to the very narrow notion of democracy in Hong Kong political intellectual culture. As Petula Ho-Sik has argued, the price to pay for a certain loyalty to the movement, which is to say for an identification with it, and perhaps an identification with Hong Kong identity circa 2019, is one's intellectual integrity and independence as well as the ability to provide critical feedback *to* the movement.[40] Identification runs opposite to critical distance. Thus 'cultural studies' of, e.g., Occupy in 2014 or of 2019 that do not interrogate them critically but instead make them seem "theoretical" and "ground-breaking" conceptually are not critical interventions so much as apologias or ex post facto justifications of social movements and political protests that failed drastically or that became reactionary.[41] Sometimes "the people" and protest movements can be wrong, even in Hong Kong, and even when posed against the P.R.C. It should not be necessary to state this, but it is.

The identity that emerged in 2019, no doubt with twists and turns along the way since the early 1970s, is loaded with affect, nostalgia, and desire, and cannot be separated from—in fact is now functionally part of—the city's nativism or localism: an imagined, even transcendent community of horizontal comradeship indeed.[42] As Benedict Anderson noted, nationalism or imagined communities are not false because they are imagined. They are seemingly universal at that: as Anderson once wryly noted, he had only met two or three "cosmopolitans" or non-nationalists in his life. But like forms of religious belief they can nonetheless be not only empowering but dangerous and reactionary, and are in any case by definition—and like liberalism—exclusionary and limited. What is or was excluded in this case in some type of 'solidarity' or humanistic feeling with "mainlanders" or those with opposite political views on the issue of the city's integration and the mainland's ultimate sovereignty. This makes the recent Hong Kong–China confrontation—unfortunately triangulated by the USA in 2019—eminently political in that dyadic, Schmittian sense where there can in reality only be one (if non permanent) winner. This was simply, even tragically, a political conflict that could not be neutralized by either protest or legislation, or the repeal of legislation. Its causes were multiple, as always, from government ineptitude and the inherent contradictions of the Basic Law (e.g., sovereignty and autonomy, integration and 'two systems,' and so on) to the dynamics of burnism/nihilism and an identity and identity politics pushed to its extremes. The intensity of the negative affect and hatred, the willingness to destroy or "burn" the city literally and metaphorically, even to rather directly court/incite arrest and violence has to be explained in substantial part by that identity formation.[43]

This was not the exact same identity as that of the 1970s (which was apolitical in comparison). But it did have its roots in this late colonial period, and the knowledge-power or discourse politics needed to perpetuate colonial rule better and the need for the colonized—like all humans—to have something, some identity to believe in or belong to. In sum, while the China field will by and large continue to ignore this, there should be no doubt that the 2019 events, and the clash of political and intellectual cultures therein, also have much to do with the region's and world's histories and politics of modern, Western colonialism and contemporary neo-imperialism. Nativism after all, and the production of a single, true authentic identity connected to place, has long been powerfully associated with colonialism or imperialism. While perfectly understandable as a response to colonial/foreign oppression or exploitation or deprivation, or even to the mere perception of such experiences, Hong Kong's would not be the first time such an identity politics proved less than progressive or humane to its own society and people as well as towards its others. Much of post-colonial studies, for example, has diagnosed nativism in just such a critical fashion.[44] Whether we call it localism or nativism, it is striking that this type of militant if not crypto-fascistic identity politics, premised on a horrifying, yet imagined threat from the other, would also take the form of a liberal or "democratic" demand for freedom, rule of law, autonomy, and so on. This is what contemporary liberalism has become, or can be articulated to. In this sense the oft-noted parallels between the 2021 Trumpist supporters storming Capitol Hill in Washington, DC and those in Hong Kong's storming of the Legco Building in 2019 do have something to show us, namely that liberalism can be articulated to deeply problematic acts and wills to power based on perceived, imaginary threats and colonizations of one's "own" places.

Thus 2019 (or Hong Kong 1997–present) is not or was not a simple story of "authoritarianism versus freedom" or, in the slightly more academic version of this media meme, a tale of people's "right to participate" (with xenophobic violence and petrol bombs apparently) versus becoming cogs in some disciplinary capitalist machine (as if Hong Kong were not already rather capitalist!).[45] It is now settled decisively, in structural terms, in the mainland's and Hong Kong government's favour. We shall see what this will in turn lead to in the coming years.

As for Hong Kong identity, within the city as opposed to what is now called its "diaspora" after the national security law, this too will inevitably change and take new forms. As the superb scholar and sociologist of Hong Kong, Lui Tai Lok, argued well before 2019, the future of Hong Kong identity in its present form (dating from the 1970s but intensely 'yellow' or nativist now), and where Hong Kong "culture" will reside (whatever this means),[46] will precisely be in its diaspora, be it in Shanghai, Western cities in Canada, the UK, Taiwan, and elsewhere. But the present argument here is that this refers only—but significantly, to be sure—to the post-1970s identity of Hong Kong and Hong Kongers as a place separate and autonomous from the mainland, and categorically different. Others will emerge, including a new dominant identity and culture. The relative hegemony of the authentic, 'yellow' one circa 2019 (hegemonic in culture, media, and education but not in government) will give way to something else. Hong Kong has always been a city of changes in many ways, despite the pan-democratic project of autonomy and preservation of the status quo. Hong Kong has dominant, residual, and emergent 'cultures,' groups, and identities and ideologies like all other major cities and places.

This changeability is sometimes reified as Hong Kong's 'culture of disappearance' a la the influential, semiological book by Akbar Abbas in the later 1990s.[47] But Abbas never meant that Hong Kong was actually disappearing or dying, just as it is not now either; and his work itself was never meant to be nativist or localist in a political way. While no fault of his own, it has always been odd to see Abbas taken as some type of Hong Kong booster in a localist sense, when he himself has not only lived abroad for years but has also spoken about not being taken as an authentic Hong Konger during his Hong Kong years due to his non-Chinese appearance. Indeed Abbas's point was simply that the identity of Hong Kong itself was always (or *sometimes* we might say instead, to avoid hyperbole) changing and never stable. As I have argued above (and as have many others) this is akin to what many of us experience as human individuals—that we have several identities and roles and modes of being, that we are always already hybridized to some extent. Of course some identities are more equal than others: connected to power or money or privilege in specific contexts. While Abbas did not delve into subject positions or anthropological or ethnographic analysis, the take-away from such an analysis would seem to be precisely that a localist or nativist identity—or a national-patriotic one—would not stick for very long, even within a single human generation.

If it is in Hong Kong's nature to always be 'disappearing'—changing and adapting—then the nativist place-based identity, firmly rooted in the local and standing against a bogeyman identity to the north whilst predicated on an alleged authenticity, is actually impossible. It stands revealed as very much the specific, post-1970s, colonial and Cold War 'social construction' that it always has been. The rise and now eclipse of that particular identity proves the point about fluidity and changeability in the long run. What is disappearing, or what will do so— eventually, in a generation, give or take—is this particular, hierarchical post-1997 form of an identity predicated not just on place and authenticity but on autonomy and nativism in an ultimately harmful, certainly xenophobic, and colonially-rooted way. And Hong Kong culture, from its own cuisine (which was always hybridized with other places of Asia and the West, and yet has always been Cantonese), to its own language and ways of seeing will still exist in Hong Kong and will continue to change and live on, as all cultures do.

Thus one should not reify the contemporary "yellow" identity that in part resulted in the protests-turned-riots in 2019 as being genuinely authentic and the one real Hong Konger identity. So too the assumption that this particular identity (and anti-mainland politics) includes virtually everyone in the city misreads not only the demographics of the city (especially its ruling classes *and* grass roots population) but also cannot explain the massive and rapid changes in the city since the denouement of 2019's protests.[48] The issue of who belongs to what Hong Kong identity (there are more than two variations) is an empirical question and should not be taken for granted, despite what the obviously partisan media and Hong Kong "diaspora" wants everyone to believe. Moreover "authenticity" may be a meaningful *ethic* on an individual level (as opposed to being, say, a careerist or opportunist), but to articulate authenticity to a cultural, social, or racialized identity is clearly problematic and even dangerous. This should not need saying. The fact that identities are made, not natural or given, and that they—or we—are multiple (we each contain multitudes, as the poet Whitman put it) should have obvious consequences for politics as much as for life. The problems of nationalism and nativism (to be discussed in the next chapter) are cases in point.

It is certainly true that mainstream mainland discourse has its own would-be authentic and dominant notion of Chineseness (as there is for American identity, etc.) and this too has changed over the years, not least from the more internationalist, communistic Mao years to that of today. But many people within China have been ignoring mainstream or dominant identities for years too, just as they do elsewhere. Of course this sometimes takes courage and a non-conformist spirit, and can involve real risks in specific instances. At any rate the political point or red line is now clear, and it is the sovereignty of the mainland and the taboo against independence or separatist speech. Obviously this marks an authoritarian turn, particularly if such speech gets interpreted too broadly.[49] But it is perfectly conceivable for Hong Kong to have its own place-based identity and more or less full cultural autonomy (including the language of Cantonese) as long as this does not get articulated to, or devolve into some type of regime-change confrontation that it cannot win in any case. One suspects that it is precisely because Hong Kong was colonized by the British and West that it wants or wanted—that some in 2019 wanted—its de facto political independence and own, de facto sovereignty. A self-other dialectic that was doomed to fail given the forces involved, but moreover one that may well not have been worth dying on the hill for. Not least because independence has never been an explicit mass demand within the city. One person's revolution may be another's putsch.

Here too, in the realm of identity politics, is where one can see an historical connection to the rise of nationalism that arguably underpins the rise of Hong Kong nativism (including a nativist or separatist identity). As famously theorized and historicized by Benedict Anderson, nationalists in Europe and later in the colonies were willing to die for their nation precisely because their imagined national/political communities were powerfully affective and existentially, if not transcendentally charged. Nationalism provided an answer or resolution for issues of human mortality, belonging or 'horizontal comradeship,' and the experience of simultaneous or non-homogenous time. All of which had previously been brought to crisis towards the end of the feudal/pre-bourgeois and/or colonial eras. Anderson also argued, albeit more controversially, that nationalism was modular and, more to the point, was in effect exported from Europe to the colonies and adopted there to drive anti-colonialism and national liberation. It is not hard to see a very similar dynamic within Hong Kong, by substituting nativism for nationalism, or a free autonomous Hong Kong for nation, and 'burnism' for a willing to sacrifice one's life. As for time or our lived relation to it (temporality), the 'revolution now' feeling would certainly seem at least to be a messianic, quasi-revolutionary disruption of empty homogenous time as well as "borrowed time."

Obviously a document like the Basic Law cannot account for, or remedy any of this. Nor can some type of natural belongingness to the great Chinese nation that many Hong Kongers have little direct experience or even knowledge of. Again, we need to recall that identity and nationalism/nativism are not merely false consciousness but imagined, meaningful, and powerful to the point of perceived transcendence and martyrdom. They are also capable of great malevolence and violence and ugliness towards others not in 'your' group. In other words they are neither fake nor innocent and call out for interrogation, not celebration or knee-jerk side-takings.

# Notes

1. Leaving aside, of course, the too easy scapegoating of "Beijing" for such discontents.
2. The circularity should be obvious here. For more information, see the review essay by Terrie Ng of several recent books, "Protesting with Text and Image: Four Publications on the 2019 Pro-democracy Movement from Hong Kong Civil Society," *China Perspectives*, 2021/1 | 2021, 55–60. Just to be clear, texts and 'culture' defined in this way are not unimportant and are welcome contributions in general, but they cannot substitute for political and inter-disciplinary analysis. What I have in mind is stated in text, but I would also index, for example, the work of British Cultural Studies as originally conceived *a la* Stuart Hall, Williams, and others. The work of my former teacher, Larry Grossberg, offers a strong critique of textualism-as-culturalism. In short, culture, and therefore cultural studies, are not always about texts and should not be reduced to them.
3. See for example Jeffrey Wasserstrom, *Vigil: Hong Kong on the Brink* (Columbia UP, 2020). Slower, more scholarly writing can also take the form of more investigative, longer-form journalism, of course. But insta-history and insta-punditry are the problem.
4. Note that we do not need pseudo-philosophical terms like 'futurity' here.
5. See Wang Hui among others, "Depoliticized Politics, Multiple Components of Hegemony, and the Eclipse of the Sixties," Trans. Chris Connery. *Inter-Asia Cultural Studies* 7.4: 683–700. The work of political economist Mark Blyth on the failures of austerity/neo-liberalism and the rise of global Trumpism should be far more known within cultural/global studies, as he provides a lucid and penetrating account of why our party systems and political structures have failed so miserably and are rejected so consistently by so many. Like Wang Hui's work it is free of the triteness informing much Western left-ish theorizing. See for example, "Global Trumpism: Why Trump's Victory Was 30 Years in the Making and Why It Won't Stop Here," *Foreign Policy*, 15 November 2006. https://www.foreignaffairs.com/articles/2016-11-15/global-trumpism. Accessed 4 May 2020.
6. We can date this from the 1970s due to the rapprochement between the PRC and the USA on the one hand, and hence a different phase of the Cold War, and on the other to increasing contact on the matter between the UK and China. It was in the 1970s that the English phrase "living on borrowed time" became more commonplace. I have discussed the Basic Law in *Illiberal China*, in the light of 2014's Occupy movement. See especially the work of Lui Tai Lok cited below. For the full text of the document, see the HK Sar government. https://www.basiclaw.gov.hk/en/basiclaw/index.html. Accessed 4 May 2020.

7. I wish to keep the identity of the conference speaker anonymous, but I trust that the paraphrase will seem familiar to others within our local milieu as it is not an uncommon take. There was a widespread belief that Hong Kong would transform China, and its 'failure' to do so may well inform some of the negative affect attached to its recent history since 1997.

8. See Lui Tai Lok, "The Unfinished Chapter of Hong Kong's Long Political Transition," *Critique of Anthropology* 40.2 (2020): 270–276.

9. As Lui notes, Friedman thought having two currencies in the city (HKD and RMB) would be unsustainable, would require capital controls/strong state intervention, and would therefore induce economic collapse.

10. Lui Tai Lok, "The Unfinished Chapter of Hong Kong's Long Political Transition," 273. The increase in two-way capital and human traffic marked a departure from the one-way years, i.e. that of only Hong Kong capital and people going north. It was also a response both to SARS and the economic impact thereof, and a political crisis against the C.E. Tung Chee Hwa around the security question.

11. Lui Tai Lok, "The Unfinished Chapter of Hong Kong's Long Political Transition," 274. See also the chapters on the Basic Law by Albert Chen, Danny Gittings, Sung Yun-Wing, in Lui Tai Lok, Stephen W.K. Chiu, and Ray Yep, Eds., *Routledge Handbook of Contemporary Hong Kong* (Routledge, 2019).

12. See the short but full text of the 1984 agreement, "Joint Declaration of the Government of the United Kingdom of Great Britain and Northern Ireland and the Government of the People's Republic of China on the Question of Hong Kong," at the Hong Kong government website: https://www.cmab.gov.hk/en/issues/jd2.htm. Accessed 4 May 2020.

13. For this general take, see John Ford, "The Pivot to Asia Was Obama's Biggest Mistake," *The Diplomat*, 21 January 2017. https://thediplomat.com/2017/01/the-pivot-to-asia-was-obamas-biggest-mistake/. Accessed 4 May 2020. Ford, like others, sees this as an inadvertent attempt to contain China.

14. See his Twitter feed of June 2020, which as of the time of writing is still online. https://twitter.com/chuhoidick. Chu is currently serving a jail sentence for participating in the July 2020 unofficial primary, for physical fighting in LegCo, and on other charges. Needless to say, while critical of the appeals for US and other foreign intervention, and of the constant filibustering, I do not wish to condone let alone applaud his and other's too-harsh sentences. The sentencing of the 47 pan-democratic activists for their primary—admittedly an attempt to dominate and shut down the legislature—is arguably the most decisive, political strike from the establishment or more accurately from the mainland. While these and virtually all the arrests have followed the letter of the law, so to speak, one wishes

3 BASIC LAW, BASIC PROBLEMS: AUTONOMY AND IDENTITY    93

that the spirit were followed more. There is a difference between someone like the Trumpist Jimmy Lai and other activists.

15. See Article 45, under Chapter IV of the Basic Law at: https://www.bas iclaw.gov.hk/filemanager/content/en/files/basiclawtext/basiclaw_full_t ext.pdf. Accessed 4 May 2022.

16. Interestingly, the Wikipedia entry on this is less tendentious and ridiculous than the usual 'respectable' media. See https://en.wikipedia.org/wiki/ 2021_Hong_Kong_electoral_changes. Accessed 15 May 2022.

17. In the somewhat convoluted Hong Kong electoral system, district councillors are not members of Legco but rather do more mundane and quotidian labor of specific neighbourhoods and committees. They are however quite important in their own right. As a constituency they could also elect one Legco member.

18. See David Zweig, "The Chief Executive Election Hong Kong Could Have Had," *South China Morning Post*, 24 March 2017. https://www. scmp.com/comment/insight-opinion/article/2081575/chief-executive-election-hong-kong-could-have-had. Accessed 4 March 2022.

19. We will later discuss the issue of the fear or perception of the loss of autonomy, which in my view has much to do with the issue of Hong Kong identity as it was/is constructed from the colonial 1970s onwards.

20. See in particular, Cornelius Castoriadis, *Philosophy, Politics, Autonomy: Essays in Political Philosophy*, Ed. David Ames Curtis (Oxford Press, 1991).

21. See Freud, *Civilization and Its Discontents*.

22. Tom O'Shea, "The Essex Autonomy Project: Critics of Autonomy," (2012) "Critics of Autonomy." Essex Autonomy Project: https://aut onomy.essex.ac.uk/wp-content/uploads/2016/11/CriticsofAutonomyG PRJune2012.pdf. Accessed 4 May 2022.

23. See a recent Hong Kong Economic Journal article by Winston Fung, "Authoritarian-Populism Spectre Hanging over US-China Relations," 18 November 2021. https://www.ejinsight.com/eji/article/id/2969627/ 20211118-Authoritarian-populism-spectre-hanging-over-US-China-rel ations. Accessed 1 April 2022. On the transformation/degradation of liberalism despite the rise of rhetoric about "illiberalism" globally, see Vukovich, *Illiberal China*, 2019.

24. Jean Baudrillard's point here was actually about sex and sexuality not identity, but I think he would not mind my extrapolation. See his *America* Trans. Chris Turner (New York: Verso, 1989).

25. See the Preface and indeed the entire monograph by Chun, *Forget Chineseness: On the Geopolitics of Cultural Identification* (Albany: SUNY Press, 2017). I am indebted to Prof Chun for his work and collegiality. To say that identity politics are group politics—which has an implicit obviousness—is not to dismiss them or debunk them but to begin to take group

politics, which is to say real politics, far more seriously. But then one needs to take the problem or 'problematic' (Althusser) of groups and class seriously as well. Figures as diverse as Freud and Schmitt are thus germane here, and not only contemporary theory.

26. See Wang Anyi [王安忆], "Brothers" [[弟兄们, 1989]. In *Red Is Not the only Color: Contemporary Chinese Fiction on Love and Sex between Women*, ed. Patricia Angela Sieber, 93–141 (Lanham, MD: Rowman & Littlefield, 2011).

27. See John Carroll, *Edge of Empires: Chinese Elites and British Colonials in Hong Kong* (Harvard UP, 2005).

28. See Law Wing Sang, *Collaborative Colonial Power: The Making of the Hong Kong Chinese* (Hong Kong UP, 2009). I should note that Law's views on the autonomy/organic nature of Hong Kong identity in this book, and his evaluations of the PRC in general, are different than mine. But he too in later work also notes the turn to an independence/segregationist split, in essence a liberal ("left" in Hong Kong terms) and right wing split within Hong Kong identity since 2003 and especially 2011. See his comments in "From local identity to the pursuit of independence: The changing face of Hong Kong localism," by Varsity in *The Hong Kong Free Press*, 11 November 2016. Accessed 4 May 2020. There should be no doubt that localist identity has become or became quite right wing (xenophobic, anti-communist, anti-mainland) in in recent years, though this has barely informed popular and academic work on Hong Kong. One can reasonably disagree over the scope and scale, but to not see it as substantial and damaging by 2019 would seem a major error and self-interested interpretation.

29. Michael Adorjan, Paul Vinod Khiatani, and Wing Hong Chui, "The Rise and Ongoing Legacy of Localism as Collective Identity in Hong Kong: Resinicisation Anxieties and Punishment of Political Dissent in the Post-Colonial Era," *Punishment & Society* 23.5 (2021): 650–674.

30. See the survey and other data in Adorjan et al., above.

31. See Gordon Matthews, "Hèunggóngyàhn: On the Past, Present, and Future of Hong Kong Identity," *Critical Asian Studies* 29.3 (1997): 3–13.

32. I use quote marks here because there should be no such thing as second or third generation immigrants: after the first generation, they are or should be real, equally belonging citizens and subjects.

33. Of course you can also easily, too easily theorize a "civic local identity" that would have read Jurgen Habermas and the like, but the point is that such ideal type cosmopolitanism rarely if ever exists in actual societies. As Ben Anderson liked to quip, I have only ever met two or three cosmopolitans in my whole life.

3 BASIC LAW, BASIC PROBLEMS: AUTONOMY AND IDENTITY   95

34. See "The Hongkongers from ethnic minorities who thank protest movement for helping them finally feel part of the city," *South China Morning Post*, 30 October 2019. https://www.scmp.com/news/hong-kong/society/article/3035258/hongkongers-ethnic-minorities-who-thank-protest-movement. Accessed 4 May 2022.

35. On this friend-enemy dynamic in regard to group-identity, See Schmitt, The *Concept of the Political* (U Chicago Press, 2007). Trans. George Schwab. [1937]. From Schmitt's standpoint in this work, the Hong Kong-China political relationship as played out within the city's protest and democratic movement, would seem to offer the perfect, and perfectly disturbing, illustration of what "the political" is by definition. My own argument has been to see the final form of the 2014 and 2019 movements as actually de-politicized in that they gave up on legislative or state action or reform and devolved into symbolic struggles. In the case of 2019, a struggle against the police or "blue" people. But Schmitt's usefulness for the Hong Kong-China antagonism is all too obvious.

36. Info on the film can be found at *Variety*, "Film Review: 'Ten Years.'" https://variety.com/2016/film/reviews/ten-years-film-review-1201748166/. Accessed 4 May 2022.

37. See the insightful take on the movie in just these terms, by Alice Wu, "Love It or Hate It, *Ten Years* points to the common enemy in Hong Kong politics—fear," *SCMP*. https://www.scmp.com/comment/insight-opinion/article/1934694/love-it-or-hate-it-ten-years-points-common-enemy-hong-kong.

38. See Liu Shih-Ding and Shi Wei, "Why Is Reconciliation Impossible? On the Clash of Emotions between Hong Kong and Mainland China," *Made in China*, September–December 2021. https://madeinchinajournal.com/2022/03/08/why-is-reconciliation-impossible/. Accessed 4 May 2022.

39. See Ip Iam-Chong's *Hong Kong's New Identity Politics: Longing for the Local in the Shadow of China* (Routledge 2020).

40. See Petula Sik Ying Ho (2022) "Connection at the Price of Collusion: An Analysis of 'Hong Kong's New Identity Politics: Longing for the Local in the Shadow of China," *Cultural Studies* 36.2 (2020): 229–251. I should note that the point here about identity circa 2019 is my own. But Ho's principled critique of the 2019 movement, or its trajectory, is important, and courageous, in the context of Hong Kong academic/intellectual politics.

41. See for example Pang Laikwan's *The Appearing Demos: Hong Kong During and After the Umbrella Movement* (U Michigan Press, 2020). Ip's book, by contrast, does not shy away from the problem of nativism and localism, even if it seeks to redeem them in some sense or at least see their silver lining.

96    D. F. VUKOVICH

42. The reference here is to Ben Anderson's classic, *Imagined Communities: Reflections on the Origin and Spread of Nationalism* (London: Verso, 2016) [1983].
43. Of course there were no doubt other emotions/affects in play, from solidarity and belonging to great sadness and so on. But the anger and hatred and sheer aggression and atavism must be recognized, even if they were largely ignored by the Freedom, Inc take.
44. See for example, Anthony Appiah, *In My Father's House: Africa in the Philosophy of Culture* (Oxford UP, 1993). Mahmood Mamdani's work on nativism is also crucial, albeit in a different context than that of Hong Kong (yet still about the British empire). See *When Victims Become Killers: Colonialism, Nativism, and the Genocide in Rwanda* (Princeton UP, 2001) as well as *Define and Rule: Native as Political Identity* (Harvard UP, 2012).
45. See for example the amusing essay by Italian journalist Simone Pieranni, "Hong Kong, the first revolt against surveillance capitalism," translated at the *positions* blog. https://positionspolitics.org/simone-pieranni-hong-kong-the-first-revolt-against-surveillance-capitalism/. Accessed 4 May 2022. What is funny is to see the mediatized 'revolt' framed as being against surveillance, a la some libertarian fantasy, and also as somehow against capitalism.
46. All cultures, Hong Kong's included are, as Raymond Williams suggested of the word itself, notoriously hard to define if also undeniably pointing to something important to people and thus to cultural studies. See Williams, *Keywords: A Vocabulary of Culture and Society* (Oxford UP, 1976). Thus "whatever this means" here is to be read literally, not as a critique. Cultures invariably copy and counterfeit one another, such that claims of uniqueness and exceptionalism are always misleading and tend to be made to police certain boundaries and identities.
47. Ackbar Abbas, *Hong Kong: Culture and the Politics of Disappearance* (U Minnesota Press, 1997).
48. For a recent example of the reification of localist, and allegedly 'authentic' and majoritarian identity I am trying to describe here, see Gregory Lee and Patrick Poon's article, "Hong Kong: The Decolonization that Never Happened." https://postcolonialpolitics.org/hong-kong-the-decolonization-that-never-happened/. Accessed 4 May 2020. Just as some de-colonization movements can be essentialist and/or right-wing, so can some versions of post-colonial analysis.
49. To take one example, demagogic politician Junius Ho once declared that anyone opposing the zero-covid policy could (should) be construed as violating the national security law. But this was never taken seriously by the government or 'establishment.'

CHAPTER 4

# Re-Colonization or De-Colonization?

*It's the Economy, Stupid.*

Unless there is a long-overdue recognition of and engagement with the colonial past as well as the present "post"-colonialism of Hong Kong, which is to say of the city's and the mainland's failures to de-colonize, then Hong Kong's discontents and unhappiness will endure *despite* the impossibility of "burnism" and independence-talk emerging again. As we have noted above, the Basic Law mini-constitution and would-be blueprint for Hong Kong-mainland integration says almost nothing about de-colonization, and in fact does not raise that term or any other related, liberatory language. Economically, it even (erroneously) promised to keep the two systems of socialism and capitalism apart. Even allowing the term 'socialism' for the mid-1980s or late 1990s mainland system of economy, it was, as we have argued, at best dubious to think that the tidal waves of capital accumulation and flow (obvious in 1997 if not 1983) would leave Hong Kong, or the mainland, intact. Intact and therefore two "systems," not one, and yet economically (and in terms of migration) mutually invested and steadily if not rapidly coming together. From the standpoint of de-colonization, the economic "front" was simply not to be opened (or conceived as a thing that must be de-colonized or re-made from its British roots).

© The Author(s), under exclusive license to Springer Nature
Singapore Pte Ltd. 2022
D. F. Vukovich, *After Autonomy: A Post-Mortem
for Hong Kong's first Handover, 1997–2019,*
https://doi.org/10.1007/978-981-19-4983-8_4

97

Of course this is because the mainland wanted to preserve Hong Kong's role as a banking and finance capital centre for mainland investment and related services, and it was already deeply immersed in daunting, radically conservative or anti-Maoist national-level changes and structural adjustments. But there is nonetheless a larger failure here in regards to de-colonization, and not least for a system that firmly sees itself as socialist. From the elite sites of power on all three borders from Beijing to London to Central district Hong Kong, it was as if the economic "energy" and abundant growth of both places would magically work to smooth out the handover and transition. If everybody is busy and happy getting rich, then who cares? As Deng Xiaoping also famously promised, the parties and horse races would continue. The image of Hong Kong as a place of parties, gambling, abundance, in a word Hong Kong as a capitalist-consumerist, contented 'paradise' that was very Chinese yet very non-political: this is actually a British colonial image of Hong Kong, which Deng and others in Beijing must have known if not also endorsed themselves. We leave to one side here the British decision to try and introduce "democracy"—partial legislative elections—in the last few years of their reign, but only after the Joint Declaration was signed in 1984. This was, however, less a response to popular demand than a deliberate, parting shot to change China as it saw fit, and in that sense not unlike what it did to deadly effect with the Partition of India when it finally had to leave fifty years earlier.[1]

For all the references to the Chinese "socialist" system, or to two systems, what we can call *economism* or the quasi-religious belief in market forces and market relations and growth/accumulation solving social and political and historical problems—in effect de-politicizing society—was the order of the day. This is also a key part of a classic if vulgar liberal-economic discourse that triumphed in the nineteenth and twentieth centuries in the West during the so-called Great Transformation as theorized by Karl Polanyi among others, and more recently by Mark Blyth in terms of austerity economics.[2] The colonial system and the capitalist market system were always articulated together in the modern period, just as finance capital more specifically did so with imperialism and militarism. This is a fairly standard insight within much of the former colonized world and within the better, critical academic disciplines, but unsurprisingly *not* the conventional wisdom within fields like Chinese history and political science and in 'global academies' like Hong Kong's. Indeed the latter, while publicly funded and largely affordable for those who get in, and consistently ranked very highly in various and tendentious ranking polls, are far from de-colonized and are closer to corporations than institutions of higher learning and broad-based education. It is easy enough to see a rough but strong homology between laissez-faire liberal economics, with not a little anti-statism and anti-collectivist sentiment a la Von Hayek or neo-liberalism, and the initial post-Mao Party-state of the Deng Xiaoping and handover eras leading up to 1989.[3] There was no debate about China launching shock therapy or austerity economics in Hong Kong, which had been practicing the latter since its origin; if anything Hong Kong was there to grease the wheels of the transition to capitalism (or the strategic deployment of it if you really prefer) in China and Guangdong in particular. Hence the early outflows of Hong Kong capital into China, the re-location of local industry to the north, and so on. It may be useful for some to recall that the post-Mao Party state, in so far as it had a socialist or Marxist-influenced economics, was decidedly not in the Maoist 'politics in command' mode but more in an economistic Soviet-esque "no class struggle but development of the productive forces" camp.[4] To be sure the role of government planning in managing the market still obtained in the mainland (as it does even at present under Xi Jinping) or rather triumphed over those who wanted a more straight-up, shocking neoliberalism; but the plan for Hong Kong's economy was essentially to have no plan at all, and to keep it separate from the mainland's, aside of course from capital inflows *from* very capitalist Hong Kong.[5]

## Towards Economic De-Colonization?

As noted before, prior to 2019 the mainland rigorously refrained from any *direct* input into Hong Kong governance in terms of the economy or much else. The point was, perhaps, to let Hong Kongers rule Hong Kong under the Basic Law. This nonetheless led to endless speculation about the underground communist party in the city, about secret control of the local government, conspiratorial united fronts, and so on. While it is certain that there has long been "spies" or security agents operating in the city at one level or another (if this is not too Cold War-esque a way to frame it), as evidenced by the quick arrests and "unofficial extraditions" of the Hong Kong booksellers, the point here is about politics and governance per se, at the level of the state/officialdom. Before 2020, this was largely a hands-off affair aside from the obvious case of the C.E. nomination process. Hong Kong was going to be left to work out its own problems, partly on principle (relative autonomy) and partly because Beijing knew full well that any direct moves would be controversial.

Suffice it to mention the importance of Hong Kong tycoons to the selling and smoothing-over of the Basic Law and the handover. Two of the SAR's four Chief Executives to date have been tycoons, and the second C.E., Donald Tsang, was indeed their close friend later convicted of taking bribes. Mainstream mainland identity politics, for their part, simply assumed that "compatriots" in Hong Kong would mostly welcome the handover due to their shared Chineseness/identity.[6] Deng Xiaoping's speeches suggest his apparent belief that Hong Kong people, like all good Chinese, would be happy to re-join the motherland once they get to know it better; and in any case all Chinese greatly desire the re-unification of Hong Kong, Macau, and Taiwan with the proverbial motherland.[7] It is as if de-colonization, from the Dengist Party's perspective was either a non-issue entirely or would simply be dissolved by an economic integration in due but assured time. As we have seen, the actually existing Hong Kong identity, from the 1970s onwards but especially with the rise of an intense, dyadic, friend/enemy localism after 1997, put paid to this myth.

The 2019 protests seem to have finally woken up the mainland and the local government to the realization that the economic question can no longer go begging. The various editorials and implied directives, official and otherwise from the mainland have now insisted that the housing shortages and precarious economic situation of many, even most Hong Kongers must be alleviated. Plans—and they are very much plans, not actualities as of 2021—range from finally bringing in more qualified doctors from abroad (something long opposed by the local medical lobby here), to land reclamations off of Lantau island, to the creation of a "Northern Metropolis" (a new urban district) closer to the border with China, with over 900,000 new flats. The Greater Bay Area had already been announced before 2019, as a regional project of economic integration along the Guangdong, Pearl River delta area and including Hong Kong as well as Shenzhen, Macau, Zhuhai and Guangzhou. As with the even grander and global Belt and Road Initiative, this is less a blueprint or model than a certain mandate to foster greater economic integration and therefore, so the theory goes, more peace and livelihood. Hong Kong indeed needs more development and livelihood, and the cultural, social, ideological and emotional discontents expressed in 2019 (and earlier) no doubt have an important, even fundamental economic or livelihood dimension. We must never forget the power of money (or the lack of it) in bourgeois society, as the young Marx put it. The slogan of the day from China is no longer the "China Dream" but "Common Prosperity," which is to say the rhetoric and later hopefully the reality of a more social democratic, equitable re-distribution of wealth in China. Hong Kong's projected economic reforms are of a piece with this. The ensuing decade or two will tell the tale, and while this will certainly be a far cry from the communist horizon of Marx or Mao or even the relative beneficence of, say, German social democracy, it may nonetheless be very significant indeed for Hong Kong as it currently exists. Richard Wong, an avowedly neo-liberal/Friedman-esque Hong Kong economist from the Chicago school of economics and a very long-time vice president, provost, and power-broker at Hong Kong university, has for example expressed worry over the new "populism" and "common prosperity" drive allegedly sweeping the mainland and perhaps coming to Hong Kong, as has various editorialists in the city's major opinion outlets, the *South China Morning Post* and the *Hong Kong Economic Journal*.[8] This is rather premature at best—and would in any case be most welcome to millions in the region— but the worry over such a redistributive and 'populist' movement *within the government* as opposed to the streets, is a useful sign of the city's mainstream intellectual political culture.[9] Clearly Hong Kong needs a better ruling class (to put it bluntly), and moreover the development of a much more socially democratic intellectual political culture. This will obviously not happen overnight. But the city could and historically has done far worse than the admittedly conservative, anti-liberal mainland system that prioritizes performance legitimacy and has a lower tolerance for inequality, as opposed to Hong Kong's free-market, "business" system that has great antipathy to social welfare and the state.

Will the housing, health and job fronts, if successful in Hong Kong (by no means assured), represent a de-colonization of the economy? No and yes. No, because it will very much be within a "capitalist" or developmental, not egalitarian context and it will inevitably involve some type of co-operation with, or assent from the powerful, elite interests of the colonial era (the proverbial business community, the real estate tycoons and so on). Yes, because it would, or could fundamentally change—as in the sense of meaningfully reform—the iniquitous Hong Kong economy that, after all, dates from that British and finance capital, imperialist era. After all, not all varieties of capitalism are the same, and the term itself, while useful in the past for pointing to a modern, historical mode of production that arose after feudalism and ancient and "Asiatic" modes of production, can become an anti-intellectual talisman for those who allow it to simply end their analysis.

Anti-capitalist analysis, after all, can be as trite as apologias for the market and globalization. It is telling that dismissals and would-be debunkings of the P.R.C. as 'capitalist'—ubiquitous on the so-called Western left—can never define that term or contextualize it in the current period of global capitalism that, after all, has long abandoned formal colonies and old-school imperialism. Likewise post-Mao 'socialism with Chinese characteristics' clearly departs not only from Marx (and even Mao) as well as, say, European social democracy at its height, but at the same time cries out to be taken seriously, if only because it is taken seriously by many in the mainland and is used to self-describe or self-understand its own trajectory. Moreover Chinese "socialism" like the "second handover of Hong Kong" is also a new discourse in the making, something to be understood empirically as a 'real-world' process but also conceptually and dialectically. (This is not the ambit of the present study, which seeks instead merely to clear the ground for such inquiries to come.)

Indeed the term 'developmental'—as opposed to non-developmental aka failed or failing economies—may still be more useful to describe China in the last decade or so, as well as what Hong Kong has failed to become (as opposed to seeing a failure to have Western-style democratic elections). For a society that has always lacked, even more than the USA, a discourse of welfarist or iron-rice bowl social democracy and so-called 'statism,' even a small movement towards distributive justice in Hong Kong—e.g. progressive taxation, welfarism—would be tremendously significant for the people living there.

Is the welfare state anti- or de-colonial? If it makes sense at all to refer to economies as colonial or non-colonial (as opposed to imperialist and extractive), then we might say such a development would make the city at least a bit less so in that it would have to push back against the egregious power of land owners and developers, on the one hand, and to address the feudal-seeming but colonial-era old money families and classes on the other hand. Basic welfarism has always implied and required a certain social contract or bond that suggests everyone should get a fair shake, and should be protected to some extent from market failures or forces beyond their control. Some notion of community and belonging, in short. Localism is one version of this, but it is or has become highly xenophobic at best. Perhaps in place of a localist identity predicated upon Hong Kong's difference and autonomy from the mainland (and a superiority to it), the localism can in future be articulated towards a more inclusive and tolerant communitarianism or progressivism. That it has lacked this in the main has to do with the promulgation of a localist identity under British rule, starting in earnest in the 1960s. Ironically it also has to do with a with a certain Sinocentrism and its racial/cultural/ethnic blindness that it shares with traditional Chinese/mainland culture. A form of ethno-nationalism that says foreigners can never be Chinese (which is to say part of the national/imperial community). Indeed this rather contradicts British legal commonwealth mentalities as well.

One of the things that happened during the 2019 protests, towards their end, was the development of the so-called "yellow economy."[10] This meant supporting/spending money at businesses (often restaurants) that were openly yellow, i.e. in support of the protesters (and their money). Far more fatefully, this also meant not just boycotting—a time-honoured form of civil disobedience in China and elsewhere—but vandalizing or even trying to burn down "blue" businesses, i.e. those whose owners were either explicitly or even just thought to be against the protests and therefore "blue" (in support of the police and/or the mainland). This campaign was indeed reactionary and nationalistic in an objectionable way, and cared not a whit for the labor or class politics involved (e.g. workers at shut-down businesses, small shop despotism versus large chain conditions, etc.). It was yet another indication of the radical yet deeply problematic, authoritarian quality of large swathes of the 2019 movement. Certainly property destruction is not equivalent to severely beating or burning a counter- protester or 'mainlander.' The concern here—as with burnism in general—is not over private property so much as the xenophobia and purely aggressive, narcissistic affect. But if we want to differentiate types of violence, as in self-defence or 'popular justice,' we therefore can and should suss out and criticize violence and hatred which seems unjustified and simply inhumane. Be it genuine police brutality or genuine, xenophobic or sadistic violence or aggression.

However one thing the brief yellow economy 'movement' did do, for those would could read it as such, was to signify that the economy should *not* be an autonomous entity. This should have been a lesson in why Hong Kong autonomy is not in fact a good or even feasible idea, as it is dependent on the mainland economy and is also itself important for mainland capital flow. In short, rather than being an autonomous realm of market forces, the economy should serve the people, be it restaurant or otherwise. In other words, there is indeed a larger, finally substantive democratic principle here: or could have become so. The form it took was burning down businesses over ideological disagreements at one extreme end, or simply boycotting mainland-sympathetic or anti- protest businesses in favour of 'yellow' capitalists. Note that such boycotts are, in general terms and on principle, a non-issue in ethical terms and even welcome in themselves.

But the more general point is that something like "common prosperity" can only make sense as a thing for government to make happen if it is the people or citizenry or 'commonwealth' who matter more than profits and the rentiers, financiers, and other parasites. Thus it is not the ethnic-ideological or "local" identification that matters here but precisely the political question of livelihood, the rational kernel within the "yellow economy" moment at the end of the 2019 event and therefore the end of the opposition movement since the handover. What is needed is not a yellow or blue economy but a more social, even populist one. Even the city's finance secretary—traditionally an arch neo-liberal or 'fiscally conservative' post—has come out for a better, fairer distribution of wealth in the city. As the Secretary Paul Chan said himself:

> Economic development is for the people to have a better life; this underlines the significance and meaning of 'common prosperity'. We must not only make the cake bigger, but also divide the cake well.[11]

This is just a speech-act, of course, and may amount to little in the long run. *But it is one that was impossible to hear before 2019.* It took the end of the anti-ELAB movement and the re-assertion of mainland sovereignty as much as the rise of Xi's own 'common prosperity' mandate coming down form the north. It is certainly not something that former Finance Secretary, John Tsang, a staunchly conversative budgeter and the longest serving one in the city's history, would have ever said. Tsang, notably, also became a darling of the pan-democrats when he launched a failed bid against Carrie Lam for the C.E. post. This is, again, a telling sign of the SAR's intellectual political culture, and of its 'democratic' values even within the political opposition. The city's ruling class of bureaucrats and ersatz politicians may never reach the quality of, say, a John Maynard Keynes or J.K. Galbraith or Lee Kuan Yew (to pick fairly modest, bourgeois examples). But it would matter a lot if there were fewer little

Milton Friedmans managing the economy and budget, and squandering Hong Kong's opportunities for development and integration and livelihood. The rise of a 'new class' may well be in the cards for Hong Kong in its second handover. We shall see. But this economic and developmental front is indeed all important, for de-colonization and livelihood. In the absence of these things, you indeed get 2019 Hong Kong, or specifically one of its major conditions of possibility.

The question of de-colonizing the economy in Hong Kong would mean, relatively speaking, some progress towards social democracy or "socialism" or "common prosperity" with Hong Kong-Chinese characteristics. It would also require ameliorating and steadily undoing the iniquitous land and money-power distribution in the city that dates from the colonial era originally, and has since become exacerbated in the so-called post-colonial era. The Greater Bay Area and Northern Metropolis projects are clearly aimed at this, as are other new housing initiatives. While localists still attached to the idea of Hong Kong's natural sovereignty might disagree, these would not seem to be the actions of a re-colonizer. At the same time, economic de-colonization has been announced more than practically launched. And it would at any rate take a generation or two. But for the second-handover to go better than the first one from 1997, the economic front will have to be successful. China, as in the Chinese government or state, has hardly extracted resources from Hong Kong, a la classical imperialism or colonialism. It has if anything neglected the city and failed to take responsibility for its well being. The mainland-Hong Kong free market—e.g. property speculation—has had free reign, but this has benefitted few.

When Hong Kong lost its manufacture base to China's opening up (just as Hong Kong capital fled northward in a far more imperialistic, extractive fashion), all that the bulk of the Hong Kong population, that got in return was tourism and a stridently localist, place-based identity rooted in exceptionalism. Not least because the undeniably popular pan-democratic cause has been nixed, it is high time for the mainland to deliver the economic goods, so to speak. As has not escaped anyone's notice, the post-Mao Party state has been exceptionally, as in world-historically, good at economic growth and expansion, to the tune of "lifting" hundreds of millions of people out of relative poverty. This has come on the backs of Chinese labor, to be sure, and has been decidedly uneven and unequal. Inequality—class inequality specifically here—in China is stark and appalling, and not only because this challenges the very idea of socialism, to say nothing of communism. But if we may bracket this for the purpose of further analysis—while never forgetting this very fundamental contradiction—few would deny the P.R.C.'s successes in economic terms and in improving or developing people's livelihood and their access to global, capitalist modernity. It is therefore highly likely that the plans for Hong Kong will work in strictly economic terms. For all its own iniquities and other problems Hong Kong already has numerous advantages compared to other cities and places within Asia and the world, including its high literacy and bilingual or trilingual demographic and excellent transportation infrastructure. But the immediate problem is that the integrated development and improvement will inevitably take a long time to materialize, and will depend on Hong Kong officials and politicians to make it work. They in fact have little experience working with their own system let alone within the mainland system. Hong Kong's ruling class has always been of the tycoon and colonial-bureaucrat/comprador variety, and if this class fraction was adept at collaborating with the British regime this does not necessarily help at all in the present context.

This too is part of the still-colonial nature of Hong Kong governance: not just the lack of a political class in general, but one that deeply understands and can 'work' the mainland system effectively. One can agree or disagree with the Chinese system being meritocratic and therefore legitimate and commendable, but there is less room for debate about whether or not it takes someone skilled in that system to not only rise up individually but to achieve results. Hong Kong has since 1997 not developed such a class of politicians and bureaucrats, due to the Basic Law.

When it comes to Hong Kong property and housing iniquities, and in addition to the real estate tycoons and their companies, another major obstacle is decidedly colonial as well as capitalist. The Heung Yee Kuk is a rural political and lobby group of so-called "indigenous villagers" whom allegedly date from the pre-British era in the nineteenth century, but who are also all of Han Chinese ethnicity. The British, in their classically fetishistic-racist colonial way, endowed them as something like a caste or native pseudo-ethnicity that legally entitled every male descendent of such an "indigenous" family (clan) to build a three story village house on Hong Kong land. Modern colonialism, it will be recalled, loved to produce ethnicities and related divisions amongst its colonized, as Bernard Cohn among others has detailed elsewhere.[12] The Kuk's feudal and conservative nature is indicated by this patriarchal patrimony, and these supposedly original inhabitants of what is now Hong Kong and the New Territories were not only few in number but also not the only such 'first peoples' of the territory.[13] Indeed on anti-colonial and symbolic grounds alone, this rural system and rather dubious ethnicized system should have gone with the last Governor. The unfairness of their privilege has long been an affront to other Hong Kongers (and to common sense) when land supply is scarce and costs enormous, and waiting lists for cramped public housing can be years long. To call these wealthy families "villagers" or even "rural" is euphemistic at best, as the best parallel would be to elite landlords whom have long evaded any reckoning with the larger community of citizens or political and ideological reform.

More to the point, the Kuk have been a classic example of institutionalized colonial collaborators since their inception in the 1920s. In recent decades they have been plagued by charges of corruption (e.g. having Malaysian nationals own new housing developments), turning unused green spaces into junkyards and dumping grounds, colluding with property developers, and in short controlling the land supply in the rural areas despite being a fraction of the actual population living there.[14] The Kuk institution holds large swathes of land that they refuse to sell back to the government (or to farm on for that matter). Recently the top court in Hong Kong, following its British era duties to the core, upheld the constitutionality of this system, as if the colonial era laws are sacrosanct. Despite its unpopularity across the yellow/blue divide in the city—a rare thing virtually all sides can agree on—the Kuk will hold sway for the foreseeable future.

This entire matter is clearly a bad colonial hangover that the local government seems unable or unwilling to tackle, despite the small percentage of people it unfairly benefits and privileges for no good reason. Here the British core value of the rule of law, aka the damage done to Hong Kong society by the former empire, is exposed in all its glory. Without a strong enough state to simply end this system, even via a generous buyout to the Kuk, the land problem in Hong Kong will remain more difficult than it needs to be. Indeed one of the major current plans to develop more housing, the Lantau Tomorrow Vision project referenced earlier, involves a massive and expensive and long-term land reclamation project. Politically, it is easier for the SAR—given its British legal system and the power of the Kuk—to create a new land mass form the sea than to simply buy or take the idle lands back from the Kuk and build affordable or even private housing. The political inability to use its own land is a telling example of the colonial baggage still weighing down Hong Kong. The state of Hong Kong politics is perhaps best illustrated by the very idea of this Vision project itself: reclamation from the sea over a decade or two, rather than fighting a fully justifiable political and legal battle against an anachronistic and absurd colonial heritage (the Kuk system) and just using the abundant land already in place. De-colonizing Hong Kong would mean the Kuk has to go, but this would require a political will and capacity that is missing at the top, so far. Thus political de-colonization would have to be in command of any economic one. It is ultimately politics or the political process that determines the economy, which is not and cannot be an autonomous, quasi-objective realm.

## POLITICS NOT IN COMMAND: POLITICAL DE-COLONIZATION?

If the economic de-colonization of Hong Kong seems daunting given the power of vested interests and the bone-deep commitment to laissez-faire within the city, then political de-colonization may seem frankly impossible. This is because from the pan-democratic/liberal perspective, also that of mainstream media discourse everywhere outside of the mainland, the de-colonization of Hong Kong could only mean "self-rule" and electoral, direct-nomination democracy. In short, the protesters are right, and on the right side of history as the American presidents like to say, and therefore they represent, directly and indirectly, the anti- or de-colonial front. Put another way, colonialism is in essence a non-issue aside from the vote and self-rule. After all colonialism/de-colonization has not been a keyword of the general movement aside from the inevitably more removed intellectual circles, especially in the academy.[15]

Since Hong Kong is already self-ruled in that Hong Kong people do after all fully run the place since 1997 (albeit without a 'yellow' or 'pan-democratic' C.E.), it is clear that direct elections—therefore of anti-Party politicians and full-on localists—is the heart of the matter.[16] As is, or was, the will-to-power of the pan-democratic or otherwise localist bloc. This take on de-colonization—that it ultimately stands or falls on direct voting—certainly has the virtue of clarity and simplicity. And when one transcodes—or inflates—direct-nomination-voting into phrases or ambiguous concepts like "self-rule" and "freedom" and even "suffrage" the symbolic and affective stakes are raised much, much higher. But is this what voting gives us in liberal capitalist societies, or even mere cities? Go in fear of abstractions. This is not to deny that something like a majority (or even a large minority) of Hong Kongers seem or seemed to want precisely this, or did so between 2014 and 2019 if not for a decade or longer beforehand. This can be true (as in correct) and yet mistaken or problematic, just as it can be true and yet impossible or unrealistic. More than one thing can be true at the same time, and if nothing else Hong Kong politics illustrates this platitude quite clearly.

For reasons we do not need to repeat ad nauseum, this faith in suffrage/nomination is also a clear, if historical impossibility for the present generations and likely many more to boot. While the Basic Law does not specifically preclude dissent or critical views of the Party/mainland, and Deng's speeches at the time of drafting even allowed for such voices to exist if they did not collude with anti-regime forces, it is now abundantly clear that it will not be bent to allow direct nomination. In fact the government has reduced the amount of seats in the legislature decided by popular vote, for much the same reason (the prevalence of anti-Beijing or full-on autonomy politicians). The pan-democratic movement is finished, with the final straw being its full-on participation in the 2019 movement, its loud and clear silence when that movement violently pursued "burnism' and occasionally attacked suspected or actual mainland people. The pan-dems, like the so-called establishment, had never really won the hearts and minds of the people so much as been their— the anti-mainland or pro-autonomy people—electoral vehicle. Recall that 2019's occupations and more violent or confrontational "be water" tactics were authored not by the pan-dems but by the younger and more localist groups and individuals who were politicized during and after 2014, and not least because 2014 too had been widely hailed in the global media and was a major, 'live' media event for several weeks. Thus the pan-democrats had really just been *tailing* the "revolution of our time" as it was not really their time, from at least the youth's or street's perspective (i.e. of those participating). Their failure to take any critical distance on the movement as it was unfolding and unfolding in a terrible way—like the scores of intellectuals and experts egging on the movement—certainly needs stated.

But it also revealed how poorly they understood mainland politics and mainland views of the Basic Law and so on, or put another way, how deep ran their contempt and/or fear and loathing of the mainland as a political entity and sovereign power over the city. Mainland rhetoric about Hong

110    D. F. VUKOVICH

Kong officials needing to love both the mainland and Hong Kong thus stands revealed as having a point, if a ham-handed one: that there was indeed a huge "hatred" problem that needs to be overcome. As for the pan-democrats notorious (or heroic, if you prefer) use of the filibuster, the so-called primary of July 2020 (in which they openly declared their intent to bring down the CE via future filibustering) was the denouement of their mode of electoral politics (get elected to prevent change) and their embrace of their own version of 'burnism.' One can regret the mass arrests that resulted from this pan-democratic plan (unwisely conducted soon after the national security law was passed) as well as the waste of time and opportunities from the decades-long filibustering of potential progress in livelihood and development. One can also understand the contempt and fear and loathing and hatred, as the older generations were certainly around when the Basic Law and handover were negotiated but played little to zero role in it: they had never been consulted, so to speak, and had no avenues of political participation during the British era. It is as if their filibustering mode of electoral politics and ritualistic symbolic protests (e.g. the June 4th commemorations) substituted for an independence, de-colonization struggle. But one that could not be named: either through fear of reprisal or mockery (of the very idea of independence for Hong Kong) or because this was never quite consciously understood but felt, affectively.

But there is a certain ruse of history here worth noting: most of their convictions from 2019 and the 2020 primary—as with those pertaining to rioting—date from British colonial laws, not the new national security ones. What if the post-1997 opposition movement, or the localist Hong Kong identity co-created by the regime and subjects of the 1970s had focused to some extent on the de-colonization of "things" such as the legal system, the education system, the popular arts and so on, as opposed to the obsessive focus on "suffrage" and Beijing's alleged re-colonization and imaginary nationalizations (or "mainlandization")? Where was the *critique* of British style rule of law and liberalism? What if Hong Kong had had an opposition that aimed at more effectively, rationally, and democratically or equitably integrating into, or benefitting from mainland China? Schooled in anti-communism and anti-leftism, what if Hong Kong's opposition intellectuals and activists nonetheless embraced Dengism not as a capitalism but as a 'socialism' or democracy or 'something else' that could be better than liberalism for Hong Kong and China? After all, before the rise of localism and a vehement anti-mainland identity the 'democrats" had expressed a desire to help China as much as Hong Kong, even to lead it to the promised land of democracy and prosperity. This was probably as delusional as thinking the handover would naturally be smooth because of shared Chineseness, but there was at least a discursive space for thinking in terms of solidarity rather than antagonism with mainland people.

Such 'what if?" questions may well sound merely fanciful. But more to the point here is that neither Beijing nor the Hong Kong camps have given much thought or time to the question of de-colonization, precisely because there was not an anti-colonial movement or history of note within the city, or subtending China-Hong Kong-UK relations. (Even Mao Zedong was content with the status quo though the early 1970s.) This is what is so striking by the adoption of such anachronistic language within the Hong Kong movement over the last decade, from public intellectual Chin Wan's popular works on British era Hong Kong as a de facto, almost autonomous city-state that is analogous to ancient Venice or Singapore, and with Hong Kong people as a de facto, separate ethnic group to boot, to the "Liberate Hong Kong, Revolution of our Time" slogan and other self-rule, Beijing-as-colonizer rhetoric. It was as if Hong Kong's very own anti-colonial movement, directed against its United Nations sanctioned, fully legal "motherland," at last appeared on the world stage. But only after the historical, technological, and economic conditions of possibility for national liberation, or indeed of 'revolution,' had already disappeared. All that was left was an intense localism-as-nationalism, albeit one that was and is defined against the (mainland) nationalism of its feared and loathed other.

Not by conscious design, of course, nor by foreign funding a la the N.E.D., but it is as if Hong Kong's opposition had been following a certain script from a textbook version of post-colonial studies, from invasion and conquest on the premise of some lie (free trade, cultural exchange, etc.) to the rise of nativism even to the point of *creating* a monolithic ethnic identity, the drive towards reclaiming or preserving local culture and tradition (restoring autonomy), to the emergence of a full-on national liberation struggle. (Equally we might say the establishment camps simply assumed the only issue was sovereignty—solved by giving it back to Hong Kong Chinese—plus the equally 'natural' progress of a modernizing capitalism.) Indeed the connection to academic post-colonial studies—or perhaps more accurately to a certain, popular catechism about colonialism and resistance that also includes Cold War

112    D. F. VUKOVICH

narratives—is not far fetched. Such terms and topics and phenomena long ago left the ivory tower, or rather had already been part of the real world of de-colonization movements and the Cold War in the global system. And thence, as with say "postmodernism" from the 1980s and more recent terms from academic or campus identity politics, to enter the global media by a trickle-down dispersion in various forms (and with no strings or original contexts attached). Such a dispersion of terms and narrative bits and the like is not a bad thing in itself, *contra* the conservative reaction to the so-called cultural wars. But in the case of Hong Kong (and elsewhere) contextualization and a historical, political realism are nonetheless paramount to reach a fuller understanding of major events like the 2019 movement/riots, and therefore to produce more useful knowledge. In short, it matters that Hong Kong is not being invaded and colonized by Beijing, and that the simulation of a nationalistic, colonial liberation movement, not to mention the Cold War of the 1950s–1980s, is not only anachronistic but highly misleading. This particular 'post-colonial' *form* indexes the absent presence of a substantively democratic or progressive, political mass movement that would turn less on perceived desperation and not at all on xenophobic hatred for example, and instead on equality and inclusion of the dispossessed and wretched of the earth on all sides of the border.

But then the opposition clearly didn't read far into the advanced post-colonial syllabus, so to speak, and hence did not engage the admittedly difficult if not intractable problems raised by, for example, 'provincializing Europe,' 'coloniality' or being-colonial, the exclusionary nature of nationalism and liberalism as communal and political ideologies, or the ethno-centrism/xenophobia of historical nativism. Perhaps above all else, the main thrust of post-colonial studies can be said to be its anti-universalism. This functions as a method and "theory" or more accurately as a critique of objective/empiricist/historicist epistemology and theory. This is in part derived from Marx, Nietzsche, or more often—for better and for worse—Michel Foucault and Jacques Derrida. But the anti-universalism is more specifically aimed at universalism as an actually existing, historical practice that was a constituent part of orientalism, modern colonialism, and the power-politics of discourse, i.e. the rationalizations and "objectivity" of foreign rule. This radical (as in root-seeking or rigorous) historicism goes further than conventional, disciplinary history as found in most academic or tertiary history departments, which themselves still turn on a certain, generic and humanist universalism. More generally, be it from Edward

Said or Dipesh Chakrabarty (or related thinkers), the anti-universalist movement, if it can be called that, seeks to situate, contextualize and relativize or provincialize Western history and also Western knowledge as particular and specific to its own contexts. This would, of course, apply equally well to Eastern or any large-scale or macro history that seeks to speak beyond particular historical minutiae. It is not that East and West or Orient/Occident are separate realms (this is the very definition of classical orientalism), but that knowledge and human agents and actions all have their roots, their own moments of genesis in specific places and for specific reason. As Edward Said (among others) always insisted, there can be no objective or universal truth or knowledge about an other culture or place or history. Particularly when the modern world is built upon colonialism and imperialism and exploitative or coercive relations between peoples and empires/colonies. This is, or was, fairly axiomatic in the heyday of post-colonial studies but the blossoming of this field in literary and cultural studies has never had a parallel within traditional, conventional disciplines such as political science or history. Thus it is worth repeating here, and not least when it comes to the inherently emotional, bone-deep matter of politics in general, and about China—the object of renewed orientalism since the rise of Covid-19—in particular.

Put another way, there are no universal forms of politics. Politics may be what makes us all human but this means only that it is an inevitably messy, complex, and 'interested' field of human endeavour and conflict (and occasional co-operation!). From this perspective, few "anti-colonial" movements in recent history have been so baldly (and falsely) universalist yet flagrantly pro-Western and avowedly democratic (or liberal-democratic if one prefers) as that of Hong Kong's; and yet turning on an undeniable and rather visceral and at times violent anti-Chinese affect and ideology. This discourse of equality and legalism/rights based talk that is simultaneously defined by hierarchy and exclusion (of the inferior yet threatening other/mainland) maps seamlessly onto the critical histories and theorization of liberalism during modern colonialism and the Cold War.[17] Of course popular culture and protest movements or slogans are not trying to be nuanced and rigorous and sophisticated in some academic or professional sense. Seeing this arise in Hong Kong—though not the extent of it perhaps—comes as no surprise if one knows the place intimately. What is more surprising, again, is the near-total lack of critical commentary amongst China studies and other experts in regard to the xenophobia and dark sides of the movement.[18] But still we must analyse them. Unless one takes the view that the civics-textbook and human rights perspectives mobilized by Hong Kong democratic politics are (or were) all merely strategic or not genuinely meant (and they certainly were heart-felt), then these views must not only be counted as "Western" but more importantly as universalist and absolute, and therefore not open to negotiation or compromise.

This is because it was a matter not of logical, rational political or philosophical belief but of identity in a bone-deep, monolithic sense, one that sutured over (in the wake of China's rise and Western imperial decline) the decline of Hong Kong's symbolic importance as the light-unto-Asia or as the "good China" not the communistic bad one. This symbolic importance of the former colony too lies behind the affect of affect, autonomy, Hong Kong identity circa 2019, and the ill-fated 'burnism' strategy. It is far more than a mere preference or committed, logically valid belief but is or was something far, far more closely and intimately held, as if a matter of life and death. In this sense the Hong Kong opposition/democracy movement has been overall strongly colonial not just in its genesis but in its substance and end. To be sure, advocates or partisans of the movement and of liberal democracy might say that is all obfuscation and that universalism or 'coloniality' is a non issue. Again from this standpoint, democratization—direct nomination and election of the C.E., aka 'suffrage' in the Hong Kong context—would be (political) de-colonization, full stop. That this would amount to political independence from Beijing is never reported by the sympathetic media or scholars, but is an uncomfortable truth.

To be sure, one other theme from post-colonial studies—one that can be construed as provocative or defeatist, depending on one's take—has been that in many ways, and despite the best intentions and efforts, political independence ultimately achieved little beyond the change in sovereignty itself. While clearly incorrect in an empirical sense, there is no doubt that these national liberation movements had major failures and limitations, particularly in terms of enduring economic and gender inequalities and the imposition of a narrowly nationalist, monolithic identity at the expense of minorities and the vulnerable within the former colony, as well as at times a retrograde re-invention of certain 'native' traditions. Ironically for Hong Kong's post-1970s opposition, and for certain anti-statist post-colonial theorists, it has been the communist—as opposed to strictly anti-colonial—revolutions that have fared better at breaking with old ideas and in terms of development and equality.

Which is to say the P.R.C. above all, and despite its own glaring failures in equality after the Mao era, its brutal handling of Tibet and now Xinjiang, and so on. It also did this despite facing arguably far greater economic and planning obstacles. The pursuit of an alternative, socialist modernity—including the single-party, developmental, 'dictatorship of the proletariat' state, is precisely what gave the P.R.C. its flexibility and adaptability in rapidly changing national, regional, and global conditions after 1949. The communist horizon (or imaginary) meant that both anti-colonialism and nationalism, whilst indisputably part of the equation (and no doubt more affective and effective than, say, straight-up Marxist rhetoric), nonetheless did not set the same limits and pressures on the post-liberation era as did, for example, the liberalism or spiritualism of a Nehru or Gandhi in the anti-colonial struggles in South Asia.

When colonialism, defined as lack of self-rule and the lack of 'native' autonomy sets the agenda for the anti- and de-colonization movements, then many other questions and problems go begging. Not the least of which is the absent-presence of a more radical, communist and anti-capitalist perspective and politics. Class equality (defined against the present iniquities) becomes an afterthought at best to the rise of nationalism or nativism as well as a powerful but negative freedom-from logic that demonizes the colonizer (as one should, it must be said) but more fatefully propagates a discourse of autonomy and individual freedom in general. Nationalism and its imagined, transcendent community thrives not despite actual social inequalities in the colony but precisely because of them. So too for nativism, a la post-Occupy Hong Kong. Yet it offers, naturally enough, no social or intuitional plan of attack against those class- and power-based iniquities within.[19] From the problem of alternatives to economic and political liberalism for development and prosperity, to the profound question of what the true meanings and desired ends of the new order should and could be, these issues were at no time posed by the British-era refugees and new Hong Kongers. Nor were they asked during the handover process dating from the 1970s onwards. The P.R.C. had and still has its own limitations and pressures from the encounter with modern colonialism and imperialism (and from its own traditions and conditions), not least getting caught up in a new 'great game' or geo-political competition with the United States above all. It has always been a far cry from utopia, and has always struggled to deal with political and other realities of modernity. But the Chinese revolution was not only against imperialism but equally as much against its own 'feudal' decay and conditions, albeit not therefore in favour of liberal autonomy. This was not a nativist revolution even if it was unabashedly nationalistic in the face of Japanese and other invasions and degradations. Where nativism invents traditions and assumes a pre-Lapsarian, authentic past, the communist movement—but also much older ones like the Taipings—instead waged its own war and cultural revolution against tradition. Chinese communism (Maoism) as well as other related strains of thought (prolet-cult intellectuals of the former Soviet Union) thus has a lesson about nativism to learn, as does the post-colonial studies' critique of tradition and nativism too. The Chinese revolution's was a much more critical, dialectical take on its own past than that found in most 'anti-colonial' national liberation struggles, whilst being less overtly nationalist as well.[20] As for authoritarianism, while the Chinese state is certainly that, the other victorious movements from the colonized world (and the former colonizers) likewise share this problem. It is certainly a real problem and danger, as Hong Kong is seeing clearly now. But many of the laws being used to rectify Hong Kong politics now, and to sort out the arrests from the 2019 movement, are very much British colonial era ones and are parallel to contemporary capitalist democracies.

Finally, as for the political de-colonization of Hong Kong via the democracy movement as it actually existed in 2019 and before, we must raise a difficult question that is rarely asked of the "revolution of our time" against mainland "colonial" rule: whom precisely would benefit from such a liberation, even assuming the mainland decided to let its enclave go without military intervention? Why would one "burn down" the city in order to save it? Save it from whom exactly, and *for* whom? How would this liberation—or even the preservation of the then reigning status quo between Beijing and Hong Kong—help the ordinary people of Hong Kong, or those who form a clear majority (i.e. the middle or working classes of Hong Kong's rather limited economy)? Even if the liberation of Hong Kong from mainland control had been achieved (bearing in mind that is was far less so controlled in June 2019), it is hard to say whom this would have benefitted exactly, aside from those who had had not just the will-to-power but the ability to win.

One would still have to deal with Hong Kong-China-global capitalism, and it is hard to say what *any* small city legislature or leader could do by flying solo in such winds. "Suffrage" in itself is clearly no guarantee for autonomy (assuming this is desirable to begin with); nor is 'self-rule.' In sum, while the anti-ELAB protest, early on, was clearly generated by a great many anonymous people ('the masses') it also derailed into an impossible anti-government or, really, an anti-police (and at a very short remove, anti-Beijing) protest that then only turned worse from a democratic standpoint. Moreover, being initially leaderless and structureless, it was quickly captured by the usual suspects of Hong Kong political theatre: the pan-democrats and localist/nativist actors, and by a local and international media that famed the flames and clouds of tear gas. Structurelessness itself can be a form of tyranny, as Jo Freeman famously put it.[21] In the end, from a de-colonizing perspective what the opposition historically and this movement in particular have offered is a universalist faith in electoral democracy (direct nomination), and a localism-nationalism predicated on Hong Kong pride and authentic identity, but wrapped up with a fear and loathing of the invading/colonizing other.

## Politics of Knowledge (Brief Reprise)

Needless to say, the spectre of China and yellow-peril discourse is always ready to hand for the media and, it must be said, for the large "yellow" demographic of Hong Kong and its civil society. In the end, then, why were the 2019–2020 events in Hong Kong the biggest political and global media event of the last several decades, at least in global Asia? It was virtually live-broadcasted and mediatized from the very beginning, and at a time of intense if "cold" trade war between the US and China above all. Secondly, we must refer to political orientalism vis a vis the P.R.C. as a state and allegedly monolithic entity. Cold War and colonial discourse have always subtended education and intellectual culture within Hong Kong, for obvious reasons, and it has functioned historically as a major site for the production of Sinological-orientalism. Or alternatively, one can say that Hong Kong has always been a fount for "liberal" or "good" knowledge production as to the truth of the communist regime to the north and the comparative advantages of free-market liberal capitalist society. To be sure, mainland views and knowledge of their own history were rarely represented in any case during the British era, or indeed afterwards except for obvious, and largely ignored propaganda outlets like *Ta Kung Pao*. However one wishes to frame Hong Kong's discourse about China, as either colonial discourse or truth-speaking, this too is set to change in the coming years.

Ironically for a Party-state that until recently has been trying its best to de-politicize its own society, it is itself the ultimate "enemy" in the friend-enemy antagonism subtending geo-politics between the two superpowers and their legions of observers. Hong Kong 2019 demonstrated this, and in turn Beijing has realized that it can no longer ignore such a politics of discourse in the SAR. The national security law has taken an iron-first approach to this question; it will simply outlaw regime-change types of groups, forms of activism, and in some cases even such speech acts (e.g. chanting the 2019 'liberate Hong Kong' slogan). The larger de-colonial issue will be to develop complex and nuanced 'takes' and knowledge about Hong Kong's integration and place within China and within the world, beyond occidentalism or orientalism. Here the universities of Hong Kong, in the present author's own admittedly particular experience, have so far missed their opportunity to help produce a new or nuanced yet non-anti-regime discourse within the city. If there was ever a chance to productively hold dialogue and conversation over the future and fate of the city as a SAR, the campuses would have been the ideal locale. If not there, where else? Yet mainland views of itself—which must be brought on board in some fashion to talk about both the PRC itself and Hong Kong-mainland relations—have not really been incorporated into the universities. Given their colonial and avowedly liberal (read: anti-communist) roots, this is not surprising or unexpected in itself. But one side effect of this, aside from the lack of nuanced understanding of the mainland in general (in political-historical terms), has been the creation of a predictable yet powerful rule of discourse and duality: Hong Kong *versus* China, liberalism *versus* communism, freedom *versus* authoritarianism, us *versus* them, and so on (and vice versa). The hegemony of anti-views may or may not fade away eventually. We shall see. But here is the rub: this will result not in the triumph of so-called mainlandization and nationalist indoctrination, or the neutralization of discontent, but in the administrative triumph of de-politicized, highly conventional, and narrowly disciplinary work, and an emphasis on corporate science, grant mongering, and so on. This has been the situation well before the national security law. That will exert its own pressures perhaps, but the drive towards purely conventional work and thought, the commodification of the scholarly and humanistic mission of the university, is a much longer and older story.

More broadly speaking (beyond academe), demonizing that state to the point of calling for an end to the Party's rule, or for Hong Kong's independence is now risky if not verboten. One might well regret this on principle: that free speech counts most at its extreme margins, and must be absolute for it to be a meaningful freedom ad ideal. But of course free speech in the absolutist sense has never existed, and should not.[22] But even if one regrets on idealistic principle the foreclosure of such free speech 'options' as denouncing the mainland regime and calling for its end, or for independence, it has never actually been useful in advancing democracy (in whatever sense) or freedom in Hong Kong or in the mainland in recent decades. There is in the historical record no end to justify those means. Moreover the pan-democratic opposition to the mainland political system, which has always turned on just such an understanding, has never enabled understanding or dialogue between the two places. One can easily, and rightly fault the Beijing regime for not being more tolerant of such anti-Party state views within its own non-SAR borders. It is not actually threatened by them. But it takes two camps to produce the political and developmental stagnation (and antagonism) that has been Hong Kong's since 1997. The so-called establishment groups and leaders have likewise failed to retort such speech except by denouncing it, and in fact they have no deep connection to the mainland either, intellectually speaking.

But of course it has been the hegemony of generally pan-democratic, liberal and localist views (and identities) that have held sway before and after the handover. This corresponds to a Hong Kong pan-democratic reading of the Basic Law discussed previously, i.e. that it implies a powerful if not de facto complete autonomy. Form this standpoint it is natural to see Hong Kong and the mainland as existing on a level plane. But we should be wary of false equivalences. In addition to the contradictions and ambiguities of that particular document, Hong Kong has never had, or been promised, or been able to realistically demand an equal seat at the table with Beijing. It is absurd to think so and yet much of the hand-wringing over Beijing's treatment of Hong Kong even before 2020 has taken just this form: that the mainland broke an otherwise fair and square contract and is the guilty party.

But the political, social, and historical realities we are trying to put on the table here do not mean that Hong Kong will simply have to assimilate, tout court, to all things mainland, from mainland identity to mainland ways of seeing the mainland. Does even Shanghai do this? "China" and Beijing look and feel different from within the mainland itself, after all. For all the fear amongst pan-democrats or nativists in Hong Kong that the city will become "just another Chinese city" (even as it rapidly falls behind others), and even as the city is now indeed more firmly under the mainland's purview, it is worth remembering that major Chinese cities, new and old, are not the same and have their own imaginaries, identities, and contradictions.

Such an assimilation would neither be desirable nor even possible since, after all, the mainland is not a monolith, and is if anything far more diverse and striated than the small city of Hong Kong itself. While there is, as is the case everywhere else, dominant national ideologies and forms of power for Hong Kong to contend with—and now a very clear red line as to independence and state subversion activities and rhetoric—one can rest assured that Hong Kong will have its own ways of seeing, its own identities, and so on. Hong Kong will always be *different* (though perhaps less exceptionalist) from the standpoint of mainland discourse and national identity, if only because its own history is different, and the post-1970s diaspora will undoubtedly maintain its own discourse for years to come.

But the SAR—the people actually living here—will nonetheless have to engage the mainland's own self-understanding, be this Chinese liberalism (of the *Caixin* media group, of academia, or the non-dissident sort), neo-traditionalism, new-leftism, or something else entirely.[23] By the same token, mainland governance must finally engage Hong Kong's own history and realities far better than it has to date, and seek to understand that part of the intellectual political culture that genuinely fears and loathes the mainland as a political if not total entity. Hong Kong *is* different and is mostly inhabited by people whom have grown up as Hong Kongers in their identity and in their discursive frameworks and ways of seeing. They have not been part of China except obliquely, or by name. This is a direct consequence of Hong Kong's colonization by the British and Hong Kong's place as a Cold War outpost as well. This requires patience and understanding from the part of the ruling/governing class on both sides of the border. This was not lacking before 2019/2020 but if anything was ironically foiled by the generally hands-off approach by Beijing. Overall it has been inept at winning hearts and minds in Hong Kong among the very sizable demographic of people who were not already "patriotic" or mainland-oriented, often proceeding as if blithely unaware of post-1970s localism. This will be the mainland's main challenge for the future of Hong Kong, and it may even learn something in the process by which it could then win/achieve more "soft power" elsewhere. In the end, it needs to tell better stories about what and who the mainland is, and what it can offer Hong Kong. So too Hong Kong's opposition, if it is to have a significant one, needs a better approach in winning the ear, if not the hearts and minds of mainland officialdom and the population at large. Assumed positions of superiority and of a hierarchical, not neutral difference, as with fear and loathing, need to be unlearned on both sides of the border.

There is much to unlearn and unpack on both sides, stemming from the modern colonial period and China's and Hong Kong's relationships not just to each other but to the same historical yet deeply ideological and difference-making phenomenon of colonialism and imperialism. The discourses and problems of nationalism, and of the production of Eurocentric knowledge and inferiority complexes are cases in point. Also rooted in the colonial and imperial past but still at work in the world today are the dynamics of an antagonistic, self-other identity-formation that has always subtended orientalism and the relations between China and the West as much as between Hong Kong and the mainland. If Hong Kong people's desires for self-determination as a society—which does not necessarily require independence or full autonomy—have either been ignored or dismissed as colonial baggage or imperialist influence by power holders in the mainland then it is equally true that Hong Kong discourse on China is deeply problematic form the mainland's perspective.

To de-colonize Hong Kong will mean to develop a post-orientalist mode of understanding the mainland and of doing politics locally, and in relation to the mainland. Hong Kong (the educators, intellectuals, writers, artists) will have to take China—the P.R.C. as political and historical entity—far more seriously than it has overall to date. As the hegemony of liberal and anti-communist views of the PRC would indicate, there has been no shortage of "critical" views of the PRC within Hong Kong educational institutions and artistic/intellectual spheres as well as activist circles. While the universities have—in the author's experience—changed not at all in this regard the danger and opportunity here lies in this type of knowledge production either disappearing slowly (and it does need to be known, and therefore taught, as it represents the dominant knowledge formation of modernity) or simply continuing as is. The latter danger is real because Hong Kong does need to understand China on its own terms, and to take those seriously, before they can be contested or revised or engaged as needed. Indeed the Hong Kong-China relationship—its politics and meaning—is something that desperately needs to be tabled and taught at university and other intellectual levels. Given Hong

## 122    D. F. VUKOVICH

Kong's relative freedom to broach such discussions and issues, it is all the more tragic that the universities have not done nearly enough to capitalize on this advantage. Not by debunking the PRC from the standpoint of liberalism but by engaging—critically as needed—the mainland's own self-understanding.

What happens in the universities matters because their power to legislate knowledge for society is often unrecognized but has real world effects nonetheless. When you too often produce knowledge that says, in effect, that the PRC or revolution was largely a disaster, that it lacks freedom and all things good and holy, that even contemporary capitalistic and 'happy' China (which Hong Kong discourse would celebrate if some other country) is a nightmare, you are not fighting the good progressive democratic fight and saving souls so much as preparing the ground for bad China-Hong Kong relations. By the same token, putatively non-political or value-free types of knowledge production about China, or China—Hong Kong relations, while certainly "safe" are also in this context not useful. But they are the gold standard in the universities now, where the real threat to intellectual and academic freedom is not the national security law but the utter triumph of corporate mentalities and entrepreneurial careerism at the expense not just of critical, heterodox scholarship but all bona fide scholarship in general.

### CAN THE PARTIES CONTINUE? WHITHER PARTICIPATION?

To return specifically to the question of a political de-colonization: what is the way forward for Hong Kong? The idea that this would mean free-elections of the CE by direct nomination, and a de facto independence or full, not just high autonomy has died. But then so too has the idea that the city would somehow just smoothly integrate over time, a rising tide of capitalist wealth lifting all happier boats, to the point where the political aspirations of Hong Kong people would whither away. Clearly the demonstrations before and after the anti-ELAB movement have shown the strong desire on the part of many to have a say in the political and other affairs of the city. This has largely been denied to them since 1860, including the post-97 decades. While there are many official "consultation periods" to various acts or proposed measures in the community, these are often merely pro forma or perceived that way in any case. (This mirrors the universities, where 'shared governance' between faculty and administrators, or within faculties, is a compete fiction.) In the fact the hierarchies and cronyism of Hong Kong society in general, from schooling and universities to all the corporations and private clubs, are if anything worse than in other parts of 'greater China' and Asia. These are defining traits of the colonial era as much as the post-British one, from walled cities and secret societies to the money- and property-based forms of distinction and class/group power today.

These are precisely the types of things that *would* flourish in a free-market, open-port based colony built on the principle of laissez-faire. Hong Kong's famously rocky soil never had much room for sprouts of democratic culture and thought, let alone institutions, and this itself may be why the opposition's "democratic imaginary" was so singularly focused on voting even when the rest of the world was living through the utter debasement and corruption of liberal capitalist democracy. If the mainland had a revolution, warts and all, Hong Kong lacked even a mass anti-colonial movement and was instead, as is well known, a space not only of flows of capital and often 'temporary' people but one of literal refuge. But the desire for participation and voice among Hong Kongers of various types, while not universal and far less than the somewhat misleading protest photos and inflated crowd-sizes would indicate, is real enough. Of course it can also be made to go away or dissipate, as it has in many other places with, for example, low voter turnout and mild-to-intense political apathy and cynicism. But ultimately this would be a pyrrhic victory for the mainland, given the need for co-operation and federation within the Chinese system, for looming environmental crises, and simply for progress. In fact even prior to the 2020 electoral overhaul by Beijing, most Hong Kong people did not vote in ordinary LegCo elections.[24] This is hardly unique to the SAR and reflects an awareness of how futile and useless most official political systems are or appear to be. But while de-politicization is easy to understand, and has been banked on for decades by the mainland and, again, most other countries, it can only be temporary in the longer run, and, again, there are any number of looming problems that demand political solutions. A more harmonious, peaceful integration will have to happen through a more subtle hegemony of winning over consent or at least *assent*.[25] This will have to happen not only through material and meaningful improvements in livelihood and the feeling of fairness or equality, but through some form of public, social participation and buy-in.

But it must be remembered that voting is just one, albeit significant vehicle for participation. Other forms of voice, community, and service as well as collective or group belonging are at least theoretically possible, and there is no good reason that Hong Kong can not have much more of this, either through what is called "consultation" with the government and civil service/bureaucracy, or through local/district groups and organizations. Currently, however, the number of popularly elected LegCo posts has been shrunk, as well as the those for local district councillors. The latter are not part of LegCo per se and have no legislative powers, but handle a lot of mundane yet important neighbourhood issues (not unlike the 'resident committees' common in China's Party-state system). It was the latter posts that swept elections in the aftermath of the 2019 protests. Thus the onus is on Beijing and/or the local government to take up this challenge and not only allow but to actively encourage meaningful participation in politics and society broadly defined, where politics is about advancing livelihood, including but not limited to socio-economic welfare and living conditions. Politics in other words is also about community, and one need not have a liberal system in place to foster this (indeed it is typically a hindrance, as communitarianism instructs). Many, even millions of Hong Kongers—like people everywhere else—have wanted to be part of something in this sense. Not of Beijing or the Party, for perfectly obvious historical reasons that themselves will fade away in the long term, but something local, where they live.[26] But the local does not have to exclude the national (or the global), and rarely does so, outside of deeply provincial identity formations.

Relatedly, the C.E. has spoken to how she wishes more young people would enter the government or civil service, as opposed to N.G.O's or activist groups, because it is there where one's efforts to improve and help Hong Kong can be most effective. The civil service, aka employment therein, is also being *expanded* not downsized in the wake of 2019, despite a clear if minority opposition to the C.E. (and vaccinations, etc.) within the civil service. This expansion is welcome in a city with little state capacity. This is the current, official vision of encouraging participation and political life as I have been trying to define it here. It will not appeal to all, nor would all be suited for it. Nor is it a single-shot solution to the lack of meaningful participation in society. But as a job and vocation this may well be one major way forward and is unsurprisingly not different from the Party-state system to the north, with its nearly 100 million members and large and diffuse bureaucracy. Given the laissez-faire, small state ethos of colonial and contemporary Hong Kong, this too would be a striking change for the future, and for the better in any society that lacks state capacity in an age of Covid, severe environmental damage, and so on. Ironically, perhaps, another benefit of the 2019 anti-government protests, if not also of the global Covid pandemic.

As for electoral and parliamentary participation, there may yet be a space for a proverbial loyal opposition in Hong Kong. Not unlike "moderate" policy wonks in Hong Kong, I have for years argued that the democratic opposition—which is or *was* the opposition to the status quo after all, or should have been—should have seen their mission as advocating for a better, more equitable and beneficial integration with the mainland, in the time-honoured and deceptively simple form of 'rightful resistance' that has animated successful protest politics in China before and after 1949.[27] Why not argue for Hong Kong, too, to be a moderately prosperous society for all? Hong Kong has a higher inequality measure—typically expressed via the Gini coefficient—than even the mainland.[28] Of course this was anathema to a democratic movement focused obsessively with suffrage or democracy in a narrow sense, and on autonomy and freedom from mainland China. Likewise for many "cultural studies" academics, it was anathema to speak of anything other than Hong Kong identity and an unspecified 'culture.' Now that that movement has been crushed (and we can say this without any *schadenfreude*), the time may be at hand for a resurrection, albeit one without the Christian-missionary zeal of the older one.

In the most recent, reformed Legco election, there were six self-identified democrats who ran for seats. But most of these were apparently traditional pan-democrats who, while amenable to oath-taking and the national security law, focused on universal suffrage, aka direct nomination. One contender broke from the Democratic Party years before, when he supported the reformed electoral package mentioned above in 2014. This might indicate a way forward for a reformist, as opposed to anti-government democratic opposition. In fact this candidate, Tik Chi-yuen, was the sole winner from the democratic lot and is part of a new "centrist" party that promises to steer a course between the filibustering democrats of the past and the current establishment. This is promising for Hong Kong's future, but is after all just one candidate at present. It will naturally take time for new parties or individuals to work out that loyal-opposition mode, to be genuine reformers rather than primarily performative 'radicals' hell-bent on preserving the status quo (if not achieving "free" C.E. elections) until 2047. Likewise for the so-called establishment parties, who now in theory have a role to play in helping

126   D. F. VUKOVICH

produce an actual establishment, aka a functional government. As is well known in the city, the establishment parties have represented nothing so much as themselves as individuals and their money. The learning curve for Hong Kong political parties will be steep. But it may also be enabled by popularly wished-for future successes in development and economic integration with the mainland and the desire to break with the past political parties.

Hong Kong has not had a significant labor party focused on working class issues and workplace demands, just as its oppositional labor unions are now largely dissolved and its traditional labor unions, as in many other countries and including the mainland, are relatively weak due to structural, political limitations.[29] While there is certainly a potential constituency of working class, poor, and simply struggling and precarious workers in the middle-class of Hong Kong, the pan-democrats (even the self-defined leftist splinter groups like the former League of Social Democrats) have never sought such folks as their base except in so far as they might support the goal of suffrage and autonomy from the mainland. In this they are, at best, of a piece with the American Democratic Party or Labor in Britain; but in Hong Kong they cannot count on, yet have never courted working class or new-immigrant voters (who would have to have residency of course). The Hong Kong working class for its part overwhelmingly votes for the Beijing-friendly establishment parties, such as the D.A.B. This too has continued in the most recent election in 2021, where the largest "pro-establishment" bloc (whatever this means) came from the public housing estates.[30] Thus the class character of the protest movement's youth and the historical pan-democrats in general—clearly middle-class aka bourgeois—remains unchanged. Nor did it change in the wake of 2014 Occupy either, as the younger localist parties and leaders like Joshua Wong et al. (e.g. *Youngspiration*) that emerged from that movement rejected a working-class politics from the get-go. This does not of course invalidate their own concerns but it reveals the boundaries and exclusions of a generationally-defined, liberal or autonomist politics.

As revealed consistently by their voting preferences, the working class in Hong Kong are not Trumpists or right-wing blue collar voters in the American or Brexit mode. And it is worth recalling that more white-collars and women voted for Trump than otherwise. Hong Kong xenophobia lies more within the democratic localists. But the working class and 'have-nots' in the city do have an obvious interest in economic growth aka mainland economic integration, and they too like some of their Western counterparts may have a certain, hard-earned critical distance from the leadership claims of liberal or leftist/democratic politicians and activists, all of whom can come off as decidedly elite and privileged and not simply freedom-loving autonomists. (As can leaders of the so-called establishment parties.) It is worth noting the fate of the Professional Teachers Union, the largest single union in the city, and one that had been founded and run for years by the late Szeto Wah.[31] He was in many ways the model democrat for Hong Kong, respected on both sides of the border as a loyal patriot of both locales, and even a staunch supporter of the 1989 protests.

But his identity was not that of the post-1970s place-based "authentic" Hong Konger who desired nothing so much as autonomy and separateness from the mainland. He was also against radicalizing the PTU in terms of it becoming dedicated to regime-change and to opposition to the Party-state on principle alone. By the end of his life he had been marginalized and—worse—pathologized and mocked by the new pan-democrats and arch localists of the next generations (such as "Long Hair" Kwok and others). In the end, by the time of 2019 the PTU placed their bets not in shop-floor or workplace issues specifically but in the regime-change game. (As did the Hong Kong Confederation of Trade Unions, a smaller and looser federation of various unions even more dedicated to civil society agitation in general.)[32] A game they were destined to lose. Here is where the latest phase of Hong Kong identity, and moreover the lack of knowledge of mainland politics and economy and stark cold brute fact reality came back to haunt not just the PTU but what passed for the putatively left-wing aka democratic movement. By 2019 the PTU were co-sponsors of the Human Rights Front's marches that invariably and predictably ended up in violent clashes with the police, with petrol bombs and attempted shut-downs of the city. Because of this affiliation (which long predated 2019) and others, and the importance of the public education system for the struggle for hegemony that the government now realizes it must fight, the union was forced to disband.

This is not a good thing for teachers or for education in the city (it was the city's largest union, at 95,000 members), but neither was the union's turn away from its primary educational and workplace missions. Perhaps part of Hong Kong's political learning curve can be a return to 'bread and butter' labor issues within its unions and/or within a future labor party. This is a very tall order for Hong Kong at present and for the near future, but a stronger labor movement, with or without a party alongside it, would be instrumental in 'de-colonizing' the legacies of the colonial economy and the ideology of free enterprise and 'market-forces' that came with it. Given the influx of mainland working class people to Hong Kong, labor organizing—about labor and workplaces!—would be one fertile ground for cross-border solidarity beyond the entrenched identity politics and regime-change ambitions of Hong Kong opposition. This too would be de-colonial work in the sense not only of solidarity (as opposed to monolithic place-based identity politics) but in moving beyond nationalism and nativism. Hong Kong has had several labor-oriented N.G.Os and activist-type research groups for years, the most important of which is the China Labor Bulletin headed by former Tiananmen, 1989 worker-activist Han Dongfan. As of June, 2021 Han remains not only free and at work with his NGO as he was before the national security law, but even upbeat in comparison to the partisans and spokespersons of burnism 2019:

> I was there in 1989 on June 4 in Tiananmen Square. I saw fire, I saw the bullets, I saw blood ... But throughout these things, Hong Kong is still Hong Kong. We are still privileged. It's a place that still has quite a big space, and don't tell yourself there's no more space.[33]

The difference here is that Han is, after all, not a Hong Konger in the nativist sense and did not grow up with that post-1970s identity of a non- or even anti-mainlander human individual. Han is very much a Hong Konger in any other sense however, having come to the SAR in 1992 after being released from his 22-month prison stint following his leadership role, among workers it must be recalled, in the 1989 Tiananmen protests. He is in a sense closer to Szeto Wah of the former Professional Teachers Union than to what has come down the road in later generations of democratic activists and organizers, let alone to the 'out of the closet' localists and 'yellow camp.' The challenge for Hong Kong, and for the mainland, will be to enable future generations more in this vein, specifically politicians, activists, organizers and simply citizens whom are more anti-colonial and de-colonizing precisely because they refuse both nativism and the myth that China is a 'harmonious society achieved' and has no major class divisions. If it should be admitted that Marx and Engels were radically wrong when they declared in the middle of the nineteenth century that 'the working men have no country,' it should also be said that Marxist or communist notions of class equality and international solidarity should never be forgotten but only aspired to. Right now, the only people speaking this language of anti-colonialism within Hong Kong (and leaving aside the social media diaspora) are top-level Hong Kong officials who—in a gesture clearly learned from the mainland –like Carrie Lam can correctly refer to their being more than one model or type of democracy, or who can refer to the city's need to decolonize and be less concerned with the British system of law.

Now that the 2019 protests and riots seem unrepeatable, it is likely that Beijing will eventually float a similar proposal as that in 2014, for a one-person, one-vote run-off election of two acceptable (i.e. previously nominated) candidates for C.E. This will be a far cry from the "five demands, not one less" goal; moreover there will be no major ideological difference between candidates. But it would be a major step forward and undeniably more electorally-democratic than anything in Hong Kong's history. It would also make Hong Kong's C.E. election as procedurally-democratic as virtually all other comparative (urban, regional) elections in the world's major cities. It can even be construed as a step towards de-colonizing the inherited system from the British era and/or the Basic Law itself. Indeed on the very day of the most recent LegCo elections under the revamped electoral system, Beijing issued a white paper on Hong Kong democracy that spoke in clear if still general terms that democracy was still on the agenda for Hong Kong and that under the new system (that bars anti-Party-state/separatist candidates) it is now getting closer to the goal of universal suffrage under the Basic Law.[34] Thus some version of the ill-fated previous electoral reform package at the time of Occupy in 2014 is likely in the cards for Hong Kong. That this Hong Kong democracy white paper came shortly after the recent national one launched by Xi Jinping, praising the virtues and legitimacy of China's version of "whole process democracy" in general, is no accident, and signifies all the more that the SAR is now firmly in the orbit of mainland political discourse and global communications.

More importantly, for Hong Kong to move forward politically, away from the late colonial British era of the 1980s and 1990s and the birth of that arguably Occidentalist procedural -democracy movement, what will be needed is the development of an actual political class in an actually functional political system: one that not only wants to, but *can* work the mainland political and social system effectively for something other than personal enrichment. In this context this means that if and when this

130    D. F. VUKOVICH

political class arises (and it eventually *must* given mainland sovereignty now) it will be a major step forward in the decolonization of Hong Kong politics. De-colonization from the standpoint of the mainland certainly, and for those Hong Kongers—arguably a large minority of not small majority—who unambiguously support national integration or being part of China (i.e. those who do not take up the *nativistic* or 'yellow' place-based Hong Kong identity, although like most city-dwellers they may certainly be proud of their city/home-town).

The lack of this political class or group is a direct result of colonialism, which ruled Hong Kong via a politics of appointment and British bureaucratic domination as much as laissez-faire economics. These legacies are very much alive in Hong Kong and can, for example, explain Hong Kong University perfectly well, among other major institutions in the city. This is a separate question from how progressive or conservative such a new 'mainlandized' political class will be, or how progressive or not the city's de-colonization will be. There is nothing that guarantees its success, or its values and ideology: in fact the absence of analysis or conversation about the values and ideologies of the new, second handover Hong Kong has ben a major concern, as discussed above. Given the strongly conservative nature of Hong Kong political intellectual culture (aside from its more libertarian, tolerant elements that also exist) it is also perfectly possible that the city's love of hierarchy and familialism, its odd mix of entrepreneurial mentality and desperate fear of change (a fear most common amongst the 'progressives' it seems), will run roughshod over any future politics of community and common prosperity.

But if the political system and Hong Kong's economy are to be better and more rationally integrated with the mainland, then the Party-state's system of "meritocracy," performance-legitimacy and the like may bode well for the city's future, or at least bode better than the heretofore model of bringing colonial-era "loyal" tycoons and upper level bureaucrats to the C.E. position, and thence to the morass of a militantly filibustering LegCo.[35] Hence one need not idealize the mainland system to see that in this context it may be better—in terms of producing more effective and simply *competent* politicians and bureaucracy—to have it incorporated locally than to maintain the post-1997 mode of failure. One country, one system—or perhaps 1.5 systems—may in the end be better for the city and its peoples, not least its youth and children.

Much of what I have been theorizing as routes to economic and political de-colonization for Hong Kong presume that it will take the form of integrating into China. The territory, after all, belonged to it prior to modern imperialism and British colonialism, and its original inhabitants and generations hailed from the place, just as the uniquely place-based, localist identity of 'authentic' Hong Konger seems to date from the 1970s at the earliest. And yet, clearly, much—but not all—of the city's population has recently wanted nothing so much as separation and autonomy from the mainland. This is an understandable, historical problem that has much to do with the intellectual and cultural (including identity) hegemony stemming from the British era. One can freely admit that this is also a socially valid, real yearning and belief system or ideology in its own right for many, perhaps even a small majority of Hong Kong people. (The latter is an empirical question that we do not have a decent answer for, liberal mediatization to the contrary.) This split is a genuinely intractable issue, for which there are no easy or painless answers in terms of policy or even thought. As noted earlier, from the essentially liberal and pan-democratic standpoint, de-colonization for Hong Kong would mean either independence from Hong Kong (which was rarely stated before 2014 but indeed felt by many) or de facto complete autonomy for it, as well as the adoption of a directly nominated C.E. election. The point here is not that this take is wrong in objective or moral terms, nor that it is opposed to the Chinese state. One suspects the Western and colonial provenance of liberal democracy matters little to them. For them, it is simply a, even *the* universal political means towards universal freedom and human rights and progress and so on. Something similar has always been said by "Western" Marxism, which likewise disputes it is Western as opposed to universal. In fact the alleged Western or Eurocentric nature of Hong Kong liberalism/democracy matters little, aside from the mere fact that such views are nowhere near as widespread within the mainland, which is where the determining power lies. The salient post- or de-colonial point is merely that politics, or forms of politics like one- versus multi-party systems, are not universal. What matters still more is that this allegedly de-colonial yet liberal-democratic theory is in this context fully unrealistic, and always has been since the 1970s at least.[36] And in any case, in the end the 2019 movement was not an anti-colonial liberation movement directed against the P.R.C but was in its own terms a democracy movement based on the point about "suffrage" and autonomy from the mainland.

Moreover it is hard to see how this would be a de-colonial outcome, as opposed to a delayed victory of British colonialism. And it would have to be asked: whom does this benefit, and in what ways? The 2019 protests were undeniably large, especially at the earliest stage, and militant and remarkable and so on. But this doesn't make them de-colonial (or progressive) in itself, just as the demand for voting rights does not mean the movement was democratic except in a formal or procedural sense. Of course procedures do indeed matter, and voting can be of great importance. But democracy can and in fact has had a deeper or more substantive meaning and range of practical measures, not least distributive justice, majority rule, equality in opportunity and life chances. One might recall that in 1989 many of the student leaders such as Wang Dan specifically ruled out universal suffrage for peasants and the riff-raff.[37] Protests, even revolutions, can be conservative and reactionary just as they can be progressive or communistic. It is by no means certain that a majority of Hong Kongers wanted such a 'separatist' outcome—and even the pan-democrats' electoral successes (running on 'suffrage') ebbed and flowed over the years.

*Thus the argument here is that de-colonization in Hong Kong— assuming this is needed and desirable—necessarily has to take the form of integration with the mainland, at least in economic and political terms.* This, as opposed to preserving its status-quo via a "politics" or rather anti-politics of autonomy and demands for electing an, in effect, anti-government or anti-integration Chief Executive. In a ruse of history, this has been ushered in by the nativist and frankly right-wing turn within that 2019 movement and the pan-democratic tradition beforehand; or more specifically, this has been ushered in by the national security law and the slow and harsh yet careful and legal undoing of the conditions as well as the groups and individuals responsible for bringing Hong Kong to that point. To be sure the 'autonomist' reading of the Basic Law was not without foundation (see discussion above), and as I have argued it is the Basic Law itself, as much as the colonial-era identity production and educational systems that are at fault, with the proximate, immediate cause of 2019 being the "burnism' and the solicitation of US imperialism for 'help.' Thus there is something genuinely tragic, if one actually cares about Hong Kong, in what happened in 2019 and the years leading up to it. This is all in addition to the original sin of colonization itself, as well as the hands-off approach from the mainland, the theatrics and grand-standing of the opposition since the 1990s, the devolutions into human-rights-regime-change politics, the foreign interference, and so on and so forth.

But it must also be said that the re-assertion of mainland sovereignty (or its speeding up, if you will) is just the beginning and will not, cannot solve the colonial problem in itself. The national security law cannot achieve de-colonization except in terms of sovereignty and through certain, albeit genuinely important legal and policing changes. So too there are real limits to how well official propaganda efforts—national education reforms, for example, or lessons on the security laws—can and will work in Hong Kong. The danger here is not the new illegality of foreign funding of political actors or movements in Hong Kong, or the repression of independence views and nihilistic anti-government/anti-social politics. These will not be missed. The danger is that the mainland and Hong Kong government will stop here, and feel that re-establishing sovereignty in these ways is enough to settle the colonial problem and save the SAR from being a failed mini-state/pseudo city-state. As with Hong Kong democrats' political Occidentalism and the city's localist/separate identity, this maniacal focus on national sovereignty too is historically and practically understandable. The Party-state cares primarily about its own security and legitimacy, given the history of imperialism and the Cold War on the one hand and the consistent "refusal" of switching over to the "universal" form of good governance known as liberal democracy. Of these, and as with all states, brute force and sovereignty take precedence. But the harder goal lies in performance or other forms of legitimacy, and the PRC has no history and no track record, and no discourse *in Hong Kong* to achieve this. It must also counter or replace colonial discourse in order to do so.

Therefore for this second handover to work, de-colonization—or re-hegemonization—will naturally have to more comprehensive and reach far deeper and yet also be far more subtle and sharp, as opposed to blunt and ham-handed. Will it even try, and can it do so? China's record at achieving soft power abroad has been largely a failure, especially in political terms, and even before the catastrophe that is Covid-19. Hong Kong is, in a sense, the "abroad" or foreign entity now being brought into the fold, and the mainland's power notwithstanding, it will need to do at least some of the work of winning hearts and minds or consent/assent. In place of the strong colonial identification with liberalism, with the West, and with its exceptional, separate status and identity in Hong Kong, the mainland will have to offer other things for Hong Kong people to take up.

Things beyond mere patriotism and loyalty on principle. But also things beyond the entrepreneurial and materialistic/consumerist bases of Hong Kong culture, which is to say of the exact same capitalist culture that has likewise inundated the mainland to an equally obvious extent. Thus the time is indeed ripe for something like a mode of governance, or ethic of governance, articulated to 'common prosperity' or the like. The apparent, double-sided dream behind the Basic Law—convergence via money into national Chineseness (the PRC dream) or political liberalization via Hong Kong magic—has come to an end.

Finally it is worth repeating that for this integration/de-colonization to work better and to be more legitimate, the SAR will eventually have to allow for politicization and participation in some significant senses. Identity is one thing and another, liveable one (or more) will arise in Hong Kong for those who feel the need to have one, but people's "practice" or ways of living in society are another. Currently in Hong Kong there is very little if any room for either 'the street' to make its voice heard (which is after all one time-tested way, albeit only one way, for 'voice' to be articulated) or for other forms of socio-political participation and community/collective involvement. (This is also why the various churches in Hong Kong have been so popular as well as powerful at times.) This has as much to do with the global pandemic (and the city's zero-covid containment strategy) as with the national security law. Of course political and public health security are working in tandem now. But at some point the covid pandemic will be at an end, just as the pan-democratic era is already.

Likewise in China under Xi Jinping there is less room for popular protest and contestation such as labor strikes; this essentially repressive and conservative turn has been further enabled by the pandemic and (necessary) social/physical distancing measures. Just as there was a perfect storm of unfortunate conditions in 2019 and beyond in Hong Kong, leading to its rapid and dramatic turn away from the pan-democratic/autonomy era (which as I have been arguing may in the end birth a new and better Hong Kong for many of its inhabitants and future generations), the rise of Xi Jinping and his new consensus within the Party-state, coupled with a re-born Cold War/trade war with the US-West and again the global pandemic, has led to a major political impasse or quagmire in the present. There is no doubt that we have seen a sea-change in Chinese and Hong Kong and indeed global politics. But this

# 4 RE-COLONIZATION OR DE-COLONIZATION? 135

lockdown situation—like the Covid pandemic—shall eventually pass. The future awaits.

## NOTES

1. See Lui Tai Lok's discussion of the 1980s drafting period, cited in the previous chapter.
2. See Karl Polanyi, *The Great Transformation: The Political and Economic Origins of Our Time* (New York: Beacon Press, 2001 [1944]). And also Mark Blyth, *Austerity: The History of a Dangerous Idea* (Oxford UP, 2013) as well as his *Great Transformations: Economic Ideas and Institutional Change in the Twentieth Century* (Cambridge UP, 2002).
3. David Harvey is only the most well known, and admittedly accessible and lucid, account of this in his text, A *Brief History of Neo-liberalism* (Oxford UP, 2007). To his credit, Harvey does not actually equate this turn in China with neo-liberalism but 'merely' the basic structures or logic thereof.
4. I rehearse some of this history and argument in *Illiberal China*, and in fact it stems from both mainland Chinese intellectuals (Maoists) and foreign scholars of the 1960s/early 1970s.
5. See Isabella Weber's book on this important period of intellectual and political, economic history. *How China Escaped Shock Therapy: The Market Reform Debate* (Routledge, 2021).
6. See Deng Xiaoping, "Maintain Prosperity and Stability in Hong Kong," 3 October 1984. http://en.people.cn/dengxp/vol3/text/c1250.html. The above is how I read his use of "compatriots" throughout, and it is clear if unsurprising that he knew little of Hong Kong identity and culture, of course.
7. See for example Deng's speech from April 16, 1987, "Speech at a Meeting with the Members of The Committee for Drafting the Basic Law of the Hong Kong Special Administrative Region," in which he notes:

> Ever since the Opium War, reunification has been the common desire not just of one political party or group but of the whole Chinese nation, including the people in Taiwan.

http://www.china.org.cn/english/features/dengxiaoping/103351.htm. Accessed 4 May 2022. Deng may or may not have been pragmatic, and he almost certainly saw himself as Marxist or socialist, but he was clearly also an ethno-nationalist thinker.

8. See the twitter feed for Richard Wong (https://twitter.com/yuechim) as well as the freely searchable indexes at https://www.scmp.com/ and https://www2.hkej.com/. Accessed 4 May 2022. Wong is also notable for his long time advocacy for privatizing Hong Kong's already-limited public housing.

9. We also should not assume that Xi's aim is some type of direct or explicit redistribution to begin with.

10. See Debbie Sze-Wan Chan and Pun Ngai, "Economic Power of the Politically Powerless in the 2019 Hong Kong Pro-Democracy Movement," *Critical Asian Studies* 52.1: 33–43. In the following paragraphs in text, I am following their lead here in trying to find something positive within the yellow economy movement, but obviously my take is not a full-on endorsement.

11. See the other comments from Chan as well, in the wake of the Fall 2021 Party Plenum that endorsed Xi's common prosperity drive, in the *South China Morning Post*: "Hong Kong must 'make the cake bigger' to achieve Beijing's goal of 'common prosperity', finance chief says," 14 November 2021. https://www.scmp.com/news/hong-kong/politics/article/3156011/hong-kong-must-make-cake-bigger-achieve-beijings-goal. Accessed 4 May 2022.

12. Bernard S. Cohn, *Colonialism and Its Forms of Knowledge: The British in India* (Princeton UP, 1996). See as well Selina Ching Chan, "Politicizing Tradition: The Identity of Indigenous Inhabitants in Hong Kong," *Ethnology* 37.1 (Winter, 1998): 39–54.

13. For the critique of the gender politics involved, see Chiu Man-Chung, "Negotiating Han-Chinese Legal Culture: Postcolonial Gender Political Discourse on Hong Kong's Small House Policy," *King's Law Journal: KLJ* 17.1 (January 2006): 45–70.

14. For critical reports, see "Hong Kong Rewards the Property Oligarchs" by Our Correspondent in Asian Sentinel, 28 February 2017. https://www.asiasentinel.com/p/hongkong-rewards-property-oligarchs?s=r and Kent Ewing, "Scrap the Heung Yee Kuk: An out-of-touch mafia-like anachronism hindering Hong Kong's development," *Hong Kong Free Post*, 31 March 2020. https://hongkongfp.com/2016/09/19/scrap-the-heung-yee-kuk-an-out-of-touch-mafia-like-anachronism-hindering-hong-kongs-development/. See also the article by Tony Kwok, former head of the ICAC, "Hong Kong Must Seize the Moment to End the Abuse of Land Rights in the New Territories," *SCMP*, 24 September 2016. https://www.scmp.com/comment/insight-opinion/article/2021923/hong-kong-must-seize-moment-end-abuse-land-rights-new. Accessed 4 May 2020.

15. Just to be clear, this is not a criticism of the so-called ivory tower but just to mark the gap between sectors of society and intellectual and more

practical labor. It also goes without saying here that much of this "post-colonial" rhetoric has taken the form of the mainland re-colonizing the SAR, that it is 'between colonizers,' that it is part of the great Sinophone resistance to the mainland and so on. My views on this type of post-colonial studies, a product of American academe and ideology first and foremost, are well known and need not be rehearsed here.

16. Of course it is an elite class of politicians, bureaucrats, and corporate lords that run the city, but the point here should not be lost: that these are all Hong Kongers. Thus the pan-democratic, conspiracist obsession with mainlandization and so on categorically misses the point and only promotes intolerance and xenophobia. The failures of adequate, let alone radically democratic, mass representation are another issue, sadly a global one of most regimes today be they democratic or otherwise. The classic language of self-rule from anti-colonial movements, as with claims for and politics of sovereignty for spaces like Hong Kong, are simply a fascinating anachronism and simulacrum today.

17. See Uday Singh Mehta, *Liberalism and Empire: A Study in Nineteenth-Century British Liberal Thought* (Chicago UP, 1999) and Domenico Losurdo, *Liberalism: A Counter-History* (New York: Verso, 2014).

18. See for example, Ching Kwan Lee's May, 2020 editorial in the Los Angeles Times, "Hong Kong is the front line of a new cold war. If it burns, the world gets burned too," https://www.latimes.com/opinion/story/2020-05-28/op-ed-if-hong-kong-burns-the-world-gets-burned-too and the various blog postings made by senior, 'progressive' China scholars in the *positions* journal e-zine. Accessed 4 June 2021.

19. Again, Anderson's treatment of these issues in his *Imagined Communities*—the horizontal equality of the nation in face of vertical class and other differences—are not to be forgotten.

20. I am speaking here of nationalism through the Mao era and 1980s.

21. See Jo Freeman, 'The Tyranny of Structurelessness," *Berkeley Journal of Sociology* 17 (1972–73): 151–165.

22. There is of course a large literature on this subject, but for an entertaining read, see Stanley Fish, *There's No Such Thing As Free Speech, And It's a Good Thing, Too* (Oxford UP, 1994).

23. It is worth remembering that Hong Kong has long had a certain relation to mainland intellectual liberalism, and to an extent with "Confucian" or neo-traditional intellectuals as well.

24. See Nury Vittachi's discussion of voting percentages, as well as the famously a-political nature of traditional Hong Kong culture, in his *The Other Side of the Story* (YLF Press, Hong Kong, 2020).

25. This distinction between consent and assent is part of Stuart Hall's important work on the concept and practice of hegemony. See the discussion by Lawrence Grossberg, "History, Politics, and Postmodernism." In *Stuart*

138  D. F. VUKOVICH

*Hall: Critical Dialogues in Cultural Studies*, eds. David Morley and Chen Kuan-Hsing (Routledge, 1996).

26. But note as well that until recently—the last decade or so—it was quite common for Hong Kongers to identify nationally or in terms of culture with China and Chineseness in a broad sense, just not with the Party or political system (about which they only knew the dark sides in any case). See Anthony Fung's 2004 article on this question for example: "Postcolonial Hong Kong Identity: Hybridising the Local and the National," *Social Identities* 10.3: 399–414. The Beijing Olympics of 2008, widely celebrated throughout the city, is a case in point. It is not only possible but likely that at some point such a dual or friendlier Hong Kong-Chinese identity will emerge again, to be taken up by many.

27. See the important book by Kevin J. O'Brien and Li Lianjiang, *Rightful Resistance in Rural China* (Cambridge UP, 2006). There is by now a large literature on contentious politics and forms of resistance in China, all of which should be useful now for Hong Kong, but this is the best place to begin.

28. See Wu Xiaogang, "Income Inequality and Distributive Justice: A Comparative Analysis of Mainland China and Hong Kong," *The China Quarterly* 200: 1033–1052. The author notes that Hong Kong's Gini measure is nearly double that of the mainland's, and yet tolerance of inequality is much higher in the southern city.

29. The Labour Party of Hong Kong was formed in 2011 by three veteran pan-democratic legislators, led by Lee Cheuk-Yan, with an eye towards bringing labor issues more to the fore within the pan-dem camp. After some success in the 2012 election (wining four seats) it lost badly in 2016, was plagued by internal strife in 2017, and is now moribund if not defunct. Two of the founders, Lee and Cyd Ho, are currently in jail awaiting trial for the 2020 "primary election" issue. The need for a labor party focused on labor remains.

30. See the report in the *South China Morning Post*, "Hong Kong Legco Election: Biggest Backers of Pro-Beijing Bloc Live in Public Housing Estates," 27 December 2021. https://www.scmp.com/news/hong-kong/politics/article/3161111/hong-kong-election-numbers-highlight-pro-establishment. Accessed May 4, 2020.

31. For an excellent essay on Szeto Wah and the fate of the democracy movement, one that argues usefully that there is plenty of blame to spread around for its failures, see the independent scholar Suzzanne Pepper, "Beijing, Britain, pan-democrats or localists: Who is to blame for the death of Hong Kong's democracy movement?" Feburary 2022. https://hongkongfp.com/2022/02/12/beijing-britain-democrats-or-localists-who-is-to-blame-for-the-death-of-hong-kongs-democracy-movement/. For more on Szeto Wah and for a straightforward introduction to the

4 RE-COLONIZATION OR DE-COLONIZATION? 139

history of the movement in relation to the mainland, see Shiu-Hing Lo, *Competing Chinese Political Visions: Hong Kong vs. Beijing on Democracy* (Prager Press, 2010).

32. See in particular)albeit with a grain of salt as always) the Chinese language entry on the HKCTU, as it has more detail than the English one: "香港職工會聯盟," at the Chinese Wikipedia entry at: https://zh.wikipedia.org/wiki/%E9%A6%99%E6%B8%AF%E8% 81%B7%E5%B7%A5%E6%9C%83%E8%81%AF%E7%9B%9F. Accessed 4 May 2022. For a report which conflates the independent unions of Hong Kong with the non-existing independent unions of the mainland, see the report in *Jacobin* magazine by Tim Pringle and Peng Pai, "Hong Kong's Trade Unions Are Under Attack," no date, https://www.jacobinmag.com/2021/10/hong-kong-confedera tion-trade-union-hkctu-dissolved. Accessed 4 May 2022. This is obviously a partisan report on behalf of "the masses" in Hong Kong and China, and its concerns with labor are, as always, well founded. But the brute fact is that independent unions in China cannot exist and will not outside of some collapse or revolution, which even then does not guarantee any improvements for "the masses" labouring under capital. One can argue that independent unions are to be preferred (and the official ones are indeed too weak and not radical at all) but not only is there a certain Cold War precedent for this, but the championing of these from afar seems less about solidarity than projection and fantasy. In the case of Hong Kong, which is radically different, my own argument has been that the more such unions delve into or become social activist and civil society groups, the less they become labor unions to begin with. The legal case against such unions in Hong Kong has been based not on their labor polities per se but on their funding and participation in 2019.

33. See the comments from Han in a Reuters report from June 4, 2021, "Hong Kong Not Dead Yet, Says Tiananmen Veteran Taking Lone Stand in Park for June 4 Vigil," https://www.reuters.com/world/china/hong-kong-not-dead-yet-says-tiananmen-veteran-taking-lone-stand-park-june-4-2021-06-04/. Accessed 25 May 2022.

34. For a fuller discussion from the mainland's and HK government's side, see "SCIO briefing on 'Hong Kong: Democratic Progress Under the Framework of One Country, Two Systems' White Paper," 30 December 2021. http://www.china.org.cn/china/2021-12/30/con tent_77961725_2.htm. Accessed 4 May 2020.

35. Of course the notion of Chinese meritocracy is also widely used as part of its official propaganda. It is certainly that, and the meritocratic politician is more of an ideal type than anything else (at best). But it is also one theory or notion of governance, and should not be simply be dismissed

140    D. F. VUKOVICH

because it has meaning in the Chinese system itself, which is something to understand not mock. My use of quote marks is meant to suggest this.

36. As argued and, it may be felt, *demonstrated* repeatedly by various historians and critical scholars (see the works of Uday Mehta and Domenico Losurdo cited earlier), liberalism was part and parcel of historical, modern colonialism. At the same time, being the dominant discourse or interpretive framework of modernity, it was also variegated and complex and taken up by some anti-colonial movements and intellectuals (e.g. in India and via Nehru) as the antidote, in some fashion or the other, to the same colonialism. There were also liberal thinkers from the metropole whom were anti-colonial (e.g. Burke but by no means J.S. Mill). One could easily argue that liberalism's record—within the former colonies especially—in this matter of de-colonization and national liberation has been either an utter failure in political terms or a decidedly mixed one. The poison never became a remedy. The case of East Asia and China in particular are further cases in point. Thus it should come as no surprise that colonial liberalism or an allegedly de-colonial liberalism in the tiny, exceptionalist space of Hong Kong (in fact an anti-statist liberalism to boot) met a similar fate. Its way forward will have to come through other means, and now necessarily through the state.

37. This was something often noted by critical scholarship at the time, from Geremie Barmé for example. Of course some of these same youth, e.g. Wang Dan himself, later changed their minds in a more inclusive direction.

CHAPTER 5

# Coda: The Search for State Capacity After Covid and Zero-Covid

As argued earlier, for Hong Kong to de-colonize would mean for it to become a functional and integrated (as opposed to dysfunctional and 'autonomous') part of the mainland; it must be so not only in economic and rhetorical terms but in political ones, including but definitely beyond national security.[1] The issue is not simply a missing nationalism or patriotism within the city, although such a requirement—that all officials, from district councillors to Legco to appointed electors, is now inscribed in a required loyalty oath to 'love China and love Hong Kong." But whether one finds this distasteful or common sense, neither conscious nationalism nor patriotism (however defined) are necessary, strictly but practically speaking, for Hong Kong to be a better governed, mutually beneficial part of the P.R.C.[2] (Though certainly nationalism will grow further in Hong Kong, as it has elsewhere, as if a perennial favourite of all modern societies.) Performance legitimacy (as it is called in the mainland) and any social contract turning upon people's livelihood requires such a substantial state capacity. Let us define this last phrase in the conventional way, as state (hence public) power to do things, to enact and implement policies and decisions other than, or in addition to the act of policing/adjudicating crime (which until recently has been the primary

© The Author(s), under exclusive license to Springer Nature      141
Singapore Pte Ltd. 2022
D. F. Vukovich, *After Autonomy: A Post-Mortem*
*for Hong Kong's first Handover, 1997–2019,*
https://doi.org/10.1007/978-981-19-4983-8_5

142 D. F. VUKOVICH

focus since 2019). Policing and security, after all, is the easiest to accomplish, if also the easiest to obsess over from either the state's or the (now defunct/repressed) opposition's perspective.

Hong Kong must develop an ability to carry out specific policies that go beyond 'rectifying' 2019 (a legal and policing mission already accomplished in large part) but that also resolve the Basic Law's central contradiction between autonomy and integration. The SAR must—finally—get on with the real work of improving people's lives and livelihoods as a part of the PRC and not only as "Asia's global city." This would not be re-colonizing the city but de-colonizing it. *The danger for Hong Kong's future – what would turn it into not another mainland Chinese city but a fairly miserable, alienated space – is that the bald and forceful re-assertion of mainland sovereignty and the securing of national security legislation within Hong Kong will be taken as enough.* Or enough, if mixed with renewed efforts at 'national education' within the public schools and other propaganda efforts thrown in for good measure.

## ON THE STATE, DURING AND AFTER COLONIALISM

Admittedly this will work to one extent or another, particularly if some of the—welcome—economic and job-creation plans pan out for those other than financiers and property developers. Not just jobs but living conditions and livelihood development are paramount for genuine security as well as for greater contentment within the populace, which has ben suffering from governmental and political/civil society dysfunction for decades now (to say nothing of the colonial years). But this will in turn first require *state*, not purely *market* capacity, or in other words— and to keep things real—a state-led market development for the city. To some ears, the argument that the wealthy global city of Hong Kong *lacks* development may sound odd, but this is true only if one is unaware of the decay, or even absence of its public infrastructure: as the pandemic has exposed with the health care system, not only health but education from primary to university levels is much smaller that it needs to and should be, given the city's coffers and size, the lack of taxation to the mainland, and so on. To say nothing of the housing crisis and housing quality (cramped flats and cubicle homes), the lack of adequate 'leisure centres' or other public facilities, and so on. This deliberate forgetting of development and *social* equality, which can only happen via the state it must be said, has been the blind spot of the democrats and aligned intellectuals celebrating or affirming the 2014 and 2019 protests, just as much as the deliberate elision of such movements' xenophobia and anti-immigrant positions.[3]

Of course, just to anticipate the "whatabout" objection from some quarters, we can readily say this is not unique to Hong Kong's political theatre but, alas, can be found virtually everywhere, as can—noted previously—the rise of nativism as well as reactionary identity—and postcolonial politics. When one combines such affect and structures of feeling with anti-statism and the absence of parties and political structures that can adequately *represent* the masses or large swatches of society, you get the bleak political scene and the failing or flailing states not only of Hong Kong but of much of the world. China has until recently at least been far more effective in at least retaining and deploying such state capacity, including the ability to mobilize people as well as resources. This has been seen clearly with the response to Covid, but a darker side obviously exists as well (including within the recent lockdowns in Shanghai). Suffice it to mention Xinjiang. Hong Kong, despite the clearly or at least arguably harsh sentencing of some of those convicted from the 2019–2020 events, is not Xinjiang and has not been securitized in the same way (nor was it so pre-emptory). And whether one regrets or approves of the second-handover and securitization of Hong Kong, the SAR, it is in any case going to go forward. There can be no turning back. We do not get to choose, but we do get to think through the transition and the recent past leading up to the present.

And yet such development in and for Hong Kong, if mixed only with propaganda and securitization or authoritarianism, may not be enough, unless some of the preceding issues are addressed: e.g., forging a new identity or series of identities for Hong Kong as a place *within* China; de-orientalising knowledge of political China and taking P.R.C. politics and self-understandings seriously; 'growing' the economy and housing supply in an equitable way; and fomenting a capable political class who are at least 'engineers' (red or otherwise) as opposed to mere tycoons, 'business leaders,' and ineffectual bureaucrats.[4] This is going to be a long process.

But to speak of the need for a better political class, or for better, genuine development, is already to speak of the state and hence an effective state capacity. A small or weak political class without a 'strong' or interventionist and redistributive state may be a neo-liberal or "anarcho" dream, but it is also exactly what Hong Kong has now, of sorts, even 25 years after its alleged de-colonization. This is not much different than Hong Kong's laissez-faire colonial governance, which was always relatively

144    D. F. VUKOVICH

"hands-off" internally and at one or two removes from London's attention and direct control.[5]

Hong Kong's brief period of welfarist policies came, as noted before, as a response to the mainland's cultural revolution and anti-imperialism and the perceived need to make Hong Kong better off, more democratic or fair than the mainland.[6] After this, from the Patten years onward through the handover and up to the present, the mode of governance was much more neo-liberal than developmentalist. Even the city's first C.E. after 1997, patriotic shipping tycoon Tung Chee-Wah, quickly dropped his initial plan to build 85,000 public flats a year after the Asian financial crisis hit the city (bowing to perceived public pressure, i.e. from mortgage holders). After this Tung et al. kept ignoring the elephant in the room: the city's principal contradiction, the housing problem. So focus turned to non-economic, non-livelihood issues like National Security or Article 23, and endless filibuster battles over "suffrage" and negative liberty, i.e. freedom *from* the mainland. In short, between 1997 and 2019 and putatively under the mainland's attention, the continued use of largely *politically* unqualified capitalists and former civil servants as C.E. has been all too familiar, and clearly ended in failure under Lam, the mishandling of the extradition bill and then the fifth wave. When we question the competence of such political leaders and officials the point is precisely that of politics or political experience on the one hand, and on the other their deep roots in the Hong Kong of British colonialism and the laissez-faire, non-state state.

While it is still fashionable, within the 'Western' left and right in particular, to see the state (as such) in purely negative if not dismissive terms, this has more to do with the degradation of liberalism since the 1970s (and of ac actual statist liberalism before this!), the hegemony yet utter social failure of austerity economics, and the general dumbing-down of political thought that has subtended the rise of dysfunctional political elites the world over as well as the rise of sound-bite social media. What is more, it has to do with the absence of political theory (or philosophy) within the general academic discourse and lines of inquiry (e.g. in cultural studies, post-colonial studies, China studies). Politics is simply not taken seriously as a field of inquiry and discipline that one must be trained or versed in, that one must labor at.[7] To practice medicine you must have a license, to 'do' economics you must have training or deep experience in that field, but to hold forth on politics you just need to hold forth. There is nothing more common, yet banal and jejune, than for example a historian or humanities academic holding forth on politics. Politics is seen as universal, and something that anyone can speak to; it is moreover something that one already knows as if on principle, or just by virtue of being human and therefore a political animal, as the ancient Greek is alleged to have said. This is not to make a case for elitism or for protecting the turf of say political science or political theory. Indeed it is not a bad thing at all for everyone—ordinary people especially—to have opinions and passions about politics. If anything more of this is needed, not less, albeit hopefully somehow without the hate-speech fuelled by social media anonymity. But there is, or should be a place for deeper command and depth of knowledge about politics and political thought in academic or professional writing. It is this latter dimension that one can find lacking, if only because it is woefully under-developed within the academy and in secondary education worldwide.

And so, in sum, for several reasons, we lose sight of the practical, brute fact, or if you prefer the argument since antiquity, that the state is the very terrain of politics and something that we humans living in complex societies *cannot not want*. Moreover in an age of looming (and present) environmental catastrophes, and now global pandemics, state-led development (or state-led markets), coordination, and welfare are more important than ever. As Jan Nederveen Pieterse has argued in a recent book on global Covid:

> By many accounts Covid brings the comeback of the state, also in market-led societies. Market forces and corporations don't fix crises, crises of public health, climate change, inequality or natural disasters, unless they provide profit opportunities.... Based on onsite examinations of pandemic health performance of 26 countries across the world, three key variables stand out in success or failure in dealing with Covid – knowledge, state capability and social cooperation. (205)[8]

While a full examination of the politics of Covid is well beyond our scope here, we must note Pieterse's point that all three of these key variables are best when they work together. Furthermore such a combined machinery, particularly with market-based societies like Hong Kong, takes many years to develop institutionally. This period of time, or crucible of history, is precisely what has been lacking in Hong Kong, even apart from its domination by free-market, non-state politics and decision-making.

146    D. F. VUKOVICH

Given that the struggle for state legitimacy via 'free' electoral democracy is over for Hong Kong (for many years to come at any rate), leaving only performance and livelihood other than repressive power, it behoves us to think of other routes to de-colonization and social progress in Hong Kong. And this question of legitimacy in Hong Kong was not articulated to state capacity in any case. The argument here is that de-colonization would require a functional and effective state, as opposed to a failed or failing, and heretofore *small* state. In short Hong Kong—a free market, non-society in Thatcheresque terms if ever there was one—has lacked state capacity for much of its history and therefore the means to provide well for people's livelihood, let alone to become a "democracy" in some bona fide, social or majoritarian sense.[9] It is worth recalling that one product of imperialism and modern colonialism was the production of 'local' states that not only were radically undemocratic and alien, if also collaborationist, but also woefully inadequate to the new world and new tasks in the aftermath of national, anti-colonial liberation. As with the cases of the communist victories in Russia and China, for example, the inherited states were obviously failed or failing, and had to be radically reformed if not jettisoned, the morning after the revolution. But all of this was far easier said than done, as history painfully shows across the globe. We need to recall that colonialism and empire entailed not just economic and technological but also *political and state under-development*.[10]

Many in Hong Kong studies see the territory as lucky to have been spared the trials and tribulations of the mainland liberation in 1949 (from famine to the chaos of the cultural revolution). This is a fair point indeed.[11] But it must be said that while the P.R.C. has now had several decades to develop or pursue its own form of state adequate to its needs, with admittedly varying degrees of success, the Hong Kong 'state' has barely begun such a journey. Or moreover has not until very recently begun to even see the need for such major reform. The fifth wave of the pandemic delayed proposed governmental structural reform. Thus while the elimination of the pan-democratic opposition and its obsessive–compulsive filibustering has resulted in far more bills and acts being passed within Hong Kong—as argued earlier, a welcome development compared to years of stagnation—the regrouping of bureaucratic divisions to better tackle the perpetual housing crisis has been set aside as of early 2022. Even the passed legislation awaits its actual implementation. Some measures have been taken via 'emergency powers' to battle the Omicron wave, such as the importation of mainland health workers and doctors. This is all to the good, and could indicate at least a commitment to increasing state capacity or 'getting things done.' There is certainly pressure from the North to do so now. But unless legislative acts and new policy directions were to be made consistently through emergency powers—not a bad idea but certainly a controversial and therefore unlikely one—then the problem of becoming a functional, developmental state remains for Hong Kong. It has only been 2–3 years since the 2019 crisis and its aftermaths. But this is long enough for us to inquire into whether it will actually happen, and if so in what form or ways? As long as Hong Kong remains committed to its small state, colonial (aka British) liberalism and to its massive resistance to change, buttressed in some quarters by an autonomist or separate-but-superior Hong Kong identity, there is little reason for optimism. Pessimism of the intellect would seem the order of the day, or at least of the many days after the rise of Covid.

The response to the pandemic, particularly in its latest, fifth wave (of the highly contagious yet far milder Omicron variant) has painfully illustrated the problem. The lack of state capacity in Hong Kong is certainly not new, and is familiar to actual residents here who rely on, for example, under-funded public hospitals and public schools, and a sparse welfare system. It has everything to do with the colonial heritage, where 'people's livelihood' was not exactly the social contract put in place by the British. Now that Hong Kong has lost or is losing its privileged and protected status as an autonomous space (putatively free of the mainland but fully open to capital), it is high time for it to stop living on borrowed time, that neurotic temporality of British Hong Kong. It is time instead to develop a state, or form of state, that will be adequate to its actual needs. Not simply as a part of China but as a political entity and society that bears some responsibility for the livelihood of *all* its people, not just the wealthy and well-connected or those from the 'right' families. How will it do so, without direct 'civic' elections? It is a tall order indeed, even allowing for the failures of liberal-democratic societies with such elections.

But the answer is obvious: trial and error, and with mainland tutelage as much as possible. One could see this as paternalistic or even as 're-colonization' in the trite cultural studies way.[12] But a better metaphor would be "receivership" and, again, tutelage. Hong Kong never had a proper *transitional* period between the British (who in effect tried to sabotage the mainland's view of the Basic Law via last-minute electoral reforms) and the present period. (We are speaking of politics proper here, and economy for that matter, and not culture and identity; the search for a transitional identity, or some form of e.g. Chineseness is something else entirely and not our concern.) The years from 1997 until Covid were largely, in effect, the time of lost generations and still-more borrowed time and limbo. But things do not stay the same or status quo in such a limbo-state; they get worse, except for those whom might benefit, which are invariably the wealthy and privileged. In point of fact Hong Kong became worse off in some crucial ways, perhaps most notably the quality and affordability of housing (and delays for public allotments), the decay and exhaustion of the public health system, and the failure to expand higher education adequately. Certainly it did not degrade in all ways. While they received bad press locally and internationally, the link to high speed rail in the mainland and the bridge to Macau/Zhuhai were welcome additions (and not the only benefits).

But such projects were clearly not enough and moreover did not and could not improve people's livelihood for a local economy based in finance and tourism and property 'development' for the already wealthy. A receivership may therefore be in order, which is to say far greater guidance and more direct leadership from the mainland.[13] This is precisely what has been starting to happen in Hong Kong in its—belated—attempts to follow a dynamic zero-covid strategy with mainland advice and direct assistance (most notably from SARS and Wuhan veteran advisor and leader, Liang Wannian). It would require more of the same in general, i.e. in non-pandemic economic and social matters, to achieve a more functional form of state or governance. This is turn requires a certain amount of competence and 'performance legitimacy,' on the part of Hong Kong's Chief Executive and officialdom. But before this it will also require a certain amount of political will and conviction. We will turn to this below.

Having already essayed the question of identity and colonial or orientalist discourse, we leave to one side here further discussion of a *cultural* or social de-colonization. While it is typical for post-colonial or cultural studies to obsess over identity and "culture" in some textualist sense (e.g. films as windows into reality) these are in the present context of Hong Kong not as important as directly political questions. For all the rise of a xenophobic "localism" and "yellow-nativism" in the past decade, Hong Kong identities are actually diverse and multiple, and could not be extinguished even if someone wanted them to be. New ones will inevitably arise, hopefully for the better and hopefully treated less as life and death differences. As for culture, understood as synonymous to ideology and belief, suffice it to mention that all that is needed is for certain parts of

Hong Kong to unlearn and move away from its xenophobic or nativistic hostility to the mainland and its people. This will happen in due time with greater integration and the development of more social relations between the two places and peoples. It need not come at the expense of Hong Kong place-based identity (and it would be hard to imagine a city without a place-based identity) so much as at the expense of the colonial baggage underpinning Hong Kong's—a goodly chunk of Hong Kong's—discourse about China.

To be sure, even two years into the pandemic in Hong Kong and the end of the oppositional movement, xenophobic and orientalist/colonial discourse about the mainland still runs deep. Perhaps the most telling recent example has been the objection, voiced by the mainstream media as well as by health care workers, about the arrival of desperately needed, Cantonese-speaking doctors and nurses from the mainland to help stem the sharp rise in deaths amongst the elderly and vulnerable population in Hong Kong. Rather than expressing, say, gratitude for such aid, one care-home worker openly expressed disbelief that the mainlanders would know how to care for the elderly in Hong Kong (and so would need thoroughly re-trained), and one local news reporter from the major outlet *Nowtv* could only ask a legalistic question about what patients could do if (*implied*: when) they suffered malpractice from the mainland professionals.[14] As distasteful as such sentiments are, one has to remember that in the wake of the pandemic and travel restrictions, the mainland has been largely closed off from Hong Kong, and therefore from the process of mixing, exchanging, and experiencing that will eventually—given time— smooth out the hard edges of xenophobia and parochialism. Or in other words, that will eventually leave only typical or 'normal' levels of such all too human sentiment, rather than the toxic surfeit that has helped spoil Hong Kong-mainland relations since the putative end of British colonialism here. Again, it is important to not over-state this dark side of Hong Kong culture (rarely admitted in any case), but it is equally dangerous to pretend it does not in fact exist in a real way. Not all forms of "identity politics" are worth dignifying, and in some cases they are better described as racism or xenophobia.[1]

---

[1] On racism, xenophobia, and yellow peril discourse within Hong Kong (directed towards mainlanders), see Sautman and Yan, 2015.

# The Fifth Wave: Incapacitation

While our purpose here has been to perform a political and theoretically-driven post-mortem on the 2019 protests/riots, we must end by further engaging the pandemic in Hong Kong, and specifically the government's halting and often maddeningly failing efforts to perform the mainland's "dynamic" or "zero-Covid" policy. In the first year of Covid, before the development of vaccines in China and abroad, the Hong Kong government undeniably succeeded in reducing the amount of infections and moreover fatalities from Covid. Here as elsewhere the zero-covid strategy of closing borders, mass testing and contact tracing, social distancing, etc., was effective if obviously harmful economically for many and certainly difficult for most. After an undeniable success in the first wave—as measured by sheer numbers of cases and fatalities—Hong Kong became in 2021 and 2022 a poster-child for, first, an unduly harsh and draconian quarantine and closed-border policy that adversely effected not only travellers and residents abroad but local businesses and, indeed, everyone. Long and arguably unnecessary school closures (especially in the Omicron era), micromanaged yet ineffective and sometimes illogical closings-and-openings that made little sense, and a lack of communication or clear messaging characterized the governmental response.. And then things turned worse.

*What the wave of Omicron infections exposed was nothing less than the very real limits of a 'laissez-faire' minimalist state (or a neo-liberal one if you prefer) and, as discussed earlier, the lack of a political class actually capable of governing*, with or without some type of charismatic, communicative authority. The government failed to come up with an exit strategy, as if the zero-covid strategy (aka suppression and containment of the virus) was not a public health and governance matter leading towards a goal, but something to be kept in perpetuity, a symbolic-heroic war against human mortality. In short: despite having almost two years lead-up time to what would arrive as Omicron, and after repeated calls by health officials in 2021 to get the elderly far more vaccinated, Hong Kong left its population, particularly the elderly and vulnerable, mostly unvaccinated and therefore highly susceptible to the worse effects of that strain (and deaths). Vaccine-teams were not dispatched to care homes, for example, until Spring 2022 after thousands of the elderly had died. Isolation centres and makeshift Covid hospitals were not built—with mainland help!—until well into the fifth wave. Even prior to Covid in 2020 the public health system was in need or more staff and more facilities. Financial incentives such as the several cash and voucher pay-outs were *not* tied to vaccination. Smartphone technology to help trace contacts and places visited by the infected was not deployed until well after the mainland and Macau had done so, for example, and were largely toothless and ineffective. Anti-vaccination beliefs, alongside anti-government attitudes, were and are widespread in Hong Kong (not unlike the USA and elsewhere of course), and even medical professionals were slow to take up vaccines (of either Sinovac or Pfizer).

To be sure certain aspects of the local culture helped produce the crisis: e.g. suspicions of Western medicine, a long history of anti-government attitudes (stemming from the British period and its shoddy governance), the typically self-centred quality of individualism. The 2019 crisis and its attendant anti-government sentiment is a major factor as well. But the point here is that the government did nothing to overcome this, and once again acted as if it did not even know its own population (e.g. Lam and others have often said that it was just a small portion of Hong Kong society that was involved in the anti-ELAB protests and that it does not reflect Hong Kong identity[15]). It is one thing for mainland China to do zero-covid because of its vast population and lack of ICUs (though it too has not done nearly as much as it could have with building up public health). It is another thing for a wealthy, privileged city run by unopposed elites and with more self-professed medical experts than ICUs to do the same. Why indeed should Hong Kong's public health infrastructure be so poor and miserly, when it is one of the world's wealthiest cities? Likewise why are there so few university or vocational spaces for the youth? "Classical" British liberal ideology via colonialism is an obvious (and undeniable) culprit, but if Hong Kong (especially its political intellectual elite) had this in spades it also lacked a populist or mass anti-colonial movement. Even the *finally* large movement spearheaded by the youth in recent years did not break free of these constraints; and its anti-colonial populism, aimed at 'communist' China, took the form of a xenophobic populism.[16] Globalization is famously adept at producing localisms, and it is not secret that in recent years—if not since 1991 and the Balkans disasters—these have been stridently reactionary. This should be a familiar story by now but in the case of Hong Kong—again precisely because of the power of political orientalism visa vis the mainland—it has not even troubled the anti-mainland, freedom versus tyranny narrative.

Vaccinations of the elderly were one thing that the otherwise overwhelmed and unsuccessful governments of, e.g., the UK and USA did well in comparison. By failing to in effect "force them to be free" (Rousseau) through firmer legal vaccination requirements and infrastructure preparation, the Hong Kong government not only failed to protect its people but displayed two things that stem from its colonial heritage: *incompetence* (or lack of 'performance legitimacy') on the one hand, and perhaps still more fatefully, *the courage of its own convictions*. It knew—as its own medical advisers repeated constantly—that vaccinations, especially of the elderly was absolutely crucial to stem the virus and to open up the economy again, not least to the mainland itself (which has a definite priority for the city). For the first waves of the global pandemic, the Chinese "model" of zero-covid worked spectacularly well (in China but also in Taiwan, New Zealand, Australia, elsewhere). This is especially striking when one compares it to the USA and U.K., places that in addition to their own ideological baggage around vaccinations and individual freedoms (to not wear masks, e.g.) were also governed by a certain neo-liberalism and consequent lack of ability to test and trace people as needed. But once vaccines were available, such places fared better than Hong Kong in getting the elderly and vulnerable vaccinated. It is this which has allowed them to open up their economies and begin to recover from Covid faster, at this stage, than Hong Kong or China (which, to be sure, were also not as adversely effected).

Why did Hong Kong fail to do so? As harsh as it may sound, one has to figure in a certain lack of competence, which can only come from having a seasoned political class and, in sum, experience ruling. Thanks to the British (era) as well as to the peculiarities of the Basic Law, Hong Kong still lacks this political class (we need not call it a meritocratic class) worthy of its name or of the name "ruling class." "Ruling" implies not only authority (e.g. forcing people, by hook or by crook, to get vaccinated) but some type of effective, functional activity. Perhaps what Hong Kong has had has been a misruling class. Such is the sad state of the city— and of the world, mostly—that ruling classes are less and less able to rule even in their own bourgeois terms.[17]

It knew, or should have known, not only that there was a great shortage of local medical staff, but a shortage of beds, ICUs, and ventilators. That at the level of infrastructure as much as at the level of command, it lacked the capacity to implement zero-covid after 2020. Here the people 'panic buying' rice and noodles and toilet paper had more foresight than the government, which should have been panic-buying ventilators, medical and laboratory staff, mobile vaccination teams, and throwing up isolation and treatment centres. In a city that is infamously crowded and dense, and one that went through the SARS pandemic in 2003–2004, the lack of isolation and treatment facilities is striking.

What the city's fifth wave demonstrated to a certainty was that Hong Kong, as opposed to the mainland, lacks the institutional and labor-power infrastructure to practice a zero-covid strategy of containing the virus through rapid—but temporary—lock-downs, contact tracing, and isolation of the infected. Even allowing for the fact that this zero strategy is at best inadvisable during the omicron wave, the point is that Hong Kong tried to do this (as part of the PRC) but massively failed due to its lack of such infrastructure and state capacity or power. Even closing off the borders without loopholes proved difficult at the beginning, and lacking an ability to actually mass test, to trace and isolate and break chains of infection, it was left with a micro-managing, corporate managerial approach that ranged from rational to ridiculously lacking scientific reasoning (closing parks, playgrounds, and beaches but not shopping malls; partially but not totally closing restaurants for dine-in, culling hamsters, etc.).

To be fair, Hong Kong *did* eventually make strides in tracing and compulsory testing through mini-lock-downs of entire housing estates and compulsory testing orders and use of smartphone technology. This is a hopeful sign and necessary for combating the spread of any such virus, regardless if the goal is "zero" or something more realistic. Yet we need to remember that the city started—unlike the mainland (Wuhan)—from ground zero. Well into the fifth wave and a high death rate spike, it finally began to directly and freely distribute home tests, masks, and medicines. But this was too little too late for the people experiencing the seemingly endless repetition of random business and leisure-place closures, the economic hardship and unemployment, the extra burdens of home-learning off loaded onto families and children, and so on. It is worth noting that there has been a large spike in suicides during the pandemic, especially since 2021.[18] This is directly and unambiguously attributable to the "zero covid" strategy, especially in that it has failed as a means of suppressing the virus's spread, and merely served to prolong the perceived torture while offering no exit plan for returning to normal life after the much milder Omicron strain. It must be recalled that during the nearly three years of the strategy in Hong Kong, primary and secondary schools have largely been closed (i.e. moved online) even without any major outbreaks. In this same time the mainland has, until Omicron now and the lockdown of Shanghai and other places, largely been open and normal aside from the international border being closed.[19] In this sense Hong Kong—the city that in previous years famously weathered SARS—has been worse off than the mainland during this crisis (and its economy has also taken a much larger hit). Why has this been the case? Vis a vis the question of state capacity, the answer is clear.

Right now, with the new economic and housing plans in very initial, slow stages (in part due to the pandemic of course), and even with a Legco that can now quickly pass legislation, this governance capacity is still weak. Beyond the lack of practical experience and communication skills that would lead to greater competence, why else is this the case?

The lack of conviction or political will, even within a government that has removed all 'suffragist' parties and filibuster possibilities, is striking. It is as if the current C.E. does not fully believe in even her own policies, as the frequent flip-flopping indicates (backtracking on school openings, city-wide testing, isolation orders, and so on). Part of this may be that as C.E. her role has been to serve two masters, as she once said after the 2019 riots: Hong Kong as well as Beijing. But as we have argued, not all of Hong Kong is "yellow" or in that anti-integration space (it may only be a small majority or large minority.[20] And in any case this camp is a genuine enemy in the Schmittian sense, rooted in an irreconcilable difference or will-to-power, and would never find the government or C.E. to be legitimate or acceptable.

Beijing's own directives (in addition to security issues) have been clear enough: address the housing problems, and contain the pandemic. And yet, the appallingly colonial Heung Yee Kuk is still firmly in place, and Hong Kong not only inevitably failed to contain Omicron but blithely left the vulnerable unprotected and the public health system teetering on collapse. So these failures cannot be laid at the feet of Beijing, unless one wants to argue that they should, indeed, take more control (which they have clearly resisted by insisting it is Hong Kong's leaders' responsibility). It is ironic that an obviously authoritarian government could not—by sticks or carrots—force more people to get vaccinated, or even force private hospitals to help deal with the crisis until very late in the game (and very partially). Even the mainland government itself has failed to adequately vaccinate its elderly and vulnerable.[21] This is a blackmark against an otherwise successful covid-containment strategy prior to 2021.

It is as if the obvious lack of confidence in the government during 2019, which was then compounded by the long pandemic and zero-covid strategy, paralyzed the CE and the system. It would be hard to act with conviction if one does not believe in one's own abilities or purpose to begin with, or fully understand the matter at hand. Again, a case for receivership can therefore be made. Above and beyond the 'discreet' level of indirect advising and occasional, official meetings across the border. What if Liang Wannian had been in charge of governmental health policy form the beginning? What if the tycoons and, say, private hospital boards, has been summoned for a 'come-to-Jesus' meeting with Party officials? In fact something like the latter seems to have indirectly happened, when Mainland Vice Premier Han Zheng told Hong Kong delegates early March 2022 that he hoped that reports of private hospitals turning away Covid patients were only "fake news"; soon after, the for-profit hospitals started acting pro-actively in the virus fight.[22]

## TOWARDS A SECOND HANDOVER, AFTER THE BRITISH AND "AUTONOMY" ERAS

Perhaps most disturbing of all, Hong Kong has since 2020 specifically, sacrificed the education and well being of its youth, and families, by forcing unnecessary school closures even amongst primary age children, who are globally recognized by medical and public health experts as the least vulnerable and least affected by Covid, and the least able to benefit from online learning. In contrast, mainland primary students have largely had school in the usual fashion for the past two years, aside from *temporary* closures. Rather than insist its elderly, vulnerable population get vaccinated, the government has chosen to instead close the schools and move them online, even though primary age youth are the least able to study effectively and learn in this way. Why was this the choice, this bizarre Confucian-esque privileging of the *deliberately unvaccinated* elderly (we can of course exclude those with legitimate medical exemptions), even when the rest of the world was striving to go back to normalcy? Aside from the moral depravity of such a move against the well being of the youth, pitting their health and development against the 'freedom' of the unvaccinated, and as with continuing to prop up the landed 'indigenous' gentry (the Kuk) under the old British system, the government feels it too politically sensitive or bold to take action against the incalcitrant, vaccine resistant demographic. The government literally has or had nothing to lose by in effect forcing/incentivizing the anti-vaxxers, and yet it did not do so until too late in the game to stop the spread of the virus. This has been to use the unvaccinated as human shields deployed against the more responsible, co-operative majority of the city, including children, families, and workers.

This is of a piece with the city's mistreatment and miseducation of its youth that led to Occupy in 2014 (which was triggered not by the old time democrats but the young activists) as well as the outbursts of 2019. To take one example, there is exactly one self-described liberal arts university in the city (Lingnan University) and a small one with an—very unfair—lack of prestige at that. The largest, entire arts/humanities faculty in the city (at HKU) is still smaller than some English departments in, e.g., the Big Ten schools of the American Midwest. And far less diverse, ideologically and otherwise. In short, the universities in Hong Kong are much smaller than they should be, and deliberately kept that way by the government and the officials in charge.

More importantly, there has long been a crisis of "liberal" or "moral" education at the primary and secondary levels of the public schools. What was called "liberal studies"—dating only from 2009 but initially conceived under the British—within the public curriculum had been a bone of contention between the yellow or localist camp and the mainland-oriented and governmental camps. The crux of the matter was both liberal ideology (about e.g. citizenship, electoral democracy) and perhaps more fatefully, the topic of current events and news within Hong Kong and China.[23] After the protests of 2014 and 2019 there was enough pressure to scrap the core area of "liberal studies" in favour of what is now called "citizen and social development" studies. Scandals about public teachers setting rather dubious graduation examination questions—justifying the Japanese invasion of China; claiming the British wanted China to *stop* opium smoking in China—while not directly related, surely did not help matters. The government and others clearly saw liberal studies as prosely-tizing liberal or anti-China politics. There were also earlier conflicts over whether or not to have "national education" and what textbook might be used (this was the issue that kick-started Joshua Wong's celebrity-activist career as a teenager). It is clear that educational reform is on the agenda, and again, it is clear that this has to do much more than now teach the national security law and the textual details of the Basic Law.

The point here is that liberal/moral/critical thinking education had only been a fledgling subject since 2009, and it definitely had a pro-democratic or pan-democratic bent to it in at least some cases. Likewise under the British there was no such core subject, though it had been discussed in the 1980s. Hong Kong/diasporic Chinese novelist Chan Koonchung has noted that for those of his Baby Boomer generation or earlier, 'moral education' came not through schooling under the British but through reading martial arts/wu xia and other literature.[24] And the point here is that if indeed it is a good thing for public schools to teach some type of—non-partisan—moral or "liberal" studies, then this is an opportunity for Hong Kong to go forward, and to de-colonize the curricula as needed, during the current 'second handover.' That this will not be called, or be *liberal* education in a specifically political sense is not the issue or even a major concern. The issue is a lack of moral/ethical education rooted in the humanities and interpretive social sciences and in critical and self-reflexive thinking. When one contemplates Hong Kong politics and the powerful yet arguably *unnecessarily* irreconcilable difference between what is called the "yellow" and "blue" camps, one feels this lack deeply. More, and better, education—holistic, moral, well-rounded— may sound like a platitude but its relative absence was present in 2019, and before and afterwards.

Obviously the present study does not endorse the worldviews and liberal/illiberal politics and xenophobia of many of the pan-democrats or younger nativist activists. But it must be said that the youth have indeed been ill served by the Hong Kong system, including the post-1997 years, in education and 'moral education' (i.e. 'liberal') in particular. "Moral education" may sound vulgar to the Western academic ear, or quasi-religious, and yet all notions of morality have their roots, and morality or valuation and judgment is a crucial cultural, social, and political matter that educational institutions ignore at our peril. If one likes, it may be transcoded into a more Foucauldian notion of discourse or the inevitability of some type of governing, interpretive framework that orients people to their world and helps them make sense of it.[25] Surely morality (or ethics more specifically) should be part of any educational system. This is not what the SAR has, or rather it does not have enough of it and in a more open and tolerant, mainland-inclusive way.[26]

But it is, far more fatefully, the peculiarities or inadequacies of the *adult's* moral or critical education in Hong Kong that poses a far graver problem. One has no other possible explanation for why the government would deprive the city's youth of a decent education in a context where there were virtually zero outbreaks or deaths from Covid until March 2022. Again, Hong Kong, like all too many other places, deserves a better, smarter, and even more humane or moral ruling class. It is as if Lam et al. simply had no idea what to do, from either a mainland or a Hong Kong perspective. They could not choose the mainland way, as it is not on the books and they know very little of it regardless, and they could not fly solo either. Not because of the lack of "suffrage' for the CE but because of the lack of state capacity and political experience and skills. So what one had is a muddle and an unintentional but undeniable production of misery, and even a spike in suicides. There is no uniquely, exceptionalist 'Hong Kong perspective' or way to guide the society and government through a crisis such as Covid or indeed as a mode of governance in general. There is the old, colonial era mode of governance through the market and a 'civil service' bureaucracy (and an ambiguous Basic Law), and there is a mainland way to be adopted and modified to work for Hong Kong specifically.

In this sense it may be that the Lam administration will stand revealed as the last colonial one. Or the early beginning of a real administration that does more than feed the market. Better yet, the last one to live on borrowed time and the impossible project of trying to have it both ways: part of China and not part of China; uniquely Hong Kong yet inescapably tied to the PRC; two systems and two countries. With a new fully Beijing-approved C.E. set to take over the reigns of the city (John Lee Ka-chiu), now with pledges to take care of housing and to benefit from and integrate with the mainland more, we shall see if the SAR can take another step forward or whether it will remain stuck in the past. So too this will depend on the mainland's capacity to actually help the city and not just securitize it.

Lee for his part is a former police officer and Security Secretary who helped implement the national security law and the various arrests that flowed later from this, and oversaw the handling of the later stages of the protests/riots in 2019. This of course helps explain his selection as the next C.E., and the selection was predictably and immediately framed by the international media as ominous and a tightening of the screws.[27] But Lee's reputation within Hong Kong is a different matter, where he has also been described as flexible and impartial, and where he had actually taken a calm and practically conciliatory approach to very hostile democratic representatives at the last major Legco meeting on 19 June

2019.[28] Lee has also voiced support for promoting economic livelihood, increasing public housing, and giving a 'second chance' to the 10,000 people (youth) arrested as a result of 2019. He has repeatedly invoked 'performance legitimacy' *a la* mainland officialdom, by saying that the government must be result-oriented and not just focused on procedures. To be sure Lee was not a politician until perhaps very recently but rather had a long career in security; he also has no significant ties with the Hong Kong tycoons and so-called "business community." All of this will make him seem, to some, like a mere pawn of Beijing. But not having a political class to begin with is precisely the colonial hangover discussed above, and it will have to change in any case. Lee might—might—be able to better work within the mainland system (i.e. the nexus between the two systems) not despite but because of this police/security background, just as the Party itself and the communist revolution before that was born out of a certain military and militant background. (Someone once wrote of political power and guns moving along dialectically.) In any case Lee's and others' emphases on not just security but results/performance and improving livelihood speak directly to a commitment to building up state capacity.[29]

We shall see. As I write, C.E. Lam and C.E.-elect Lee have worked together to launch some of the governmental reorganization and expansion announced before the Omicron wave. Several bureaucracies will be combined, and civil service jobs increased over the coming years (there are 10,000 fewer such posts now than in 2003).[30] This may sound mundane but is certainly welcome if one is interested in increasing state capacity and thence livelihood or development. Of course bigger is not necessarily better, as some concerned political scientists have noted already, but let us get real and remind ourselves that there has never been a decent welfare state with a range of public services without a big government. Let us leave the "third way" rhetoric of neo-liberal democratic thinking—'the era of big government is over' said the USA's Bill Clinton—in the dustbin of history, given the outcomes of austerity economics.[31]

Of course the heart of the matter is not the individuals and biographies involved but the social and historical crises and opportunities at hand. In so far as the unrest of 2019 has been officially and unofficially explained in part as due to economic inequalities and hardship especially amongst the youth, it seems likely that the Hong Kong government will try more substantially than ever to tackle such issues and become a more or better developmental state/SAR. This would not be a liberal future—it is liberalism as much as colonialism or imperialism that brought the SAR to the brink—but it may be a better one.[32] If this is what, in the end, the chaos and anarchy of 2019 brought, it will not be such an awful result after all. If nothing else, the seven months of 2019's anti-ELAB hastened the future and telescoped two or more decades of a political quagmire into a handful of years. At least one now can no longer deny that the SAR and the sovereign will necessarily have to evolve and develop together (albeit not with Hong Kong as some type of imaginary equal partner), and that the era of Hong Kong's faux autonomy and exceptionalism is now over. This marks an overdue codification of reality.

In the end perhaps it is after all the ideological (or cultural) legacies and aftermaths of modern colonialism and empire—in their clash with an older 'feudalism' and non-Western world—that weighs like a nightmare on the brains of the living, in Hong Kong as elsewhere. Aime Cesaire, writing his *Discourse on Colonialism* in the aftermath of World War II and the rise of Nazism and Fascism, famously theorized how the violence and de-humanization of colonialism and conquest had prepared the ground for the holocaust, just as it had also wiped out entire worlds of possibilities that might have emerged from the non-bourgeois, non-Western worlds of the past. Racism and colonialism dehumanized the West as much as the East and global South. Cesaire, following Georg Lukacs, spoke of "thingification" and reification within the rationality and practice of colonialism and capitalism. Surely this has affected our political rationalities or governmentalities as well. So we might argue similarly as Cesaire for the question of governmental or state competence, or the question of the ruling classes within the former colonies and metropoles. Perhaps the final, rotten fruit of the era of modern colonialism and imperialism has been the sheer incompetence and lack of capacity of too many of the world's states and modes of governance. They are all—including the SAR and mainland—now threatened by the global Covid pandemic, as well as the limits of neo-liberal or simply liberal or austerity economics. China is hardly immune from a certain 'liberal' commitment to market economics and moreover to over-emphasizing the economy as opposed to society.[33] As has not escaped anyone's notice, and even before the pandemic necessitated (everywhere) a certain increase in social and political control, the P.R.C. under Xi has also ratcheted up its policing and other authoritarian powers. We need neither deny nor endorse this, and still maintain the analysis in these pages.

Let us recall that two things can be true. The P.R.C. has remained nonetheless at least a different variety of capitalism (or what many mainland analysts would call a 'socialist' or statist system) and one that has performed well in comparison to other places and systems despite its massive size and massive challenges to governance and prosperity.[34] Whatever words we use here in short hand to name the system, it is clear that it has been, and can further be, a developmental state or system from which many have benefitted and from which many others can learn or use to their advantage. And vice versa. Let us recall, then, for those still crushed by the elimination of "suffrage" and autonomy and (liberal) democracy in Hong Kong that those particular systems, where they actually existed, have not exactly helped with this problem of a rotting or dysfunctional political class and state, and a decline in livelihood. Hong Kong's challenges going forward in this second handover and beyond are multiple, and daunting, despite its wealth and global presence. But at the risk of cliché, let us recall the slogan from Antonio Gramsci: Pessimism of the intellect, optimism of the will.

Independence has often gone awry. The former imperial powers of the West are in denial over their decline and importance on the one hand, and on the other over their responsibility for what they have wrought. This is as true in Hong Kong as it is elsewhere.

And so we may conclude our post-mortem by saying: Hong Kong has not died but is struggling to be born, again, as a fully *post*-colonial SAR.

## NOTES

1. Again one must note that the question of de-colonization is not an objective or scientific one, but it is a political one in that it poses the question of who or what groups are to benefit by the de-colonization and new system. One could—many do—argue that de-colonization for Hong Kong means it would either be explicitly independent or entirely self-ruled whilst somehow still being part of China (or being simply independent of it). We need not beat a dead horse here and proclaim this unrealistic, and against the legal sovereignty of China. The other issue is precisely that of capitalism and inequality. If colonialism in Hong Kong begat its infamous inequality and conservatism—and essentially there was no Hong Kong prior to colonialism—then perhaps undoing that a bit would also be to de-colonize the place. Hong Kong would always be dependent on the Chinese and global economies in any case.

2. As discussed before, a palpable ethno-nationalism lies behind everything Deng Xiaoping ever said about the return of Hong Kong and Macau to the mainland: "What is a patriot? A patriot is one who respects the Chinese nation, sincerely supports the motherland's resumption of sovereignty over Hong Kong and wishes not to impair Hong Kong's prosperity and stability," he said. "Those who meet these requirements are patriots, whether they believe in capitalism or feudalism or even slavery. We don't demand that they be in favor of China's socialist system; we only ask them to love the motherland and Hong Kong." Politics were never exactly 'in command' of this adroit yet largely conservative, deeply nationalistic, and market- and wealth-oriented revolutionary of post-Mao China. Quoted in "Hong Kong's new loyalty oath requires all lawmakers to love China – and the Communist Party," *CNN World Report*, 24 February 2021. https://edition.cnn.com/2021/02/23/asia/hong-kong-patriots-election-intl-hnk/index.html. Accessed 4 May 2022.
3. See for example, blog posts by Pang Laikwan, "Hong Kong's Sinkhole," at the Verso Books website, 11 October 2019. https://www.versobooks.com/blogs/4452-hong-kong-s-sinkhole and Rebecca Karl, "Thoughts From Afar on Hong Kong," 31 December 2019. https://positions politics.org/thoughts-from-afar-on-hong-kong-rebecca-karl-1-january-2020/. Accessed 4 May 2022.
4. The reference here is to Joel Andreas's *Rise of the Red Engineers: The Cultural Revolution and the Origins of China's New Class* (Stanford UP, 2009). Of course Hong Kong will have to have its own version of such "red and expert" technocrats, and 'red' here is not the old hue.
5. This is exactly what enamoured Milton Friedman and the Hoover Institute—an influential right wing think tank in Hong Kong—about Hong Kong, that it fit there ideological worldview and economic thinking perfectly (which is not to say it fit the city's realities perfectly). See for example Neil Monnery, "Hong Kong: A Two-Stage Economic Experiment," *VOX, CEPR Policy Portal*, 30 June 2017. https://voxeu.org/art icle/hong-kong-two-stage-economic-experiment. Accessed 4 May 2022. That the ruling of Hong Kong was often perceived by the colonial governors as regrettably happening at-a-distance from London's concerns, is a common theme in some of their memoirs and in standard Hong Kong histories.
6. In addition to Steve Tsang, *A Modern History of Hong Kong* (London: Bloomsbury Academic, 2019), see Lui Tai Lok and Rey Yep, "Revisiting the Golden Era of MacLehose and the Dynamics of Social Reforms," *China Information* 24.3 (2010): 249–272.
7. Of course political science is no answer either, but is largely a fount of straight-up state department style liberalism and faux 'objectivity' at the cost of theoretical and interpretive acumen.

8. Jan Nederveen Pieterse, "Learning from Covid: Three Key Variables," *ProtoSociology* 38 (2021): 211–228.

9. As the British Prime Minister once put it in 1987: "And who is society? There is no such thing! There are individual men and women and there are families and no government can do anything except through people and people look to themselves first." To be sure, this is merely conservative ideology, and as Karl Polanyi among others always reminded us, a society left entirely to the market and rich individuals would scarcely be able to reproduce itself. See Margaret Thatcher, "There's No Such Thing as Society," extracted at: https://newlearningonline.com/new-learning/chapter-4/margaret-thatcher-theres-no-such-thing-as-society. Accessed 4 May 2022.

10. See Rollin F. Tusalem, "The Colonial Foundations of State Fragility and Failure," *Polity* 48.4 (October 2016): 445–495. Alexander De Juan and Jan H Pierskalla, "The Comparative Politics of Colonialism and Its Legacies: An Introduction," *Politics & Society* 45.2 (2017): 159–172. And Jonathan Di John, "Conceptualizing the Causes and Consequences of Failed States: A Critical Review of the Literature," *Crisis States Working Papers Series No. 2*, Development Studies Institute (DESTIN), L.S.E., 1–51.

11. For the case for Hong Kong's luck in this sense, see John Carroll, *Edges of Empires* (Harvard UP, 2005).

12. See among other, more recent invocations of re-colonization the essays collected in Rey Chow, *Ethics After Idealism* (Indiana UP, 1997). A more fact-based approach to the question can be found in *From a British to a Chinese Colony? Hong Kong before and after the 1997 Handover*, Ed. Gary Chi-hung Luk (UC Berkeley Press, 2017).

13. Certainly we all know academic departments who have weathered a receivership for their ultimate benefit, and still others who desperately need one but instead just reproduce themselves in the worst way. Given how malleable (if contradictory) the Basic Law is, this document should pose no real barrier either.

14. See the video report, "Omicron Spreads Rapidly Through Hong Kong Care Homes as City TOPS Global Covid Death Rate," *South China Morning Post*, 7 March 2022. https://www.scmp.com/video/coronavirus/3169585/omicron-spreads-rapidly-through-hong-kong-care-homes-city-tops-global; "Hong Kong's NowTV apologises after state-backed paper attacks reporter for asking authorities about mainland medics," Hong Kong Free Press, 17 March 2022. https://hongkongfp.com/2022/03/17/covid-19-hong-kongs-nowtv-apologises-after-state-backed-paper-attacks-reporter-for-asking-authorities-about-mainland-medics/; and also Nury Vittachi, "Mind control and Molotovs: Hong Kong's

Special Pandemic Challenges," *Friday Everyday*. https://www.fridayeve ryday.com/mind-control-and-molotovs-hong-kongs-special-pandemic-cha llenges/. Accessed 4 May 2022.

15. See the interview with Lam on the Radio Television Hong Kong public broadcast, 23 July 2021. https://www.rthk.hk/radio/radio3/pro gramme/backchat/episode/761945. Accessed 4 May 2022.

16. Of course populism has also historically been associated with anti-semitism, in the West and Russia. One is tempted to see 'mainlanders' as 'the Jews" of 2019 and the years beforehand, complete with 'pogroms' such as setting fire to and nearly killing Lee Chi-cheung, a 57-year-old father of two daughters who had protested the protesters.

17. On this question of the incompetence and rot current ruling classes, see the inestimable Doug Henwood, "Take Me to Your Leader: The Rot of the American Ruling Class." https://www.jacobinmag.com/2021/04/ take-me-to-your-leader-the-rot-of-the-american-ruling-class. Henwood analyzes the American one but the problem of rot—and lack of repre-sentative power—is a global one with its own characteristics in context. In case it is not clear, when one criticizes the quality of the current ruling class and wishes it were better, one is not thereby advocating class domination but speaking to how it is better to be ruled by a competent and comparatively humane ruling class than a bad one.

18. See for example "Hong Kong's Suicide Index Hits 'Crisis Level' in Covid Fifth Wave," *The Independent*, 30 March 2022. https://www.indepe ndent.co.uk/asia/china/hong-kong-covid-lockdown-suicide-cases-b20 47058.html. Accessed 4 May 2022. This has been widely noted elsewhere in Hong Kong as well.

19. The spread of Omicron or other strains within the mainland is beyond our scope and time-frame here, including its own failures to vaccinate adequately. But as even some reports from the mainland have argued, the corona-virus has become endemic and therefore new strategies must be developed to 'live with' the virus.

20. There is no social science data that rigorously analyses this essential ques-tion, and now it is not something likely to happen in the future. But as argued elsewhere, and by others, the democratic parties combined usually pulled only 50–60% of the popular vote (and were often below this threshold within the Legco due to the functional constituencies). The deeply yellow/xenophobic elements were far less than this, and such parties did not arise until after Occupy's failures in 2014.

21. By the time of the quarantining of Shanghai in Spring 2022, only 60% of the elderly (above 60) have been vaccinated, according to various mainland reports.

22. See the report, "Vice Premier Han Zheng Warns Against 'War Weariness' Towards Covid," *The Standard*, 6 March 2022. https://www.thestandard.com.hk/breaking-news/section/4/187818/Vice-Premier-Han-Zheng-warns-against-%27war-weariness%27-towards-Covid. Accessed 4 May 2022.

23. For more background and detail of liberal studies in the SAR, see Robert Spires, "Hong Kong's Post-Colonial Education Reform: Liberal Studies as a Lens." *International Journal of Education Reform* 26.2 (2017): 156–175. And Wenxi Wu, "Politics, Textbooks, and the Boundary of 'Official Knowledge': The Case of Liberal Studies in Hong Kong." *Pedagogy, Culture, and Society* 29.4 (2020): 1–18.

24. For more see Chan Koonchung, *Living Out the Contradiction of Our Time: Social Innovation and Good Society*, Trans. Alan Chan and Richard Hsiao (Jockey Club Design Institute for Social Innovation, Hong Kong Polytechnic University, 2014).

25. I have pursued such a theorization of discourse-in-society in my previous two books, *China and Orientalism* (Routledge, 2013) and *Illiberal China*. See also the work of Gao Mobo, e.g. *Constructing China: Clashing Views of the Peoples Republic* (Pluto Press, 2018).

26. In the current climate it is perhaps worth noting that "mainland-inclusive" does not mean pushing patriotism or nationalism, but simply bringing on board its own self-understandings for the conversation.

27. See "Hard-liner Who Led Crackdown on Protests Is Favorite to Run Hong Kong column New York Times on this https://www.nytimes.com/2022/04/06/world/asia/john-lee-hong-kong.html. Accessed 4 May 2022.

28. See the "Official Record of Proceedings" 19 June 2019, on the Hong Kong government website to get a sense of this, and of what LegCo had become by 2019. https://www.legco.gov.hk/yr18-19/english/counmtg/hansard/cm20190619-translate-e.pdf. Accessed 4 May 2022.

29. I should note that the draft of this chapter was written before Lee was mentioned as a candidate. The point is, again, that these new emphases represent not only 'mainlandization' but were brought forward by the protests of 2019 themselves.

30. See "The bigger the better for Hong Kong government revamp? Public policy experts divided over expansion plan for bureaus." https://www.scmp.com/news/hong-kong/politics/article/3178125/bigger-better-hong-kong-government-revamp-public-policy. Accessed 18 May 2022. See also the plan itself, "Re-organisation of the Government Structure." https://gia.info.gov.hk/general/202201/12/P2022011200312_385382_1_1641962319224.pdf. Accessed 21 May 2022.

31. See Blyth, *Austerity: The History of a Dangerous Idea*.

32. And again, it may be an *illiberal* future in the pejorative sense (as opposed to simply being non- or anti-liberal), the rise of not only authoritarianism but a certain vulgar, deep conservativism and aggressiveness, as evinced for example by the career of Hong Kong politician Junius Ho.
33. I discuss this issue of 'liberal economism' in *Illiberal China*, 2019.
34. Again, the real issue here is not one of semantics but whether or not the mode of economy or governance is developmental (where needed) or making things better or worse, and for whom. The moral posturing and virtue signalling over whether or not China is socialist or capitalist—as if these terms are self-evident to begin with—or Good or Evil is simply anti-intellectual. Clearly, they—as in on-board intellectuals and many citizens—see it as some sort of socialism, perhaps because it is a single-party state, is paternalistic, or is *responsible* in a good way, has massively raised living standards since 1949, and so on. In this sense "Chinese socialism" is an interesting, valid, even compelling question for sociological and intellectual/theoretical inquiry. One can certainly say this is not the type of socialism or definition of socialism they like or think worthy of the name (we have noted the appalling class inequality). But who really represents the orthodoxy here, and who are the heretics or poseurs? True socialism or true communism as it exists in the heads of primarily Western, aka American academics, is simply not helpful for understanding the world, or for changing it for that matter. Much the same could be said about true capitalism, true liberalism, true markets, and so on. Given the vortex that is China studies and public opinion out there, we hasten to add that of course the PRC for all its successes has also had massive failures and 'mistakes.'

# SELECT BIBLIOGRAPHY

Abbas, Ackbar. *Hong Kong: Culture and the Politics of Disappearance* (University of Minnesota Press, 1997).

Adorjan, Michael, Paul Vinod Khiatani, and Wing Hong Chui. "The Rise and Ongoing Legacy of Localism as Collective Identity in Hong Kong: Resinicisation Anxieties and Punishment of Political Dissent in the Post-Colonial Era," *Punishment & Society*, 23.5 (2021): 650–674.

Anderson, Benedict. *Imagined Communities: Reflections On The Origin and Spread of Nationalism* (London: Verso, 2016 [1983]).

Appiah, Anthony. *In My Father's House: Africa in the Philosophy of Culture* (Oxford UP, 1993).

*The Basic Law of the Hong Kong Special Administration Region of the People's Republic of China*, May 2021 Edition. [1984]. https://www.basiclaw.gov.hk/en/basiclaw/index.html. Accessed 4 May 2022.

Baudrillard, Jean. *America*, Trans. Chris Turner (New York: Verso, 1989).

Blyth, Mark. *Austerity: The History of a Dangerous Idea* (Oxford UP, 2013).

———. *Great Transformations: Economic Ideas and Institutional Change in the Twentieth Century* (Cambridge UP, 2002).

Carroll, John. *Edge of Empires: Chinese Elites and British Colonials in Hong Kong* (Harvard UP, 2005).

Castoriadis, Cornelius. *Philosophy, Politics, Autonomy: Essays in Political Philosophy*, Ed. David Ames Curtis (Oxford Press, 1991).

Cesaire, Aime. *Discourse on Colonialism*. Trans. Joan Pinkham (New York: Monthly Review Press, 2001 [1950]).

© The Editor(s) (if applicable) and The Author(s), under exclusive license to Springer Nature Singapore Pte Ltd. 2022
D. F. Vukovich, *After Autonomy: A Post-Mortem for Hong Kong's first Handover, 1997–2019*,
https://doi.org/10.1007/978-981-19-4983-8

168  SELECT BIBLIOGRAPHY

Chan, Selina Ching. "Politicizing Tradition: The Identity of Indigenous Inhabitants in Hong Kong," *Ethnology*, 37.1 (Winter, 1998): 39–54.

Chun, Allen. *Forget Chineseness: On the Geopolitics of Cultural Identification* (Albany: SUNY Press, 2017).

Cohn, Bernard S. *Colonialism and Its Forms of Knowledge: The British in India* (Princeton UP, 1996).

Dasgupta, Sravasti. "Hong Kong's Suicide Index Hits 'Crisis Level' in Covid Fifth Wave," *The Independent*, 30 March 2022. https://www.independent.co.uk/asia/china/hong-kong-covid-lockdown-suicide-cases-b2047058.html. Accessed 4 May 2022.

Deng, Xiaoping. "Maintain Prosperity and Stability In Hong Kong," 3 October 1984. http://en.people.cn/dengxp/vol3/text/c1250.html. Accessed 4 May 2022.

———. "Speech at a Meeting with the Members of The Committee for Drafting the Basic Law of the Hong Kong Special Administrative Region," 16 April 1987. http://www.china.org.cn/english/features/dengxiaoping/103351.htm. Accessed 4 May 2022.

Di John, Jonathan. "Conceptualizing the Causes and Consequences of Failed States: A Critical Review of the Literature," *Crisis States Working Papers Series No.2*, Development Studies Institute (DESTIN), L.S.E., 1–51.

Fish, Stanley. *There Is No Such Thing As Free Speech, And It's a Good Thing Too* (New York: Oxford UP, 1994).

Ford, John. "The Pivot to Asia Was Obama's Biggest Mistake," *The Diplomat*, January 21 2017. https://thediplomat.com/2017/01/the-pivot-to-asia-was-obamas-biggest-mistake/. Accessed 4 May 2020.

Freeman, Jo. 'The Tyranny of Structurelessness," *Berkeley Journal of Sociology*, 17 (1972–73): 151–165.

Freud, Sigmund. *Civilization and Its Discontents*, Trans. James Strachey (New York: Norton, 1989 [1929]).

Grossberg, Lawrence. "History, Politics, and Postmodernism," in *Stuart Hall: Critical Dialogues in Cultural Studies* (Routledge, 1996), Eds. David Morley and Chen Kuan-Hsing.

Henwood, Doug. "Take Me to Your Leader: The Rot of the American Ruling Class." https://www.jacobinmag.com/2021/04/take-me-to-your-leader-the-rot-of-the-american-ruling-class.

Ho, Petula Sik Ying. "Connection at the Price of Collusion: An Analysis of 'Hong Kong's New Identity Politics: Longing for the Local in the Shadow of China," *Cultural Studies*, 36.2 (2020): 229–251.

Honderich, Ted. *Violence for Equality: Inquiries in Political Philosophy*. 3rd edition (Routledge Press, 2014).

Ip, Iam-Chong. *Hong Kong's New Identity Politics: Longing for the Local in the Shadow of China* (Routledge, 2020).

SELECT BIBLIOGRAPHY 169

*Joint Declaration of the Government of the United Kingdom of Great Britain and Northern Ireland and the Government of the People's Republic of China on the Question of Hong Kong.* 1984. https://www.cmab.gov.hk/en/issues/jd2. htm. Accessed 4 May 2020.

Kwok, Tony. "Hong Kong Must Seize the Moment to End The abuse of Land Rights in the New Territories," *SCMP*, 24 September 2016. https://www.scmp.com/comment/insight-opinion/article/2021923/hong-kong-must-seize-moment-end-abuse-land-rights-new. Accessed 4 May 2020.

Lam, Carrie. "Interview on Backchat Program," Radio Television Hong Kong, Public Broadcast, 23 July 2021. https://www.rthk.hk/radio/radio3/progra mme/backchat/episode/761945. Accessed 4 May 2022.

Law, Wing Sang. *Collaborative Colonial Power: The Making of the Hong Kong Chinese* (Hong Kong UP, 2009).

Lee, Ching Kwan. "Hong Kong is the Front Line of a New Cold War: If it Burns, the World Gets Burned Too," *Los Angeles Times*, 28 May 2020. https://www.latimes.com/opinion/story/2020-05-28/op-ed-if-hong-kong-burns-the-world-gets-burned-too. Accessed 4 May 2022.

Legislative Council of Hong Kong. *Official Record of Proceedings*, 19 June 2019. https://www.legco.gov.hk/yr18-19/english/counmtg/hansard/cm20190619-translate-e.pdf. Accessed 4 May 2022.

Liu, Shih-Ding and Shi Wei. " Why Is Reconciliation Impossible? On the Clash of Emotions Between Hong Kong and Mainland China," *Made in China*, September–December 2021.

Lo, Shiu-Hing. *Competing Chinese Political Visions: Hong Kong vs. Beijing on Democracy* (Prager Press, 2010).

Losurdo, Domenico. *Liberalism: A Counter-History* (New York: Verso, 2014).

Lui, Tai Lok. "The Unfinished Chapter of Hong Kong's Long Political Transition," *Critique of Anthropology* 40.2 (2020): 270–276.

Lui Tai Lok, Stephen W.K. Chiu, and Ray Yep, Eds. *Routledge Handbook of Contemporary Hong Kong* (Routledge, 2019).

Luk, Gary Chi-hung, Ed. *From a British to a Chinese Colony? Hong Kong Before and After the 1997 Handover* (UC Berkeley Press, 2017).

Mehta, Uday Singh. *Liberalism and Empire: A Study in Nineteenth-Century British Liberal Thought* (Chicago UP, 1999).

Monnery, Neil. "Hong Kong: A Two-Stage Economic Experiment," *VOX, CEPR Policy Portal*, 30 June 2017. https://voxeu.org/article/hong-kong-two-stage-economic-experiment. Accessed 4 May 2022.

O'Brien, Kevin J., and Li Lianjiang. *Rightful Resistance in Rural China* (Cambridge UP, 2006).

O'Shea, Tom. " The Essex Autonomy Project: Critics of Autonomy," (2012) "Critics of Autonomy." *Green Paper Report of Essex Autonomy Project,*

# 170 SELECT BIBLIOGRAPHY

pp. 1–26. https://autonomy.essex.ac.uk/wp-content/uploads/2016/11/Cri ticsofAutonomyGPRJune2012.pdf. Accessed 4 May 2022.

Pepper, Suzanne. "Beijing, Britain, Pan-Democrats or Localists: Who is to Blame for the Death of Hong Kong's Democracy Movement?" February 2022. https://hongkongfp.com/2022/02/12/beijing-britain-democrats-or-locali sts-who-is-to-blame-for-the-death-of-hong-kongs-democracy-movement/.

Pieterse, Jan Nederveen. "Learning from Covid: Three Key Variables," *ProtoSociology*, 38 (2021): 211–228.

Polanyi, Karl. *The Great Transformation: The Political and Economic Origins of Our Time* (New York: Beacon Press, 2001[1944]).

Purbrick, Martin. "A Report on the Hong Kong Protests," *Asian Affairs*, 50.4 (2019): 465–487.

Reuters Staff. "How Reuters Counted a Quarter Million People at Hong Kong's Protests," *Reuters.com*, 18 July 2019. https://www.reuters.com/article/us-hongkong-extradition-backstory/how-reuters-counted-a-quarter-million-peo ple-at-hong-kongs-protests-idUSKCN1UD0ZT.

Sautman, Barry and Yan Hairong. "Localists and 'Locusts' in Hong Kong: Creating a Yellow-Red Peril Discourse," *Maryland Series in Contemporary Asian Studies*, Vol. 2015: No. 2, Article 1. https://digitalcommons.law.uma ryland.edu/mscas/vol2015/iss2/1. Accessed 22 May 2022.

Scarr, Simon, Manas Sharma, and Marco Hernandez. "How Many Protesters Took to the Streets on July 1?," *Reuters Graphics*, 4 July 2019. https://graphics.reuters.com/HONGKONG-EXTRADITION-CRO WDSIZE/0100B05W0BE/index.html.

Schmitt, Carl. *The Concept of the Political*, Trans. George Schwab (U Chicago Press, 2007[1937]).

Solomon, Jon. "Hong Kong, or How Social Struggles Can Reinforce the Cartography of Capitalist Enclosure," 14 January 2020. *Critical Legal Thinking*. https://criticallegalthinking.com/2020/01/14/hong-kong-or-how-social-struggles-can-reinforce-the-cartography-of-capitalist-enclosure/. Accessed 4 May 2020.

South China Morning Post Team. *Rebel City: Hong Kong's Year of Water and Fire*. Zuraidah Ibrahim and Jeffie Lam, Eds. World Scientific Publishing Co and South China Morning Post Publishers Limited, 2020.

Spires, Robert. "Hong Kong's Post-Colonial Education Reform: Liberal Studies as a Lens," *International Journal of Education Reform*, 26.2 (2017): 156–175.

Staff Report. "Vice Premier Han Zheng Warns Against 'War Weariness' Towards Covid," *The Standard*, 6 March 2022. https://www.thestandard.com.hk/bre aking-news/section/4/187818/Vice-Premier-Han-Zheng-warns-against-% 27war-weariness%27-towards-Covid. Accessed 4 May 2022.

Thatcher, Margaret. "There's No Such Thing as Society." https://newlearningo nline.com/new-learning/chapter-4/margaret-thatcher-theres-no-such-thing-as-society. Accessed 4 May 2022. Originally published in *Women's Own*, 31 October 1987.

Tusalem, Rollin F. "The Colonial Foundations of State Fragility and Failure," *Polity*, 48.4 (October, 2016): 445–495.

Vittachi, Nury. *Other Side of the Story: A Secret War in Hong Kong* (Hong Kong: YLF Press, 2020).

Vukovich, Daniel. *Illiberal China: The Ideological Challenge of the P.R.C.* (New York: Palgrave, 2019).

———. "A Sound and Fury Signifying Mediatization." *Javnost: The Public*, 27.2 (2020): 200–209.

Williams, Raymond. *Keywords: A Vocabulary of Culture and Society* (Oxford UP, 1976).

Wu, Wenxi. "Politics, Textbooks, and the Boundary of 'Official Knowledge': The Case of Liberal Studies in Hong Kong," *Pedagogy, Culture, and Society*, 29.4 (2020): 1–18.

Wu, Xiaogang. "Income Inequality and Distributive Justice: A Comparative Analysis of Mainland China and Hong Kong," *The China Quarterly*, 200: 1033–1052.

# INDEX

**A**

Autonomy, 1, 3, 4, 6, 7, 10, 11, 13, 17, 18, 20, 25, 33, 37, 42, 45, 50, 51, 58, 59, 61, 63, 65, 66, 69–76, 80, 82–84, 86–89, 93, 94, 100, 103, 109, 111, 114–116, 119, 121, 122, 125–127, 131, 132, 134, 142, 160, 161

**B**

Basic Law, The, 2–5, 7, 10, 11, 15, 16, 18, 25, 26, 28, 35, 40, 42, 47–50, 59–62, 64, 65, 68–71, 84, 86, 90–93, 97, 99, 100, 106, 109, 110, 119, 129, 132, 134, 135, 142, 147, 152, 156, 158, 163

"Be water", 3, 24, 34, 109

Blyth, Mark, 60, 91, 98, 135, 165

Borrowed time, 3, 40, 58, 65, 90, 91, 147, 148, 158

Burnism (Laam chau 攬炒), 18, 26, 31–34, 40, 51, 90, 97, 103, 109, 110, 114, 128, 132

**C**

Capitalism, 4, 7, 15, 31, 47, 62–64, 68, 70–72, 74, 75, 96, 97, 99, 101, 102, 110, 111, 116, 160–162, 166

Chief executive office, 39, 148

Civil Human Rights Front (CHRF), 13, 26, 27, 29, 30

Colonialism, 2, 9, 15, 24, 32, 41, 50, 51, 60, 62, 64, 73, 75, 79, 81, 84, 86, 105, 106, 108, 111–113, 115, 121, 130–132, 140, 144, 146, 149, 151, 160, 161

Colour revolution, 41, 47–49, 68

Crowd size estimations, 58

© The Editor(s) (if applicable) and The Author(s), under exclusive license to Springer Nature Singapore Pte Ltd. 2022
D. F. Vukovich, *After Autonomy: A Post-Mortem for Hong Kong's first Handover, 1997–2019*,
https://doi.org/10.1007/978-981-19-4983-8

## D

De-colonial, 3, 102, 108, 118, 128, 131, 132, 140

De-colonization, 4, 7, 60–62, 64, 96–98, 100, 101, 105, 108, 110–112, 114–116, 122, 130–134, 140, 143, 146, 148, 161

Democracy, 1, 3, 5, 10, 13, 18, 20, 21, 40–42, 44, 45, 48, 50, 51, 58–60, 64, 69, 70, 74, 85, 91, 98, 101, 102, 105, 108, 110, 111, 114, 116, 117, 119, 123, 125, 129, 131–133, 136, 138, 146, 156, 161

De-politicization, 123

Development, 5–7, 11, 19, 26, 39, 57, 69, 73, 74, 99–107, 110, 114, 115, 126, 129, 142, 143, 145, 146, 148–150, 155, 159

Discourse, 2, 3, 7, 9, 10, 12, 13, 50, 54, 55, 72, 73, 75, 76, 80, 84, 86, 89, 98, 102, 108, 112, 113, 115, 117, 118, 120–122, 129, 133, 140, 144, 148, 149, 157, 165

Dongfang, Han, 128

## E

Education
 moral, 157
 university, 33, 101, 121, 142, 151, 156

## F

Filibustering, 18, 19, 25, 52, 92, 110, 125, 130, 146

Foreign funding of Hong Kong protests, 6, 28, 36, 111, 133

Foreign/resistance training, 44

## G

Greater Bay Area Plan, 5, 69, 100, 105

## H

Hegemony, 2, 6, 18, 47, 48, 87, 91, 118, 119, 121, 123, 127, 131, 137, 144

Heung Yee Kuk, 106, 154

Housing crisis, 142, 146

## I

Identity, 7, 14, 19, 41, 48, 50, 59–61, 63, 70, 72, 76–81, 83–90, 92–96, 100, 103, 110–112, 114, 117, 119–121, 124, 125, 127, 128, 130–133, 135, 138, 143, 147–149, 151

Illiberalism, 93

Imperialism, 2, 9, 13, 36, 42, 43, 46, 48, 49, 57, 60, 86, 98, 102, 105, 113, 115, 121, 131–133, 144, 146, 160

## K

Knowledge production, 117, 121, 122

## L

Laissez-faire (liberal economics), 1, 3, 7, 18, 32, 64, 99, 108, 123, 124, 130, 143, 144, 150

Lam, Carrie, 25–27, 29, 36, 37, 42, 82, 85, 104, 129, 144, 151, 158, 159, 164

Lantau Reclamation Plan, 5, 107

Lee, Bruce, 24, 53

Lee, John Ka-chiu, 158

Legislative Council (LegCo), 18, 26–31, 36, 52, 87, 92, 93,

123–125, 129, 130, 138, 141, 154, 158, 164, 165

Liberalism, 1, 3, 12, 13, 32, 41, 43, 47, 63, 72, 74–76, 80, 85–87, 91, 93, 99, 110, 112, 113, 115, 120, 122, 131, 133, 135, 137, 140, 144, 147, 152, 160, 162, 166

Liberal studies, 156

"Liberate Hong Kong, The Revolution of our Time" (光復香港, 時代革命), 24, 36, 47, 111, 118

Localism, 18, 19, 51, 64, 79, 85–87, 94, 95, 100, 103, 110, 111, 117, 120, 148

## M

Media
  and mediatization, 3, 50, 51, 54, 65, 131
Mongkok Fishball Revolution, 19
Moral Education, 157

## N

Nationalism, 12, 20, 32, 43, 49, 51, 65, 86, 89, 90, 103, 111, 112, 115, 117, 121, 128, 137, 141, 162, 165

National security law, 1, 11, 15, 17, 19, 23–25, 27, 36, 37, 42, 46, 65, 66, 69, 87, 96, 110, 118, 122, 125, 128, 132–134, 156, 158

Nativism, 4, 19–21, 51, 64, 83, 85–90, 95, 96, 111, 112, 115, 116, 128, 143, 148

Neo-liberalism or austerity, 160

Northern Metropolis Plan, 5, 100, 105

## O

Occidentalism, 3, 118, 133

Occupy Central With Peace and Love, 16

Omicron (fifth wave in HK), 2, 147, 150

One country, two systems, 11, 27

Orientalism, 9, 12, 13, 20, 41, 60, 80, 112, 113, 117, 118, 121, 151

## P

Pandemic, 1, 2, 60, 125, 134, 135, 142, 145–150, 152–155, 160, 164

Participation, 60, 109, 110, 122–125, 134, 139

People's livelihood (aka 'common prosperity'), 7, 19, 58, 101, 104–106, 130, 134, 141, 146–148

Place-based identity, 81, 88, 89, 105, 128, 149

Police
  ordinances, 22–24
  violence, 5, 36, 38, 39, 59
Political
  under-development, 146
Post-colonialism, 2
Professional Teachers Union (PTU), 127, 128

## S

Second handover, 3, 5, 102, 105, 130, 133, 157, 161

Socialism, 4, 62–64, 70, 71, 77, 97, 102, 105, 106, 110, 166

State
  state capacity, 2, 4, 7, 124, 125, 141, 143, 146, 147, 153, 154, 158, 159

## T

*Transitional* period, 147
Tycoons, 68, 100, 101, 106, 130, 143, 155, 159

## V

Violence, 15, 18, 22, 23, 26–32, 34–39, 43, 47, 51, 52, 86, 87, 90, 103, 160

## X

Xenophobia, 4, 10, 19, 21, 30, 34, 43, 59, 85, 103, 112, 113, 126, 137, 143, 149, 157

Xiaoping, Deng, 57, 67, 98–100, 135, 162
Xinjiang, 115, 143

## Y

Yellow economy, 103, 104
Yellow versus Blue camps, 6, 14, 107, 157

## Z

Zero-covid strategy, 148, 150, 153, 155

Printed in the United States
by Baker & Taylor Publisher Services